I0423138

Early in his life in Iraq, Dhirgham Jawad Kadhim earned a B.A. degree in English literature. This enabled him to further his education in the UK. He chose to attend a post-graduate course in management studies at Buckinghamshire College for higher education, High Wycombe. He continued his self-education through readings, participating in conferences that advocate human rights, in particular the rights of women among the minorities in the UK. In the meantime, he became concerned about the violence that prevailed around the world in the name of religion. Hence, he published his book, *Terrorism under the Banner of Islam* in 2017. However, and though he is over occupied with his writing, he continues to follow up with deep concern the issues of gender equality, and the environmental tasks and their impending developments.

Dhirgham Jawad Kadhim

# TRAGIC WEDDING

AUSTIN MACAULEY PUBLISHERS™

LONDON • CAMBRIDGE • NEW YORK • SHARJAH

Copyright © Dhirgham Jawad Kadhim 2024

The right of Dhirgham Jawad Kadhim to be identified as author of this work has been asserted by the author in accordance with sections 77 and 78 of the Copyright, Designs and Patents Act 1988.

All rights reserved. No part of this publication may be reproduced, stored in a retrieval system, or transmitted in any form or by any means, electronic, mechanical, photocopying, recording, or otherwise, without the prior permission of the publishers.

Any person who commits any unauthorised act in relation to this publication may be liable to criminal prosecution and civil claims for damages.

This is a work of fiction. Names, characters, businesses, places, events, locales, and incidents are either the products of the author's imagination or used in a fictitious manner. Any resemblance to actual persons, living or dead, or actual events is purely coincidental.

A CIP catalogue record for this title is available from the British Library.

ISBN 9781035831463 (Paperback)
ISBN 9781035831470 (ePub e-book)

www.austinmacauley.com

First Published 2024
Austin Macauley Publishers Ltd®
1 Canada Square
Canary Wharf
London
E14 5AA

I acknowledge the tremendous effort exerted by my publisher, Austin Macauley to produce my novel *Tragic Wedding* in such a wonderful form.

# Presentation

The 1990s have witnessed several advances in the subject of women's rights in the UK. Issues like discrimination at work, rights to maternity leave and equal pay have been brought to the open and officially recognised by the authority and the public. However, brutalities like underage marriages and arranged marriages continued to take place unnoticed. This practice is prevalent among Asian and African communities in the UK.

Parents or senior members of the families often chose the spouses for their offspring. Young men may have a spot of opinion in such an arrangement, but young girls have no say, none whatsoever. If a girl tried to oppose the family's plan, she would be condemned as outrageous, or even deserved, in their opinion, an honour killing.

Unfortunately, no clear legislation by the UK authority touched upon this issue till 1996, when the Family Law Act was introduced. However, this law was hard to implement in communities that mix up their traditions with their religions. Consequently, the Act was followed by the amendments of 2007, "Forced Marriage Protecting Order." Then came the amendment of 2014, which stated that FMPO constitutes a breach of the criminal law. However, that Act also retains its civil/family law nature, as FMPOs are issued according to the family court's practice. Very few if none of the offenders have been prosecuted under these Acts. Mainly because victims may fail to report the offenders of their own families to the authorities.

On the other hand, there would be a blurred line between what is an arranged marriage and what is a forced marriage.

Persuasion, fake promises together with false enticement are tactically used by families to break the young girl's will and achieve their heartbreaking submission, as consent by girls is ostensibly given. The expected outcome of that social cruelty is that British-born young girls are often obliged to marry someone entirely alien to their culture. That kind of practice is like a death sentence, usually imposed by primitive parents who resided in the UK generations ago but have never been fully incorporated or socially integrated with their British culture and British social values.

It is like unplugging young trees from their natural habitat and replanting them in hostile environments. Most of the times, some young ladies or even underage girls in the UK face this fate silently with almost no deterrent in the system that stands by to protect their precious lives.

That is precisely what happened to young Jameela the year she was finalising her studies at secondary school and was hoping to pursue her ambition in further education.

That was 1984 when there were no proponents in the UK to legislate against this hideous hidden crime. Jameela's arranged tragic wedding is the theme of my novel. Events of the novel are taking place between Henslowe Central, west of London and the tribes' land west of Afghanistan. I leave the rest to the readers to live the sad dramatic events and their somehow final positive conclusion that is in the end of the story.

# Chapter One

"Halt. Don't move. Don't talk. Don't look left. Don't look right. Now stroll behind the Mujahid. Keep going. Five meters. Ten meters apart and keep going." The voice was a militant type, loud and commanding. It came from nowhere and everywhere. Luckily, I understand Dari, a local Farsi dialect spoken by most Afghan people. It is the native language of my parents. They often speak it at home in Hounslow Central. Therefore, I understood the commands of our capturers. Ashu, my adventure's companion, was like a deaf in a party, as the saying goes. Maybe she managed to understand a few words, but I didn't think she could make a full sense of what was going on.

Wisely, she kept calm and followed my movements. We had encountered two gunmen. Both were heavily bearded, putting on white turbans dropping generously on their foreheads, almost covering their eyebrows. They have dressed in the traditional Afghan style; white baggy pants and grey long shirts dropping down to their knees. They looked alike. They were very similar to each other; as if they were twins who sprang out from a grotto at a nearby hill. One moved to lead the way in front of us and the other one was following us, watching over us from behind. Ashu, my friend was shuffling along behind me. I wondered then how long she would last be standing up before collapsing facing up this unpredicted drama? I deliberately slowed down to give her the chance to get closer to me.

Once she got near enough to hear me, I whispered to her to stay calm and just do what I do. Simultaneously, I managed to sneak a glance backwards. I could see that the gunman behind had appointed his gun in our direction. After ten minutes of walking, I noticed that the gunman in front had shunned his gun up to his left shoulder. Then he pulled a walkie-talkie from his belt, held it close to his mouth and started talking loudly. I could hear him very clearly as he was repeating his calls: "From patrol number 001 to headquarters. Can you hear me?"

I couldn't hear what the one at the receiving end was saying. All that I was hearing were unclear susurration. Hence, I listened cautiously to what our lead saying. He was repeating the phrase; "Yes master."

After another ten to fifteen minutes of our slow movement; creeping behind our mysterious "commander." I started to feel my mouth drying up and find it hard to swallow my saliva. However, and despite my physical stiffness, my mind used to drift and shift most of the times to my friend Ashu as I was so worried that she might make a wrong move that could be misinterpreted by the gunmen and put us in deep trouble.

In the meantime, and despite my preoccupied mind with Ashu, I tried to concentrate on the fragmented messages of the gunman that he was transmitting through his walkie-talkie. I was terrified when I heard him confirming through his transmitter to his master that the infiltrators, they captured were two, and they looked like women. He said that with a confident voice and resumed his stealthy walk.

Eventually, we reached a hummocky bushy area. Our "lead" turned to the left and we had to follow. After twenty minutes of walking in our new direction, we reached another rather small hill. Our "lead" wet around it and we did what he did. On the foot of the hill, we passed some damaged military vehicles, three of them were resting on their sides and two were sitting on their tops. Although I was weighed down by what was around us, I managed to throw another look at the strange-looking shrubs that went parallel to our footpath. The growths were about two feet high.

Some looked green-red, and some looked deep green covered with appointed sharp thorns. My impression was that we were drifting in a strange land; a very strange land or we could have stepped into a wild train. The red dust overhead had covered the area. In my right hand, I can hardly see some dusty spiky bushes forming two lines around the base of the hill, they went as far as I could see in that stony valley. At the base of that small hill, I could see a few skeletons of burnt-out military vehicles and two rusty old cannons settling on their sides; the type of guns we could observe in classic war movies.

In my left hand, we passed along a brick wall. It looked like the remains of an old castle that had been abandoned sometimes in the past after either a lost battle or after a natural disaster. The bricks of the wall were dusty, and I thought they had lost their original colour, as well as their shape. They looked eroded and easy to push to the floor. Our "lead" continued our walk following the length of the wall. Suddenly we heard a blast of a machine gun in the distance followed by a heavy bombardment. Our "lead" stopped walking and repeated loudly: "Don't worry, don't worry, the battle is too far away, too far."

Then he appointed me with his walkie-talkie to look behind in the direction of my friend. I looked back to see Ashu was crouched down on her small suitcase while her backpack moved from her shoulders to the top of her head. I went back to her and hunkered down in front of her. I put my both arms around her shoulders and whispered with passion: "Are you alright, Ashu?"

"No," came the answer, "I wouldn't be able to walk any further." Then she added, "I wet myself."

I could not see the gunman who used to follow us from behind anymore, he just disappeared. But the gunman in front had paused for a short while, and then he came a bit closer, and asked, "What was the problem?"

I told him with a shy voice that it was a woman's matter. I didn't know if he fully understood what I meant, but he appointed at a nearby gap in the wall, and in a commanding voice, he ordered me to leave our suitcases unlocked behind and help my friend to go through that gap in that wall. I helped Ashu to stand up. After she was trembling for a few seconds, eventually she gained her balance and manage to lean on me, and we moved very slowly in the direction of that designated gap. We had trouble walking as one side of Ashu's black robe had gone slack. The two overall black robes were provided for us by the officials in Islamabad airport.

Upon our arrival in Islamabad, we were received by two officials: a lady and a man from the Pakistani special service, and a representative of the charity organisation that planned our trip. They took us to an aside office in the airport. In that room, they welcomed us and offered us some soft drinks and biscuits. The lady was modestly dressed in a nicely designed black scarf covering her head and dropped around her thin shoulders. She was silent while the two officials were giving us detailed information regarding the rest of our intended journey.

One of the government's representative top concerns was our safety. He assured us that most of the warlords of the regions if not all of them; were funded and supported by the Pakistani establishment. Therefore, they wouldn't dare to act against someone who was sent there under its discretion. The officials opened his briefcase and reached to a sealed letter. He handed it to me and advised us to keep it sealed and only hand it to a chief of a group if we feel there was an imminent danger or a potential threat to our lives.

After the two gentlemen had left the room; the lady opened a wooden box that was placed in the right corner of the room and pulled out two black robes. She laid them on the long table that occupied the centre of the room and recommend to us in a very definite voice, that those overall black robes with attached head covers would be the only acceptable appearance for women by the public in the land we were going to trip.

It was a problem that time to find a robe that would fit Ashu's petite short figure. Therefore, the lady arranged to trim the hem of the robe that was chosen for Ashu by stitching it a few inches up. Now, in the struggle of our clumsy walking on that narrow path; some of the stitches of Ashu's robe was broken, and one side of the hem went slack, and every time we tried to move further Ashu would trip on it. That was why it took us almost half an hour for a relatively short distance to get inside the fence. Once we were inside the fence, I took a panoramic look around me.

I was astonished to see that the atmosphere that was within the fence looked drastically different from that outside the fence. The height of the fence was not even all around, and it was surrounding an area, I estimated it covered a square mile. In the distance, I could see some trees that stands across a green pasture. It was difficult to tell from that distance; what kind of trees they were? But the pasture looked fresh and was well looked after. There were several bungalows adjacent to each other, possibly six of them in a row along the wall from inside the fence.

We crept slowly till we reached the first bungalow on our right. We sat on the floor, resting our backs on the bungalow's wall. Ashu looked exhausted. I was very tired too, but I thought it was time to make a few necessary adjustments before a change of circumstances that might cripple us and tie our hands up. We didn't know what was coming next and what kind of challenges we would face. That was why I thought we should be prepared for all the possibilities ahead. Ashu starched her legs and closed her eyes. But before she was fully relaxed; I nagged her gently and urged her to open her backpack for me.

Quickly, I picked a fresh knickers from her backpack. It happened that they were black as well just like the ones she had already soaked. I reached to a small plastic container in my backpack and emptied it from its contains; some medical cotton and deposited the wet knickers inside. While I was busy doing this, a very frustrating question was nagging in my head. Had we fallen into the wrong hands? Maybe yes! If yes, would they consider us as trespassing enemies? In that case, there would be a possibility that they would try us at a "Sharia Court." I imagined Ashu entering the court, stumbling on her robe's hem.

Immediately, I ask Ashu to adjust her position to enable me to stitch up the slack part of her rim. Then I started looking for a pool and a needle in my backpack. Needle, yes. I found a set of them but no black pool insight. However, there was no spare time to fritter away. Thus, I started stitching Ashu's loose hem with white thread. I imagined Ashu standing in front of the 'Sharia judge' with a black robe decorated with white stitches. First, the thought made me very sad, and then it caused me; almost, to burst into laughter. Ashu felt my trembling hands on her side. She managed to open her drowsy eyes for a few ascends to examine my face. She was astonished to see me trying to repress inappropriate and ill-timed laughter. She showed me her empathy by drawing a vague smile on her visage, and then she went back into her semi-trance.

Ten minutes' job and one of the problems were out of the way. But the nagging question was still hammering in my head; "Where did we go wrong?" Out of my puzzlement, I took a hollow look at Ashu, as if I wanted to make sure that she was still next to me. I felt depressed to see her starching her legs on that dusty floor while resting her head on her backpack and producing whistling noise through her nose, a sign of her exhaustion. We were both very tired. We were in the second stage of our journey, and I believed we had been on the move for more than eighteen hours. And here I am.

I managed to snooze for ten or fifteen minutes, which could be more than once. But right then, I was fully conscious, thinking, and mentally revising our adventure right from the start. It is getting late, but still daylight. I took a lazy look around, but I didn't see any movement. I felt depressed, and I dozed off again. And suddenly, I felt Ashu started nudging me softly and whispering my name, "Look. Look, Kameela."

Initially, I thought I was dreaming. It took me a few seconds to regain my full consciousness. I adjusted my body by supporting my shoulders on the wall. I rubbed my sleepy eyes gently and looked to see what Ashu was appointing at, but I couldn't see much. We had been next to this wall for maybe more than six hours. Although it was still daylight, the atmosphere was rather dull. Red dust over our heads had covered the horizon, and my vision was getting blurred. There were three lines of tree in the far distance. They overlapped evenly, except for some little gaps that appeared here and there. Ashu kept telling me to look. And I kept repeating, "Where?"

Kameela, Ashu said, "You better have your eyes tested when we get home."

"If we would ever get home," I said it without thinking, maybe it came out of my frustration. Ashu's reaction came spontaneous, "Why Kameela, we have not done anything wrong!"

It came to my mind to say, "As if all those people who had been eliminated in this land done something wrong." But that sentence did not come out of my mouth. Ashu was still holding herself together, and I should not dishearten her any further.

Ashu was almost losing her temper with me. She adjusted her position and said, "Do you see that third row of the trees in the far distance which looked like a mirage?"

"Yes, Ashu I do."

"Fine, Kameela follows them with your eyes to the right end of that little gap between them."

"Oh, yes," I whispered with excitement. As it was stated in our manual that was provided by the organisation, there was a clear description specifying that after passing the Pakistani borders, we should enter an enclave that was under the control of a group of 'Mujahideen' who were led by the moderate Islamist leader, Mullah Abdul Rahman. We were told that the enclave was on adjacent terrain of the tribes' land and had direct access to Pakistan from the southeast borders. Mullah Abdul Rahman was in full communication with the Pakistani authority that oversees our trip, which was in coordination with our charity organisation.

However, the minutes after our driver had abandoned us, saying that he was not allowed to go any further and we had to walk across the hilly land to reach our destination, and we did, I felt we had entered a lawless land. Now there was some hop. Our eyes were fixed on the two figures moving in our direction. They were getting nearer and nearer. Now even we could recognise their faces.

We can see a lady in a black robe that had extended up to cover her head and a short guy with the traditional white sloppy shirt and baggy pants and white turban. The man was pushing a wooden luggage cart carrying our suitcases as well as some other things wrapped with white towels, maybe some food and water. I sneaked a look at Ashu, and I could see a vague smile on her face, maybe indicating that our agony was coming to an end, at least for the time being.

# Chapter Two

Yes, now we can see some hopes on the horizon. I would say hopes because since we were led by a gunman from the front and shepherded by a gunman from behind, we had lost control over our destiny. We were powerless, waiting for something to happen, anything that could move things forward; regardless of the outcome, negative or positive, we would deal with it, and it would be better than hollow feelings of waiting for the unknown. When the lady and her companion, our unexpected visitors, got closer, we both tried to stand up, showing respect. After sitting all those hours on the floor, I felt clumsy and very stiff to stand up quickly, but after I had attuned my position, I bent on Ashu and helped her to stand up; and yes, she did while I glanced a light smile on her face, maybe it was just a sign of relief.

"Good evening, doctors. I apologise on behalf of Mullah Abdul Rahman, the lord of this land, and in my name Sister Nashmeea Swaad, for what you have experienced already. Communication in this land is very sluggish, hence we just received your credential from Islamabad, and Mullah Abdul Rahman ordered immediate welcoming hospitality for you."

Ashu and I were astonished. Our eyes kept glimpsing, sometimes at each other and sometimes at Sister Nashmeea, trying to comprehend what was happening and to understand this sudden change of luck. "Thank you very much, Sister Nashmeea." Sometimes we say it separately, and sometimes we say it together.

Unfortunately, doctors, according to the formality that was adopted by Islamabad authority, you had been brought here via the official route, which took you almost fifteen hours. They avoided what we call the gangway that would have taken you less than six travelling hours.

While Sister Nashmeea showed us her sincere empathy, she gave a signal with her right hand to the small guy with the white turban to execute his instructions according to a prearranged plan. He pulled a rusty key that was attached to a thin green robe hanging to his neck and unlocked the lock of the huge door of the one-room bungalow, the same bungalow that we had been leaning on its wall all that time. Then he slid a metal bolt that attached the huge door to a metal ring that was fixed to a solid piece of wood embedded in the wall and pushed the old heavy door wide open.

Sister Nashmeea asked us kindly to enter through that door. As we went through the door, I noticed that the room was huge, maybe 10mx6. It was darkish and a bit damp and smelled of some sort of disinfecting odour. It had no windows, a part of a high small lookout at the top of the back wall very close to the ceiling. I could see two mattresses, made up with green sheets and topped up by two green pillows, and one military-type blanket folded neatly at the end of each of them.

There was a small metal table with two wooden chairs close to the middle of the left wall and a small metal table in the far corner. On the other side of the room, close to the corner of the right wall, there was one-foot square tin covered by a piece of cloth. Later, we understood that it was a homemade temporary mobile toilet.

Sister Nashmeea requested us politely to take our seats and ordered the small guy to unload the cart. He put our suitcases close to the wall, and the towel-covered parcels on the table. "Sorry, doctors, I knew that you had come from a civilised world, but we hoped that you would put up with us as everything we had here was poor and primitive."

She said that and moved in the direction of the small table at the far corner of the wall and pulled from its top a small antiquary oil lantern. She twisted it open to one side. Then she reached for a small box of matches in her side pouch and lit that old lantern in a smart swift move. That produced a good enough light for us to see each other and to see what was on our table. Sister Nashmeea asked the little guy to bring another chair from the next-door bungalow, so she could join us at our table.

Then she started unfolding the wrapped box and put its contents on the table. That was our feast that was made of pieces of grilled chicken, tomato soup, a thick loaf of bread, together with a few golden colour metal cubs engraved with some script from the holy Koran around their rims. She opened a carton box, then she pulled a large metal jar of water and a teapot and placed them on the table, repeating, "You must have been very thirsty, doctors." Among other things with those wares, there was a plastic ewer full of water, I suppose it was for washing and ablution.

I was wondering what had happened to the little man with the white turbine. He brought the chair for Sister Nashmeea and left quietly, almost invisible, sneaking through that wide door. But now and suddenly, he appeared just outside the opened door and mumbled a few words. I couldn't fully understand what he just said, but I guessed from the movements of his hand that he indicated that they had arrived.

Sister Nashmeea stood up and said very firmly, "Although one of the fighting groups who called themselves Taliban had taken the domain by surprise and overpowered the rest of the fighting groups, they did not care about law and order in the terrain, they occupied. The lawlessness that prevailed in the aftermath of the civil war had produced hundreds of thieves and opportunists of armed gangs who searched the area aiming to steal and rip off defenceless people around. That is why we were very vigilant in using these couple of miles as a buffer zone between our settlement and the open land towards the east. So, please do not venture outside, and I will show you how to lock your door from inside, and never open it to anyone unless you hear my voice asking you to open it for me.

Over the night, you might hear some noise caused by a few wild animals, mainly jackals wandering around from the nearby bushland looking for food. If they were prissiest, you can scare them away by making some noise. By the way, possibly, you would spend one-two more nights in this bungalow till we would have your accommodation and your practicing place ready. Then you would be within the borders of our secured village. There you would be at ease, and everything would be different."

Then Sister Nashmeea smiled and said, "Well, I call our settlement village." After Sister Nashmeea showed us how to lock our door from inside, she asked the little guy with the white turban who was still waiting on the door to come in and pull his kart away. After he had left, she told us that she would be with us early morning, then she wished us good night and pulled the door shut behind her.

As soon as Sister Nashmeea left the room, Ashu jumped, trying to lock the heavy door. Well, she reached for the iron bolt, but she could not push the door close enough to the wall to push the bolt in place. I moved to offer my help and teased her by saying, "Team effort Ashu, team effort all the way."

Now we can somehow relax. We went to the table where some cold food was still there. "It didn't matter, hot or cold, I was still hungry," Ashu said and started nipping again. Suddenly, Ashu stopped eating, she looked me in the eye and said, "Did you hear something?"

"No, what?" I answered. "Oh yes, some scratching noise on the door. They must be the jackals. Ashu, just go and clap next to the door."

"No, you do it. I was scared."

Ashu might had said that half-joking, but I wouldn't let her down, I moved my ass, and we both went close to the door, clapping and shouting, "Go away." I heard some creatures were racing away.

"Now, it was time to get some sleep," Ashu said. "No, Ashu, not me, you should know that I had been suffering from chronic insomnia for years, many years. It had started the day they had taken Jameela; my sister away under the name of marriage."

Yes, at last, we had some privacy after almost twenty-four hours in the open. We both took off our black overall-robs and hugged them on two big nails we found on the back wall. Ashu took off her jeans and her shoes and reached out to her backpack and produced a nice silver-striped pair of pyjamas. She put them on and without changing her grey t-shirt. Then she rushed to stretch her tiny body on the top of the left mattress. She unfolded her blanket and pulled it over her legs. "I like your pyjamas Ashu," I said.

Ashu liked my compliment, and she explained that it was her mother's present for her last birthday. "I envy you," I said, "I wouldn't trust my mother's taste to buy me any clothes. The last time she bought me a casual dress as a present, I begged her to take it back to the shop and give me the money to choose the one that I would like."

Ashu burst into laughter and asked, "What was wrong with it?"

"Ashu, please, don't ask a silly question." Ashu sat down on the edge of her mattress bed, insisting to know what was the colour of the dress that I did not like as a present from my mother. "Okay, Ashu, had you ever seen the puddles that would be left in the park after a heavy rainy day? A day later, they would be full of yellow-greenish staff of alga. Jameela and I used to hang it on sticks and call it a frog waste."

Ashu went into a laughing fit. I took off my shoes, dropped my jeans, pulled my small yellow notebook from my backpack, and started thumbing it in the dim light of the old oil lantern. Only me, no one else, could read through those confused scripts in my notebook. I came across some names of people and places I wrote down, hoping to bring me nearer to my sister Jameela's whereabouts in the tribes' land.

"Ashu, were you asleep?"

"No, Kameela, not yet." I was not sure about the timing of my question; nevertheless, I went on asking, "Do you think the time was right to involve Sister Nashmeea with our hope to reach out to Jameela?"

"No, Kameela. Not yet. That would divert the whole issue of our arrangement. Let us give it some more time and approach Jameela's case very carefully. Let us make it looked like as if it was a secondary issue of our mission."

"Wise, Wise Ashu, I wouldn't know what to do without you." Ashu would like my spontaneous compliments, but this time, I got no response. I stopped talking, I put my little yellow book aside and listened carefully to find out that I was talking to myself. The very low whistling of Ashu's nose had started, and I thought it was my time to try to sleep. No way! Since the tragic wedding of my sister Jameela, Sleeping had become a few hours of struggling before I passed out. Silent monologue after silent monologue would start in my head. I believed I was close to the tribes' land, I am physically close to Jameela. I might be no more than a couple of miles away from where she was. But where was Jameela right now? Was she happy? Was she sad? Was she alive?

The thought sent a chill down my spine. "No," I said to myself, shelf the thoughts of Jameela right now. You were close to the land of your mother's culture. Didn't she used to say that relieving oneself in the open air as we used to do in the tribes' land was much heather than doing it in a small, closed room? Do I dear to try that? Do I dare to venture outside this dull room for a pee? No way. Would I expose my ass to the jackals? No, I am safer to do it quietly in the tin.

My mind kept wandering forward and backwards, till it settled exactly where I was. In that dim light. I took an affectionate look at my sleeping friend, Ashu and asked myself, how did it all start? Ashu attracted my attention as quiet, timid, and somehow clever, or at least that was my impression. When I met her in my first year in our primary school. I liked her, and I liked to befriend her, but I never thought that our friendship would go that far.

Although our families were related to the same origin of the world where traditions and religion engulf all aspects of their lives still, class and status had their impacts too. My family had come from the tribes' land where life was rather primitive and belonged to pre-civilisation; almost in everything. Ashu's family originally had come from a city where relatively speaking, they had access to modern life, and they had achieved it before they had arrived in the UK.

However, both families would celebrate common traditional occasions like fasting during the month of Ramadan, or the Muslim celebration of Eid. Most of the community might act similarly, but on normal ordinary days, families of different social backgrounds would keep their distance from each other. Hence, Ashu's family and my family hardly ever got involved in our friendship. Going back to the early days of our friendship, I would go back to the second year of our primary school. That day, during the log break, while I was busy flipping my notebook near the main entrance, by the hall of the school, I noticed one of the girls running in my direction.

I closed my notebook and asked her, "What was the matter?"

She told me that my friend was sitting by herself, crying in the empty classroom. I rushed to that classroom to find my friend sitting in a dark corner of the room and sobbing continuously. I reached for some tissues in my pocket and started to dry her tears up and calm her down. It took me a while to find out from her that a girl from our class; called Linda had insulted her for no reason by calling her f****n paki.

After she had calmed down, I left her and went to the headmistress, and I explained to her that I believed that the kind of insult my friend had received from that classmate 'Linda' was nothing but a racial remark. The headmistress fully agreed with me and asked me to leave the matter to her to sort it out. A few minutes after the second class had started, the headmistress appeared at the classroom door. She excused herself and stood next to the blackboard. She stared at the pupils' faces for a few seconds, and then asked in a very firm voice, "Who was Linda Brown?"

A girl with red hair and a freckled face stood up in the back of the classroom. The headmistress ordered her to collect her books and come in front of the class. The girl had come forward with her note's book under her left arm. She stood up, facing the headmistress, while her back was facing the class. "Listen, Miss Brown," the headmistress said, "I am going to give you two options: either you apologise wholeheartedly to Miss Abdul Rahman Khan for your stupid racial remarks, or you leave the school right now, and you wouldn't come back unless

I have an arranged appointment to see you in the company of one of your parents."

Linda started sobbing inconsolably, she turned her face to the pupils in the classroom and through her tears, she managed to say, "I am so sorry, Miss Abdul Rahman Khan. I sincerely apologise for my stupid remarks."

Surely, that unexpected small drama had shocked the entire school. Kids started advising each other to be very careful with their words and to avoid racial remarks in their conversations. But that event had drastically impacted my relationship with Ashu. Since that incident, Ashu and I had become hand in glove. We hardly separated. By the end of our classes, Ashu and I used to wait for my sister Jameela at the school's cafeteria. Jameela used to finish her classes forty-five minutes later.

Once Jameela would come down and meet us, the three of us would move together towards the town's centre. Intentionally we would extend our journey around the block next to the school so that we could pass my uncle's corner shop, where my father used to alternate with my uncle by attending the shop to earn some cash that was known within the community as "under the table." Thus, the government benefit we used to receive would stay intact. When my father used to glimpse us coming in the distance, he would signal a smile and pull something from under the counter. It was our daily prize. It would be either a bunch of mixed sweets or a pack of "Maltesers." He used to hand it to Jameela, and she would split the treasure between us.

Usually, I used to keep complaining and moaning till I got the lion's share. Jameela, Ashu, and I hardly separated. We were always together at school and out of school. At home, Jameela, and I would always mention Ashu in our conversations. My mother had become so curious and liked very much to meet our friend. One Thursday, Jameela and I arrived home a bit late. "Where had you been, my sweet daughters?" My mother asked. And then added, "It was nearly two hours since you had finished your school time."

Jameela explained that the weather was nice, and we decided to walk our friend home. My mother was pleased with Jameela's answer, and she went on to say, "Listen, girls; tomorrow would be Friday, and I'm going to cook chicken curry, the best I ever cocked in my life. Hence, I like you to invite your friend for dinner, so at last, I would have the chance to know her."

Jameela and I started clapping and jumping around. My mother had rather a strange attitude toward people she would meet. She makes up her mind from the first encounter; either she would like them, or she would remain indifferent, without showing them any disrespect or unpleasant feelings. Hence, the minute she met my friend, she adored her. She hugged her and said in an emotional tone, "What is your name, darling?"

My friend replied timidly, "Aysha; aunty Khadijah Khanum."

"Oh no, sweety, that is my mother's name, God bless her soul. But to beautify her name, we used to call her Ashu. Don't you think darling that the name Ashu would sound much nicer?"

"Yes, it would Aunty Khanum," my friend answered smiling bashfully. Since then, Aysha had become Ashu. Her nickname 'Ashu' had become so popular even among her own family. Ashu had become a loveable member of our family. "Thanks, Allah, for giving me a third daughter at a late age," my mother often used to proclaim.

From that day onward, Ashu had to put up with all my mother's repeated stories. My mother was pleased to increase her audience by a new listener in addition to Jameela and myself. My mother loved to recall her youth time events in the tribes' land. Whenever my mother had the chance to see us sitting together for dinner or tea, she would start telling one of her five stories. Jameela and I gave her stories' names and numbers.

Once, she would start saying, "You would know, daughters, I never had met your father before our engagement." Hence, Jameela and I would signal to each other by putting our index finger up, indicating to each other that we were going to hear story number one, my mother's favourite story.

My mother would remember vividly the smallest details of her engagement and wedding procession when her family agreed to marry her to my father and how his family approached her family requesting "the hand" of their daughter Khadijah Khanum, daughter of Shareef Khan, to become the wife of their son; Abdul Rahman Khan, son of Mullah Nasri Khan, as honourable traditions would require.

Usually, when my mother would reach that part of her story, she would go silent for a few seconds and start steering at the opposite wall as if she was attempting to sink back in time, to remember the atmosphere of those days. Though every time my mother telling would come similarly in the thyme but not the same in details. In the process of her narrating, my mother would smile and glance at our faces to see if all of us, her audience were still keen on her tedious story. Then she would resume her subject. However, before she would start again, and in case she went back to the beginning, one of us, usually me would remind her that we had reached the time when the family of Abdul Raheem Khan had sent their delegation to her family. Then she would say, "Oh yes; the delegation was composed of two groups, seven men and five women, arrived by midday at the gate of our family's huge house. They came by two wooden buses they hired from the nearby village to impress the people in our neighbourhood. We received them with due respect."

Then my mother would recall the events of that day as if they had happened yesterday, not more than twenty-five years ago. With a deep and long sigh, she seemed to be prepared for a lengthy, interesting episode. She would shift her eyes to the wall again for a few seconds and look back at us again as if she wanted to attract our full attention to what she was going to say. "You know, my darlings, as it happened that my father was not available then, as he was trading or rather negotiating some cattle's deals at a nearby village. So, my mother sent for my uncle to welcome the men and settle them in our gust courtyard within the enclosure of our house that was built specifically for those kinds of occasions. He welcomed the men and served them our traditional welcoming coffee while my mother was welcoming the women's group to a separate room.

Although almost everyone in the village could guess the purpose of our visitors, it was bad-mannered to ask them any direct question till they spoke out and declared the purpose of their mission. My father arrived an hour later, and it seemed that he was fully informed by the villagers about our visitors and even the purpose of their visit. Typical of our community in the tribes' land. You cannot hide the news in that small society."

Here, my mother described with a glimpse of joy in her eyes how her father went straight to the guest in the gusts' court and greeted the visiting delegation, by telling them to glorify Allah and his prophet, an indication of goodwill or even a declaration of his agreement to their request.

Then, my mother would resume her story by saying, "However, the story had come to me later that my father had stood up and directed his question to the father of the bridegroom-to-be and asked him to specify the amount of dowry he intended to present at the wedding to his daughter. The minute Mulla Jamal mentioned the thousand Afghani, my father stood up and declared: No, no, no, A thousand Afghani was not the dowry for Khadijah Khanum; daughter of Abdul Nadeem Khan. That is the common dowry in the village. My daughter was not like any other common lady. She is my daughter. You know, Mullah Jamal, the village would keep talking about this for the next ten years to come." After five minutes of whispering among Mullah Jamul's group, an elderly man in the group stood up and said, "It was in the honour of both families the dowry would be fifteen hundred Afghani."

When my mother got to this part of her story, she would repeat her traditional quotes: "You see, daughters, how parents care about their daughters?" That is why Allah says in the Quran: "A good daughter should never say no to her parents."

My mother's encyclopaedia contains five stories, Jameela and I had heard them time and time again. They summarise her lifetime on the tribes' land and the relatively short time of her life later in the city of Kabul. When she would come to that stage of her life, she believed that she was uprooted from her natural habitat, the tribes' land. And if there was anyone to be blamed for that unforgivable mistake, that would be my uncle Siraj-al Deen. He was the one, according to her story, who convinced my father to move to the city where he claimed that the economy under the leftist regime was booming. My mother wasn't happy about that move, but a good wife would never say no, to her husband.

However, troubles started, when my uncle, who was an activist among the farmers in support of the leftist government at that time in the history of Afghanistan, accidentally discovered that my father was under the surveillance of the agents of the regime. My uncle used his contacts and with persuasion and bribes, he managed to smuggle my father and my mother to Islamabad, where they had sought refugee status through the British consulate.

Ironically, a few months later, after the fall of the Marxist government in Kabul, my uncle obtained a written decree sentencing him to death issued by the new government under the Islamist groups. Inevitably he followed the same root as my father did with the difference that he managed to smuggle hundreds of thousands of dollars, the budget of the farmers' union, and claimed it for himself abroad.

Ashu might find my mother's stories somehow interesting as she would hear them for the first time, but that did not apply to Jameela and me, as we had heard them ten times over.

Suddenly my thoughts had been entrapped. Something had happened close to me here in the bungalow. It was Ashu. Unexpectedly, started kicking and making funny movements on her mattress bed. She started producing some funny noise and was gabbling unclear words. Luckily, I left the old lantern on a fling with just enough light to see Ashu's face. I moved closer and put my right hand on Ashu's forehead and my left hand on her right shoulder, and wisped gently, "Ashu, my dear. Are you alright?"

After one minute, Ashu lifted her head slightly, then she opened her eyes and gave me a very strange look as if she wanted to make sure that it was me who was repeating her name. Then she slung her head again on the pillow and murmured, "Nightmare, nightmare." I believe the time was about two o'clock, when I finally exhausted my self-thinking and fell asleep.

# Chapter Three

It must be early morning when I heard some light knocking on the bungalow's door. I struggled to open my drowsy eyes. I rubbed my eyes very swiftly and looked to my side to find Ashu sitting on the top of her mattress bed and searching for something in her backpack. She stopped what she was doing and directed her eyes and her attention to the door. Then the voice of Sister Nashmeea came on, firm and very clear from behind the door, "It was me, doctors, Sister Nashmeea, please open the door."

"Yes, Sister, just one second," answered Ashu. We both stood up very quickly, and as we used to sleep with our t-shirts, all that we needed then was to put on our jeans. I went to the door, and with some difficulty, I managed to slide the metal bolt aside. Then I half-opened the heavy, bulky wooden door. "Good morning, doctors. I hope everything was okay."

"Yes, Sister, thank you very much," I replied. Then Sister Nashmeea handed me some folded black garments and explained that she had brought us two casual headscarves to put around our heads when we have men around. "It would be much easier than sticking to your overall black robes."

I took the garments, unfolded them, and handed one to Ashu. They were nice silky textures, and we both curved them neatly around our heads. Sister Nashmeea pushed the door wide open, and the same little man with the white turban whom we had around before, appeared, pushing the same wooden cart into the room except; that it was loaded with more things that time. Two young girls covered with overall black robes from heads to toes followed him, and they started to collect the remains of our yesterday's food. Had they finished removing everything, they started cleaning the table and unloading what looked like our breakfast.

Sister Nashmeea was watching the girls while they were working with her sharp eagle eyes. They unloaded what they had brought on the table; a bowl of a few boiled eggs, two plates of fried eggs, a jar of honey, and one identical thick loaf of brown bread like the one we had yesterday. Ashu stood in the middle of the room, not showing any emotion, while I was standing next to the table, moving my eyes between Sister Nashmeea and the things on the table, remembering one of my mother's favourites saying, "When you were hungry, all foods would look delicious."

Sister Nashmeea looked contented with the service offered by the two girls. She looked around the room and said, "doctors, for some urgent matters, I would leave you for a while. Enjoy your breakfast, please, for now. The time now is about ten am. I would be back about midday. The guard and the two girls would stay in the bungalow next door. If you need anything, they would be at your directive. You excuse me now." Then she emerged through the door and vanished in the distance.

Ashu jumped from her chair and went close to the opened door; she pushed it carefully just to narrow down its wide opening and stood up to follow Sister Nashmeea with her curious eyes. Two minutes later, she moved back and stood close to me, whispering, "Did you know, Kameela, two gunmen appeared from the left and walked behind Sister Nashmeea as she was making her way in the direction of the trees? And they looked very similar to the guys who apprehended us when they found us wandering around."

I throw a meaningless gaze at Ashu as if I was saying, "Nothing new." I meant that was not extraordinary. Meaning that it was not surprising to see Sister Nashmeea was well protected in her movements. More relevant at that moment for me was that I was not very hungry, but I enjoyed the taste of the fresh country eggs and the natural forest's honey. However, after all, my struggle to sleep the night before impacted me deeply. I felt I needed a short sleep, a nap. For one hour. Ashu was watching me starching my body over my mattress bed, exhausted and more than ready to sleep. "Wait, Kameela, didn't you think we should lock the door first?"

"I don't think that was necessary, we were safe in her. Would you please Ashu waking me up when Sister Nashmeea arrived."

One hour and a half passed like five minutes. When Ashu whispered my name close to my left ear, I opened my eyes to see Ashu crouching next to my head, holding my headscarf, and Sister Nashmeea standing at the door. "Are you ready, doctors? I have a man with me." We both stood up with our headscarves on. Sister Nashmeea entered the room, followed by the little man who was carrying a medium-size bronzy try.

"If you were used to London's sweets, I would think it was time that you would try our local ones." She said it with a wide grin on her face. The little man started pushing the breakfast stuff aside and placed the tray on the table.

I had a look at the tray and said, "It seemed the local sweet, Sister was the same as our Afghan sweet in London. It was the same delicious baklava that we used to serve there on special occasions." In the meantime, I was picking one chunk of the baklava and placed it on one of the saucers. Ashu picked a small piece and pushed it straight into her mouth.

After she finished chewing it, she accredited her compliment to Sister Nashmeea by repeating, "Thank you, Sister, it was my favourite taste."

The baklava festivity lasted for about five minutes. Once the jokes and the tasting were over and the little man left the scene, Sister Nashmeea put on a series face and occupied the middle chair of the table, Ashu, and I sat facing her from both sides. Sister Nashmeea paused for a few seconds and moved her eyes between Ashu and me. Then she adjusted her seat and said, "doctors, you might be astonished at how I had been conversing with you in English. Though you never asked, I felt obliged to give you some explanation. I know that my English was not perfect, but it was good enough to explain to you some essential facts.

Some of those facts were to do with me, and some were to do with our situation here in this land." She explained that she was the niece of Mullah Abdul Rahman. Her maternal uncle, who was the absolute ruler of our enclave. She told us that as a large, influential family in the region, their geographical location had drastically impacted their lives. "You might find it hard to believe doctors. We were here at the end of what was geographically called the stripe of the Pashtuns' belt. We would speak Pashto as well as Dari, language, both languages were spoken by all the people around us. So, if we moved uphill to the west, we would be taken as Pashtuns. But if we would go down the end of the borders to the east, we would be Pakistanis. However, if we divert slightly to the west in that corner of the borders, we would be Iranian. But if we would stay where we were, naturally, we were Afghan."

Ashu glanced at me for a second, and then she directed her eyes to Sister Nashmeea and said in a low voice, "But Sister, since as I believed, there was no authority that would run census neither the officials who hold statistics regarding the inhabitants of the region, it would be possible for any of the people here to claim any of those three nationalities whenever it would be suitable for them."

"Yes, indeed, doctor." Sister Nashmeea responded to Ashu's remarks with a semi-grimace on her forehead and added, "But that had disadvantages too. By that, I mean that the lawlessness of the region left it open to bandits and skilful criminals without any following up or subsequent punishments. My father was a livestock dealer. His business used to take him deep into the tribes' land. On one of his trips, he was followed by some vicious bandits who murdered him and seized his cattle. I was five years old then. I remember very well how my mother started ululating and slapping her face while my uncle Mullah Abdul Rahman was holding her arms and begging her to calm down and accept the will of Allah.

My brothers, Sardar who was three years old, and Shinwar who was two at that time, were screaming and clinging to my uncle's rob from behind. The crowd of the settlement surrounded us, but suddenly my ears were blocked, and I couldn't hear anything anymore. I could see the coffin of my father and the frustrated movements of my mother, but the whole thing started to look like a silent movie in front of my eyes. Some ladies from the crowd tried to comfort me by holding me down, washing my face, and giving me some water to drink till I gradually regained consciousness."

When Sister Nashmeea reached that stage of her tale, I felt two hot tears had left my eyes and start rolling down my fat cheeks. Before I reached to the ends of my scarf to dry my tears, Ashu jumped from her chair and ran in the direction of the far corner of the room, covering her face with her headscarf. I could hear her non-stop whimpering despite her effort to suppress it. It might be a minute of silence passed before Sisters Nashmeea managed to pull herself together and dried up her moistened eyes at me and said with a low, rattling voice, "I am so sorry, doctors. I did not mean to crop up your emotion. In this land, we had a lot of sad memories."

I took a fast glance at Sister Nashmeea and then I directed my attention to Ashu. She was quiet, but still giving us her back. I asked her with an affectionate voice to come back and give Sister Nashmeea the chance to resume her briefing. When the three of us were together again, Ashu apologised for her bursting out crying. "I am sorry," Ashu said, staring at the table. I offered her a mage of water and tapped her on the back.

However, our companion, Sister Nashmeea, was eager to give us a full account of her part in this complex situation. When she noticed that emotions were down, and we all went calm, almost back to normal, she said, "Fine, doctors. Let me tell you some positive events that we could say, came about as an indirect result of that tragedy. It happened that my father had no brothers. Hence, and according to the traditions of the land, my uncle Mullah Abdul Rahman had become our protector and natural guardian from an early age. He kept my two brothers close to his operational religious practice, and then they joined his semi-militant group.

In the meantime, he integrated them gradually into his land dealing activities. But he planned different destiny for me. He took me with him on a trip to Islamabad. And he arranged with some relatives there to enrol me at a girl's school. Once I finished my secondary school terms, he arranged for me to live at a student residency in the new female wing that was established then at The International Islamic University of Islamabad. He advised me to earn a degree in Islamic Sharia Law. However, after just over two months of my studies, I found that the subject my uncle had chosen for me was terribly boarding. I did not need a lot of persuasions to gain my uncle's agreement to change my subject from Sharia law to English literature.

My four years at Islamabad university, together with my interaction with other students, had left a great impact on my life. There weren't so many gills in the new girl's wing of the University. Most of the girls who occupied the wing were from Islamabad. It took me a while to understand the city's mentality and to make a few apparent friends. I found it hard to fully integrate with the city girls. I saw them as a bit earthly and too direct in their approach to life. I used to spend the weekend at Aunt Shabnam's house, who happened to live with her family in Islamabad.

After my graduation, I left the university hostel and moved to my aunt Shannon's house. Aunt Shabnam was a childless middle-aged lady, and her husband was working as a clerk at the municipal of the city. Both, relatively speaking, were fairly educated and they saw me as an adorable symbol of their roots, and a live link to their countryside origin. They called me daughter, and sometimes they persuaded me to talk just to enjoy listening to my untamed Dari accent.

As you might have noticed, doctors, there was no telephone line in our hamlet. The walkie-talkie that our people used mainly for military purposes had no more than three miles range. To make a very necessary phone call from our area, we had to travel fifteen miles away, up to the city of Lashkar, the centre of the Province of Helmand. So, two weeks after my graduation, I was surprised to receive a handwritten message from my uncle informing me that he was coming to Islamabad in a few days, and he had some important matters to discuss with me.

The message made me rather anxious as I was hearing in the news that a wide national Islamic front had been formed to lead the bloody struggle against the Soviet invading army, and I assumed that my uncle and his group would be active participants in that formation. However, I kept telling myself to stay calm and wait till I found out what my wise uncle was on about."

After taking a fast glance on the door, Sister Nashmeea resumed her telling by saying "It was Friday morning when my aunt Shabnam knocked on my door, calling me for an early breakfast. I found it was a bit strange as Friday was not a working day and I was not a student anymore. Yes, Aunt Shabnam, I am coming. It took me a few minutes to put myself in order. My door was half-open when Aunt Shabnam proceeded to tell me that she had some good news. They just received a cable informing them that Uncle Mullah Abdul Rahman was arriving in Islamabad that afternoon."

By half-past eleven that morning, Aunt Shabnam, Uncle Shinwar her husband, and I were in the coach station of Islamabad. The couch station was amazing. You could call it a chaotic coach station. Vehicles of all shapes and all colours and all types came and went. Small crowds were scattered around large and small spots in the station. The floor was uneven and full of dirt and dry spots of engine oil. Some men with dark blue working uniforms were holding pencils and small notebooks in their hands, trying to register the time that some coaches had arrived and the others that were departing.

They used to blow their whistles now and then. There was no precise time for my uncle's arrival that we knew but we had to be there and wait. I believed we had arrived at the station rather early. The time was passing slowly, very slowly. The atmosphere was humid and dusty. I felt unwell. I sensed somewhat giddy. Aunt Shabnam noticed my agony. She asked me if I was alright? I gave her a vague look without saying anything. She alerted her husband, and then she grasped my hand and helped me move close to the main entrance of the huge station. She helped me to sit on a small wooden bench, and her husband went to reach out for some water.

After Aunt Shabnam helped me to wash my face and made me drink some water, I felt much better. It was almost six o'clock in the evening when a long-converted military vehicle entered the compound of the station. The car was moving slowly, surrounded by a crowd of civilians and a few armed police. Some people near us uttered the Mullah, the Mullah. The three of us moved with the crowd trying to keep as close as possible to that hardly moving car. I could see a few clergy dignitaries among the welcoming people, I could tell from their appearances and their headdresses that they were of high positions, but I couldn't tell their ranks. The car came to a halt at a nearby corner bay, and my uncle alighted from the passenger seat. The driver alighted too and opened the back door of the long car and signalled politely to us to get into the car.

Aunt Shabnam moved first, but halfway into the car, she retreated to push me in front of her. Once I was inside the car. I got the surprise of my life. It was my mother sitting there covered in a black dress from top to toe opening her arms to hug me. My reaction was, oh my God, mom, it was you. My mom and I hugged each other and shed a lot of tears before we calmed down. A few minutes later, she asked me in a throttled voice the question: "When would I be home?" Of course, I had no answer. Most likely, she knew it would depend on my uncle's plans.

So, my answer was to kiss the back of her right hand, meaning I missed you too. After that emotional gesture, we both went silent. My uncle climbed back to his passenger seat, and after twenty minutes in the movie, we came to a checking point. A few army officers were sitting outside a fabricated cabin with the picture of the national Pakistani flag on top. One of the officers left his seat and came close to the window of the driver. The driver put his window down and produced an identification card. The officer took a serious look at the card, and then faced my uncle and gave him a military salute. Then he singled to the officers at the gate to lift the floor joist.

We passed through, but I was deeply impressed by the respect and recognition that my uncle enjoyed in those surroundings. For me, it was a confusing short journey. I was excited to see my mother next to me. Every ten-fifteen minute she would hug me and kiss me on the cheek. Hence, without anticipation, might after an hour or so of travelling, I realised that the car had stopped in front of Aunt Shabnam's house. Though I have been living close that house for the last four years, I felt as if I were seeing it for the first time.

While Uncle Shinwar, Aunt Shabnam's husband, folded his seat up, making room to Aunt Shabnam to descend from the car. I took a good look at the high-security fence that separated the house from the main road. The house contained five bedrooms. One of them near the main entrance of the house designated for visitors who were not related to the family. Inside, at the far end of the house, there was a nicely furnished self-contained room; nominated for VIPs guests. However, initially, we all went to the dining room except the driver, who was directed by Uncle Shinwar to the visitor's room near the entrance of the house. Before we started our extensive meal, my uncle reminded Shinwar to arrange for a full tray of food and take it to the driver's room.

Traditionally the floor of the dining room was furnished with beautiful homemade carpets; I couldn't tell if they were made of silk or fine wool close to the texture of a natural silk, surrounded by nicely decorated pillows. I was astonished to see all that variety of food in the middle of the room. I had no idea how and when Aunt Shabnam had managed to prepare all this inviting fresh food. I felt guilty that I did not help in preparation for the job. Later, I understood that the food was arranged by a special order, served by a nearby first-class restaurant.

The food in the dining room was organised like a circle in the centre of the room. My uncle took his place in the middle of the utter side of the circle. We all took our places around him from both sides, waiting and looking at my uncle, till he uttered rather loudly, In the Name of Allah, the Gracious, the Merciful. Then he started eating. Habitually, we all repeated his prayers behind him and reached down to the food and started eating. That was the ever most delicious feast I had in my life.

I was not surprised to see that Aunt Shabnam arranged for a second bed in my room for my mother. You could imagine doctors; my mother and I hardly ever slept for the first two nights. Taking and talking but about what? Digging out memories, mostly sad memories. All about our past, as we had no indications about the future. We hardly saw my uncle for a few days. It seemed he had some important meetings had previously arranged. We used not to ask him about his affairs unless he would tell us what he wanted us to know. You could imagine doctors, my mother and I hardly ever slept for a few days, and Aunt Shabnam was serving us a late breakfast.

One day, when we heard the big get of the garage was wide opened, and my uncle appeared entering through the other door of the house, as usual reciting through his teeth his usual prayers. My mother and I stopped eating and stood up conveying our due respect, which we always do when we see my uncle coming along. My uncle took a fast look, greeted us with a gesture of his right hand, and went straight to his designated apartment. My mother and I rushed to finish our breakfast, but we were still in the dining room when Aunt Shabnam appeared at the door. She got me a bit anxious when she told me that the Mullah, as she used to call my uncle, wanted to have a word with me, I looked around and, asked "Where?"

Aunt Shabnam, with a light smile on her face, said, "In his VIP room." I rushed to the other side of the house till I got next to the main door of my uncle's room. I cautiously knocked on the door and waited for a few seconds till I heard his voice calling my name, an indication of his permission to receive me. I moved in to find my uncle sitting on the top of his bed, thumbing an old book he had placed on his lap.

It looked like a very old book. I could tell from its thin yellow pages, and even I could sniff the familiar scents of this type of books. My uncle put a feather shape marker in between the pages, closed the book, and put it aside next to him on the bed. Then, he looked at me for a few seconds with obvious affection reflected in his eyes.

He cleared his throat and asked me in a soft voice, "How was our daughter?"

I answered with a smile by saying, "Very well; indeed, everything was fine under your protection, dear uncle."

"Good, good," he murmured. And then he resumed his conversation by saying, "You might know how much I trusted you and depended on you, dear daughter?"

Spontaneously I answered, "yes, uncle, of course, I knew that."

"You had been away from home for a while and now I think it was time to assign to you a very important task."

While Sister Nashmeea was fully occupied telling her story, suddenly, the little man with the white turban appeared at the door pushing his wooden cart, followed by the two familiar young girls wrapped in black and keeping law profiles as they used to do their jobs like robots. The little man stopped there on the doorstep, waiting for permission from Sister Nashmeea to make his way in. Sister Nashmeea gave us a fast glance at Ashu and me. When she noticed that we both had our headscarves on, she then gave the little man a signal with her right hand to enter the room. He pushed the pushcart, which was full of a variety of food, close to the dining table.

While the two young girls started moving the food from the cart to the dining table, the little man pulled a walkie-talkie from the top of the cart, holding it high in his right hand, and started moving it from left to right, and from right to left; indicating to Sister Nashmeea that there was a message for her. Sister Nashmeea excused herself, took the instrument from the little man, and rushed in the direction of the door. She disappeared from our sight for a few minutes. Then she came back to tell us that there was an emergency, and she was so sorry to leave us for a while. "Enjoy your lunch, doctors. I will be back as soon as possible."

# Chapter Four

When the girls and the little man left the room, Ashu and I stared at each other for a few seconds with amazement. Again, Sister Nashmeea was telling her story in such a manner as if she was reading from a book. We both felt as if we were being hypnotised while Sister Nashmeea was telling her story.

Once again, we were only the two of us in the room. Ashu gave me a long look as if she wanted to read my mind. As I exchanged her staring silently, she looked at the dinner table and said, "No appetite, I have no appetite to eat." Then she told me that she started feeling stressed. She said that she needed to move or would go for a walk. "How long would we stay like prisoners in this dull room?"

"No, Ashu, we were very close to the objectives of our mission. Walk up and down the room or work out by practicing some press-ups. One wrong move and all that we had achieved already would be washed out." Ashu responded wisely. She said, "Yes, Kameela. You are right, I would always need your wisdom, amiga."

Those words from Ashu gave me great confidence and encouraged me to suggest to her that I thought it was the right time to involve Sister Nashmeea in Jameela's case. I felt that the time was right to admit to Sister Nashmeea that the strong motive behind our charity mission was to explore the destiny of my sister Jameela. I suggested to Ashu that we should explain to Sister Nashmeea our concern about our sister, Jameela, who was wedded under duress from London to the tribes' land; almost nine years ago, and we lost contact with her for the last three years.

Then I explained to Ashu that I was almost certain that Sister Nashmeea would offer her help. Ashu didn't have a ready answer, she looked unsure about what to say. To break her silence and to give Ashu more time to come up with a suitable answer, I urged her to eat some food, and we got through some boiled vegetables that looked reddish, like chard, but we did not know what it was. It tasted good and we munched most of it without hesitation.

Once we finished our dinner, Ashu stood up and rushed to the huge gate of the bungalow, trying to lock it down. When I saw her struggling to place the door close to the frame of the wall, I went and teased her by saying, "Be a humble short lady and ask for help." After we managed to lock the door, we went back to the dining table; not to eat, but to discuss our situation and have some consultations among ourselves regarding our plans.

Suddenly it came to my mind that, initially, we had planned that Jameela, and her plight should come first in our arrangement. That was the real motivation for our volunteering adventure, and this was a pressing fact. I looked Ashu in the eye and said quietly but firmly, "Listen to me, Ashu, isn't time to discuss Jameela's issue with Sister Nashmeea? We were on the edge of the tribes' land where Jameela, my sister, was supposed to be held. Sister Nashmeea knew a lot of people on the surrounding terrain, and I believe she had the right contacts, and knowing her good nature, I would be sure that she would understand our concern and would rush to help us in this matter."

Before Ashu commented on my suggestion, I asked her to go back to her notes that she scrambled at our meeting with Dr Shashi, the director of the organisation, For Overseas Volunteering and Raising Donations, to find out if there was any indication regarding the duration of our mission. Ashu lifted her eyes to the ceiling for a few seconds and then she looked at me and said, "No, Kameela. I did not remember anything of that sort in that meeting, but I remember a clause in one of the applications forms we filled had indicated that the duration of our mission would be within the scope of three months, subject to extension, if necessary. However, I managed to scribble a few shorthand comments in my notepad, let me go back to them and see if I would make some sense out of them."

Ashu reached out to her backpack while I started watching the door. "Did I hear some kind of noise outside the door?" Ashu went quiet for a few seconds. She looked at the door listening carefully, and then she looked at me and came up with a mockery comment, "Wishful thinking, amiga, wishful thinking."

Then she went back fishing for information in her notes book. I was watching her while I was trying to say something funny about her untidy bag. But before I said anything. We heard some light knocking on the door. It was Sister Nashmeea; telling us she was back. It was me who rushed to the door depriving Ashu scoring one more attempt to her usual unsuccessful previous attempts to open that heavy door. Sister Nashmeea appeared at the door with a light smile on her face.

We both stood up and greeted her with a similar smile. She led us to the dining table with her right hand on her heart, a local gesture used to express trust and familiarity. "Please sit down, doctors," and as usual, Sassier Nashmeea occupied the middle chair around the dining table. Ashu and I sat around her, staring and waiting for what she was going to tell us. She apologised for her unexpected absence for about an hour and said, "We had to be very vigilant doctors. We emerged from a well-defined war to enter an undefined one. All fighting groups used to direct their arms toward the communist government and their supporting invaders, the Soviet army, but now, the Soviet army was pulling out, and the communist government in Kabul was in disarray and with all those powerful weapons around, every fitting group would try to hold control over the others; hoping to get a full share in the potential Islamic government.

Hence, now, and then, we had some intruders who were sent by surrounding warlords trying to assess our awareness and our defiance strategy. I had to rush when our guards captured two armed guys encroaching from the eastern borders. After half an hour of interrogations, I had concluded that they were no more than some opportunist abandons looking for unprotected livestock to steal. That was not my specialty, I diverted the case to our committee of the Sharia law."

At this stage, Ashu commented, smiling, "So what would have been our fate, Sister, if our credentials didn't arrive in time from Islamabad?"

"No, it could have been worse," Sister Nashmeea elaborated jokingly, "That is to say, a few days in jail first."

Ashu's response was humorous too, as she said, "Even if I had confessed on the spot?"

Sister Nashmeea returned the joke by saying, "We wouldn't have trusted your confession, doctor. We would have put you in jail for a few days first to extract the truth."

Sister Nashmeea stared for a few seconds at Ashu. Then she shifted her eyes in my direction, adjusted her seat, and said, "I should go back to the main subject before I where left you last time, and enlighten you about that very important talk I had with my uncle, and what had come out of it. My uncle did not surprise me when he mentioned that I had another aunt, her name was Sameeha, and she lived in a city called Coventry in the United Kingdom. I told him I had heard from my mother about her, who mentioned her to me a few times in the past and used to praise her manners and sophistication. I also knew that she was five years younger than my mother and got married at the young age of seventeen. I knew there was a story behind her hasty departure from the country with her husband leaving their land and property behind, just like what people in a trebled country often did.

But to cut their long story short, I never knew why and what had happened to their family till my uncle had put an end to that mystery. He told me that in 1978 when the communist party took over Kabul by a swift military coup, your aunt's husband was holding the position of the chief of staff of the ministry of enterer affairs. Of course, he and the rest of his family went into hiding after the takeover of the leftish junta. An employee in the intelligence section of the ministry managed to smuggle for us a list of those that were to be eliminated by the new regime. Abdulla Shaded, your aunt's husband, and his family were on top of that list.

With the help of the Pakistani Inter-Service Intelligence, we managed to smuggle Abdulla Shaded and Aunt Sameeha to Islamabad, where they managed to contact the British consulate seeking political asylum. It seemed that the British embassy then had already obtained the same secret list that included the names of those who were meant to be eliminated by the allies of the communist regime. Hence, their political asylum status was granted. My uncle then stated that my aunt's family had settled down in the city of Coventry, and he had visited them twice already. He could not remember the year, but he remembered his latest visit a few years ago when he took my aunt Shabnam with him as she needed then some medical treatments.

To that point, I couldn't work out my uncle's aim of his telling till he started talking about the injuries that the Mujahideen were suffering because of the Soviet's airpower's attacks. Then my uncle spelt it out very clearly, explaining to me that at that time, we in the Islamic Front agreed to wedge up a war of attrition, and that would go on for years to come and would require setting up a modern medical Canter under his direct planning and supervision.

Hence, my uncle had decided to put me against that task. He told me he was thinking of enrolling me in a medical course, namely nursing, in Britain in the city of Coventry, where my aunt Sameeha was living. I wanted to look my uncle in the eye, but he got busy thumbing his book. Instead, I took a deep breath to hide my excitement and managed to mumble softly, 'The way you see it, uncle, I would do my very best to execute your plan and your aspiration.'

'Good, he replied, That was my daughter. It would take two weeks to arrange your documents. You would be in the company of your aunt Shabnam who had the experience of travelling to Britain before. She would stay with you for a few weeks to settle your enrolment fees and cover your other expenses. I would arrange for a messenger to contact you and your aunt Sameeha; now and then to inform me about your progress, and to let me know about your needs.'

You could imagine doctors. What could I say? I was over-excited. Overwhelmed. Or just stunned."

At this stage of her story, Sister Nashmeea stared at the wall and closed her eyes for a few seconds as if she was trying to relive those moments again. Then she opened her striking brown eyes wide and adjusted her seat, and stared at Ashu first, then she stared at me as if she was trying to see our reaction to her story in our eyes. Did she notice our utmost interest? She might do.

Looking at the wall again, she heaved a deep sigh and said, "Eventually and after a short silence, I managed to say, I would do my utmost to be up to your expectation, dear uncle. That was at the mid of August 1989. When my uncle explained that the timing of my trip would be more than perfect, as scholarly courses in Britain usually would start by mid-September. Time might fly, and the last two weeks of August had passed like a light dream. The night before our departure, we packed our suitcases and had everything ready. Aunt Shabnam did not forget to include some small badges of local herbs and spices that were known as typical marks of our national dishes.

Had I slept that night? All I remember was the knocking on the door and the voice of Aunt Shabnam telling me that it was four am, and we should be ready within an hour as the minibus that my uncle had arranged for us the night before to drive us to Islamabad airport was already there. Our flight was scheduled for eight-thirty am, and we should attend at the airways deck by 4:30 am. After a hasty breakfast Aunt Shabnam directed the driver who was waiting near the main gate to our suitcases that he collected and placed on a wooden cart and loaded them into the minibus.

My mother was standing in the doorway. She gave Aunt Shabnam a hug and whispered prayers from the holy Koran, and she hugged me with deep affection. Before she resumed her prayers, she begged me not to sit close to the door in the airplane as she heard that doors of airplanes might break open in mid-air. Before we left the house, we went to my uncle's apartment. His bedroom was opened. Aunt Shabnam knocked at his door. He lifted his head and nodded to us to come in. We both entered his room and went closer to his bed. Aunt Shabnam lifted his right hand and kissed it twice. I did the same. He passed his hand over my head and murmured some short verse from the holy Koran and wished us a safe journey.

Islamabad's airport was not too far from Aunt Shabnam's house. It was no more than twenty minutes' drive through which we passed some landmarks that I had never seen before, but did I remember later what they looked like? No way. I was on the bus, but mentally I was miles away. The minibus was passing rather strange trees, and rather unfamiliar buildings, but they all passed in the margin of my mind. Heathrow, Coventry, its famous Cathedral, and the impressive building of the university were the images that kept flashing in my head. My suitcase was light and small in comparison with my aunt's one, but just the same, the driver added it to the trolley that he picked from a nearby bay. I supposed it was left there by a careless passenger.

The atmosphere inside the airport of Islamabad was rather tense. Armed soldiers were walking around in groups of three, and I noticed that some civilians were occupying some corners of the departing corridor, pretending to be passengers, but something in their looks told me that they were too far from being real passengers. They looked in all directions, and they looked alert if any passenger accidentally got separated from his hand luggage. Aunt Shabnam was not as observant as I was, she was busy revising some notes she prepared earlier containing the names of the spices she arranged.

One thing was for sure. Though it was my first time to fly, I was not scared. Well, I believed that I was ascending. Therefore, I was getting close to Allah and his protection. Do not laugh doctors, that was what I felt."

Sister Nashmeea's story regarding her first flying experience was very interesting. She gave us an insight into the reaction of a third world's youth getting involved in our advanced world. While Sister Nashmeea was telling her story, Ashu and I exchanged eyes contacts several times, particularly when Sister Nashmeea expressed her shock when she found out that time in London was five hours behind the time in Islamabad.

Upon arrival to London, Sister, Nashmeea did not hide her admiration and astonishment regarding the high level of organisation and the smooth communications between the various sections at Heathrow airport.

"I just followed the steps of Aunt Shabnam. Everything passed smoothly with minor delays. Once we passed the gate with the sign that reads nothing to declare, we faced a small crowd scattered behind a thick robe. Among them, were Aunt Sameeha and her husband.

I recognised Aunt Sameeha from the first look. She was the middle daughter among her sisters in my mother's family, and she looked like a young version of my mother. My aunt Sameeha hugged me first, and then she hugged Aunt Shabnam passionately. She helped us to put our luggage on a trolley and took us to a waiting point. Minutes passed to see Aunt Sameeha's husband, Uncle Abdullah Shaded, as I politely called him, parking next to us. Both aunties helped him to pack our luggage in the boot of his car, then he drove off along the M40 to Coventry."

Once again, Sister Nashmeea was talking and telling her story as if she was reading from a book till, she was interrupted by Ashu asking her about her studies of English literature and if it was of any help in her communication with her surrounding in Coventry? "That's what I thought in the begging, but no, no doctor. Not in the first two weeks. We used the language at the University of Islamabad to revise for the exam. Memorising the characteristics of old English poetry wouldn't help a young lady to be flaunted in conversing or understanding a local accent in the noisy, crowded marketplace in Coventry. Initially, I thought the people used to talk too fast with a strange accent. That did not last for long. Gradually, I found that most of the people were friendly and eager to help."

We didn't realise how time had passed so fast. It was like a wake-up call when the two little girls appeared at the door, alerting us that it was dinner time, and we should put on our headscarves so that the little man with the white turban could enter the room pushing his wooden cart that was loaded with food. Once the girls finished unloading the food and organising the table, they followed the little man outside the room. The three of us started eating our overdue dinner. I had noticed that Sister Nashmeea was eating with very little appetite. She looked as if she was physical with us, but mentally she had been flung thousands of miles away.

Every few minutes, she would stop eating, stare away from the food, draw a long sigh and repeat softly, "Coventry. What should I tell you about Coventry doctors?

Aunt's Sameeha house was a two-minute walk from the city centre, and buses numbers 17 and 17a used to take me very close to the university's campus. Aunt Sameeha drove me around and showed me the bus's route, and after a few trips to shops and supermarkets, my commutation skill improved, and I felt much more confident about my spoken English. Then came the formality of the registration. Of course, Aunt Sameeha helped me filling the forms, and she had to wait for me at the cafeteria of the university while I went for the interview. The first week went very fast. The lecturer was a very pleasant middle-aged lady.

There were no more than twenty-two students in the class: fifteen girls and seven boys. When I was asked to introduce myself, I claimed that I was of Pakistani nationality trying not to contradict the information on my passport and my registration forms. Most of the students looked local except one guy who looked like one of our people. His light dark skin and melancholic wide brown eyes could tell a lot. He was sitting in the left corner of the row behind me. I used to sneak a fast look at him, every time I had the chance to do so during the lecture, trying not to attract his attention. When he introduced himself, he said his name was Nabeel Khaleel. Originally, he came to the country as a political refugee from Chile.

Exactly, by the second week of the course, I was down in the cafeteria of the university, sitting there waiting for my tea to settle and cool down to take my first sip, and while I was staring at some notes in my notebook, I heard that deep shy voice asking permission to join my table. I lifted my head to see who was the guy who asked to join me my table? Yes, it was him, Nabeel. When our eyes met, he repeated his request by saying, 'Can I?'

I tried hard to hide my excitement, and managed to say, 'Please, of course, you can.' I said it with an obvious welcoming voice. Since that Wednesday, Nabeel and I have been together during every break. He was smart talkative, open-minded, and great conversational. He was born, as he informed me, in Chile to Lebanese parents and got involved at an early stage of his life with a leftist student organisation that was implicated in the struggle against the dictatorship of Augusto Pinochet. However, he explained to me that when a secret document of the Pinochet regime leaked to the public, and his name appeared among those who should be eliminated by the regime's security, he fled the country.

It was a rather complicated story, but the outcome was that he had got his refugee status there, in Coventry.

Nabeel was a committed and great believer in his cause. For me, he was a fresh window through to a new world. Agree or disagree with him, it was a pleasure to discuss with him. Nabeel did not believe in religion as such, except for its call for justice.

Otherwise, he was a strong believer in human rights and a devoted advocator of women's rights. I had to admit that I sometimes disagreed with some of his ideas regarding religions, but I also had to admit that deep down inside I used to think that he could be right, when he used to express his doubt about the theory of creation as it was specified by religions."

Sister Nashmeea stopped talking and picked the teapot from the table and cautiously touched it from the side, "It is still warm, I didn't like my tea to be too hot."

She slowly poured some tea into her mug. Then she rolled her eyes between Ashu and me silently. By that glance, she might have made sure that we were both following up on her tale and very keen to know the rest of her story.

Sister Nashmeea reached to her mug, she rubbed her nose with her left hand, and pulled a sip of her still worm tea. She took a fast glance, first at me and then at Ashu. Then she fixed her eyes on her mug and said.

"You know, doctors, I was brought up in an Islamic environment, and believed in my uncle's teaching: it was fine to explore a variety of theories, but one was not obliged to adopt any new one or change his conviction easily. You see, doctors, I learnt a lot from Nabeel, but I fixed to my original identity, a Muslim woman from Afghanistan.

From my short time living in Coventry, I also learnt, that our communities abroad represented a typical sample of our societies at home. They all carried a bit of curiosity, and most of them were fond of gossip. I was not aware of the one or two Pakistani girls in the course. I wanted to practice my English and explore different cultures. Therefore, there were no motives for me to befriend any of them. However, it seemed I was not excluded from their topics at home. They found in my friendship with Nabeel an exciting subject, and they would create some tells around it."

Ashu put her left hand on the table to attract Sister Nashmeea attention and said, "I am sorry to interrupt you, Sister, but it sounded typical of our community in Hounslow Central. Our people were the same even if they went to Mars."

We all smiled. However, Ashu, by her comment, managed to relax our tense atmosphere.

"You were right, doctor, so it didn't surprise me when Aunt Sameeha asked me, in a shy manner, a sneaky question about my friendship with Nabeel. Well, I suppose that friendship became obvious when we had the summer break. Coventry had beautiful parks and were open to the public. So Nabeel used to phone me now and then and invited me for a walk around the leafy parts of the city. It was a great romantic pleasure to sit on a wooden bench in the shed of the trees discussing and liking our milky ice creams."

At that stage of Sister's Nashmeea story, Ashu and I started looking at each other. When Sister Nashmeea paused for a few seconds, Ashu looked at me and said, "Wow, nice, we had all that natural charm around us in the UK, and it would pass unnoticed."

Sister Nashmeea dropped a fast comment, "Oh well a relaxing nature would call for good company." She said it with a meaningful smile.

At that moment, Sister Nashmeea had loosened her headscarf a bit around her neck. Then she cleared her throat and said.

"And you know, doctors, the common proverb: good things never last. First, the obstacles came in the form of advice from Aunt Sameeha. It was Friday afternoon, when I took one of my course books to the back garden of Aunt Sameeha's house, and I sat on one of the plastic chairs and started thumbing my book casually. Before I settled on a subject to read, Aunt Sameeha came with a plate in her hand. She pulled a chair and sat next to me. Before I said anything, she handed me the plait saying, it is time to test the cake baked by your aunt. I looked, and it was a beautifully decorated piece of cake with a fork.

Of course, I thanked Aunt Sameeha and put the plate in my lap. After a few bites of the cake, I gave Aunt Sameeha a sincere compliment. We talked about a variety of things, and then the subject touched upon my subjects in the course. Everything was normal till Aunt Sameeha said I am glad that you had a friend in your classroom, otherwise, the school would be boring. But darling, you should be careful. A friendship between a male and a female could eventually develop into something serious, and you would suffer then if that relationship could not be fulfilled.

Aunt Sameeha was talking without looking at me. I gathered some courage and said to Aunt Sameeha that if she meant it might be developed into marriage. I promised her that the thought of marriage never crossed my mind. She agreed with what I said, 'But she said you would not be a spinster for the rest of your life. In our Islamic culture, we would believe that marriage is a fulfilment of religion.'

Then she looked me in the eye and elaborated, 'In your case, about that guy, it would be impossible that your uncle would approve of you marrying a non-Muslim fellow.'

Here I opened my mouth wide and looked Aunt Sameeha in the eye, and asked if Nabeel was not a Muslim? She was fast to say all the Pakistani community in Coventry knew that fact. I was astonished and told Aunt Sameeha that Nabeel and I discussed the issue of religions several times, but neither he nor I ever mentioned our religions. I believe it was rather our sophisticated approach to keep our discussion impersonal.

Surely that chat with Aunt Sameeha had its impact on me. It made me thoughtful and apprehensive, but it had no impact on my attitude toward Nabeel, who had become a part of my life during my time in Coventry. Time went on, and I was pleased to attend my second year of the course. Nothing changed till I received that letter from my uncle. It seemed that a fellow passenger had posted it from London.

However, despite the bad handwriting and the lousy layout of Aunt Sameeha's address on the envelope, the letter was received. Aunt Sameeha noticed that on the top of the sealed envelope was the word 'Nashmeea.' Aunt Sameeha concluded that the letter was for me, and it was personal. She handed it to me upon my arrival home. The letter was from my uncle. It was short and informative.

My uncle was telling me that so many developments had taken place during my absence, and he felt that my presence next to him for that time had become more than pressing and more than necessary. Then he urged me to leave everything behind and take the first airplane to Islamabad as soon as possible. A request from my uncle that I can't possibly argue or even debate.

I put the letter aside and stared at Aunt Sameeha, who was holding a pot in her lap and sorting out a pile of vermicelli, preparing them to be cocked. She stopped what she was doing and directed her full attention to me. Before she opened her mouth to say something, I told her that my uncle wanted me back home. She opened her mouth in surprise and hushed up for a while. Then she gave me a very serious look and asked me when I would be ready to travel?

My answer came straight. I was ready, Aunt Sameeha, right now. Ready without any delay. My travelling from Islamabad to London was made easy in the company of Aunt Shabnam. But Aunt Shabnam travelled back to Islamabad after she stayed with us in Coventry for two weeks. Now I should travel back to Islamabad on my own. The first leg of my travelling would be easy. Aunt Sameeha and her husband would arrange all the necessary bookings, and they would drive me to Heathrow airport in time.

Aunt Sameeha noticed that I was a bit puzzled. So, she told me not to worry. She explained to me that once she got the details of my flight, she would phone Aunt Shabnam and ask her to receive me at Islamabad airport. Within one week, I was here at the edge of the civilisation, at the geographical boundaries of the tribes' land."

Ashu asked Sister Nashmeea curiously, "Did you meet Nabeel before your departure?"

"Yes, of course, I explained to him that the only way to reach me was to write to me by the care of Aunt Shabnam's address. I explained to him also that I Wouldn't be close by to answer his messages promptly. It could be months before I put my hand on his letters and months before I get somebody who could deliver my letters to an area with a post office service. He expressed his understanding and presented me with a nice book called The Prophet, a kind of a prose-poetry by Khaleel Gibran, a poet of Lebanese origin who lived in the States and was acclaimed worldwide recognition. It was a wonderful book. I used to keep it next to my pillow and go back to it whenever I felt a bit depressed. After I would read a few quotations from the book, I would feel great."

Ashu looked at me first, to see if I had any exclamation or a relevant comment. When she noticed that I was not all there, and my eyes rather empty or you might say, blank, she directed her eyes to Sister Nashmeea again and asked in a shy voice, "But sorry, Sister, what was that book all about?"

Sister Nashmeea looked like she was happy with the question, as I could read from her face. "The book doctor was about life, life itself. It was very touching in its poetic style and its spiritual, romantic language. Unintentionally, I found myself repeating, or even memorising some quotations from the book. For example, unconsciously, sometimes I find myself mumbling the quotation, 'Make sure always to leave a space in your togetherness and let the winds of the breeze of heavens between you.' Or 'When love signals you to follow him do, though his ways are hard and steep.'"

Ashu brought me back to the reality of the room when she said with obvious admiration, "Wow, Sister, I like it. I like it. I wouldn't dare to ask you to lend me your copy, that would be grossly unfair, I would buy myself a copy as soon as I can."

Sister Nashmeea was flattered to hear Ashu's comment. She covered her forehead with her right palm and closed her eyes, trying to remember more quotations from the book, but Ashu intercepted her thoughts by asking her, with

47

astonishment in her voice, "How did she move from Islamabad to the settlement?"

Sister Nashmeea smiled broadly and said, "The gangway, through the gangway." I didn't think that Ashu understood the answer, but she nodded her head, pretending that she got the idea. My concern was the reasons that obliged Sister Nashmeea uncle to ask her to cut her studies and come back hastily to the troubled land. So, Sister Nashmeea got the idea when I asked her about the changes she noticed in the scene upon her return. There, Sister Nashmeea put on a serious face, and said, "There were drastic changes, doctor."

Suddenly, the little man with a white turban appeared outside the door, appointing at Sister Nashmeea with his wacky-tacky. Sister Nashmeea excused herself and rushed in his direction, while hastily looking backwards rapidly and wished us a very good night.

# Chapter Five

I had been lying down on my mattress bed for at least half an hour, jogging my memory, trying to find out what I almost had lost truck off. I needed help to work it out what day of the week I was. I thought, but I was not sure; that the day was our fourth day in that dump, boring bungalow. Ashu was already agitating, but I constantly calmed her down by telling her that we had to understand that Sister Nashmeea was a consultant in her uncle's team. Hence, I believe that she was waiting for his instructions to set up our program. It looked like Sister Nashmeea was involved in several issues of her uncle's complicated daily schedules. In the meantime, I started to feel that Sister Nashmeea had become rather a close friend.

I was almost sure of that and had taken it for granted. I started to believe it was the right time to ask her directly about what was planned for us. I was debating if it was the time to drop the formality and talk to her number of things, freely and openly without hesitation or lateness. I tried several times to share my thoughts with Ashu, but Ashu used to listen to me attentively, and used to keep her thoughts to herself. She used to repeat, "Yes, Kameela, but was there any way to speed things up?"

Then she used to add, "On some occasions, I felt I was close to caving in."

In a situation like that, I would hold her hand and say, "Please, Ashu, you should give me an opinion. We were close to the target of our mission; please don't spoil it at that advanced stage."

I was over-occupied with the most pressing issue of our mission. It was my sister Jameela's mysterious destiny and her puzzling fate. After all, that was the real reason behind our complicated adventure in this troubled terrain. At this point in my silent debate, I felt I was just waiting for the right time to open the subject with Sister Nashmeea.

I would be direct and ask her, or rather beg her to use her influence and her uncle's contacts with the dignitaries of the tribes' land and take me to Jameela, or bring Jameela to me, though I knew that would not be an easy task. It could

49

be no more than a couple of miles between Jameela and me, geographically speaking, but they were the longest two miles on earth.

Yesterday, I watched Sister Nashmeea closely while she was engrossed in her telling. From my observation, I concluded that she was enjoying her subject. She might think that our presence in her terrain; could help to open a worldwide window for her country's dilemma. That was what had come to my mind. Of course, that was before she was interrupted and summoned to her chief or most likely to her uncle in the middle of our meeting. Though she rushed out for the call, but I noticed a sign of irritation on her face.

As usual, later, it was Ashu and I who were left staring silently at each other. After a few seconds of silence, I had to confess to Ashu that I was feeling tired or rather mentally exhausted, and I needed to refuge to my mattress bed as soon as possible. I felt; that was the only way I would compensate for some missing sleeping hours. Ashu was sitting on her mattress bed, thumbing through her messy notebook. I interrupted her rather cheekily by saying, "Listen amiga, tell your jackals friends not to disturb my sleep tonight."

Ashu rushed to say, "Don't you worry, Kameela. You scared them away. I didn't hear them around for the last three nights." Ashu dropped her notebook and went to her mattress bed too. As usual, once Ashu put her head on the pillow, her shrill sound of whistling would start, indicating that she had passed out.

What about me? And despite my tiredness, I would struggle in my mattress bed for hours, exploring thought after thought and fighting away undesirable images till the small hours of the morning. Eventually, I believed I must have slept for a few hours, or I should say I had passed out for a few hours. When I opened my eyes, I could see a frail ray of light striking through the high lookout in the back wall of the bungalow. I sensed that it was still early morning. My feeling told me that Sister Nashmeea would visit us early that day. However, I was feeling tired and short of sleep, but I thought that was not important.

Despite my exhaustion, I was hoping to keep going just to see an end for our monotony. Of course, my sister Jameela was occupying the centre of my mind. Though I started to feel rather anxious. Nothing in our surroundings could give us a hope except Sister Nashmeea's cooperative and understanding attitude. However, things were moving slowly, and we were cautious not to say or ask any question that might abort our aim prematurely. So, Ashu agreed with me that we better wait before raising the question regarding Jameela. It was better to see what was planned for us first.

In essence, we were no more than captives, and since our foots had touched that land, we lost our willpower. Hence, we used to listen very cautiously to what Sister Nashmeea was telling us. She was the only hope that might help us achieving our target by contacting my sister Jameela.

When I heard Sister Nashmeea's voice close to the door telling us to be ready, a phrase that was always meant to alert us to put on our headscarves, as we always did in the presence of a man. As I expected, the man was the same little guy with the white turban, which looked like the soft white mushroom; I used to see in the local fields in Hounslow Central at our primary school's picnics in springtime.

The little man, as usual, never looked left or right. He was always up to the job. He moved like a robot, assisted by the same two teenage girls ready there to help. It would take him a couple of minutes to clear the table of the old staff and re-load it with what he would bring with him on his wooden cart.

Once the little man and the two girls finished arranging the food, they would systematically bow slightly; with their right hands on their hearts and speed out of the bungalow. Then, as always, Sister Nashmeea would join us for our breakfast and try to cheer us up. That was her good nature and that would stay with her most of the times. For example, that day; was reflected by her comment on Ashu's remark. When Ashu said that the tea was too sweet that day. "The sweet for the sweet doctor," Sister Nashmeea said with a broad smile on her face. Then she said, "Apologies, doctor. It was three years ago when we had that sugar scarcity in our settlement, and the guys in the kitchen started adding sugar to the tea while it was brewing. Though I doubted their method, which they called sugar rationing. Oh well, who could argue with the chef?"

However, despite Sister's Nashmeea hummer, I felt that she had something important to tell us. She adjusted her seat more times than usual and glanced at the door more often. When she noticed that we were not busy eating anymore, she reclined against the back of her chair and concentrated her look at the opposite wall, and said, "You know, doctors, my uncle was an excellent strategic man, but when there was a war that bred a civil war, things easily could go out of hand, and plans should be changed or adjusted accordingly."

When Sister Nashmeea finished her sentence, I sensed like butterflies invaded my stomach. Several questions occurred in my head. The most terrifying question that alarmed me rigorously was if the time of our mission was coming to an end. What about my sister Jameela? Would we leave without her news after getting so close to her possible location? I was only speculating.

I decided to stay calm and see what Sister Nashmeea was trying to explain! Sister Nashmeea was not in a hurry. She stretched her lips and said, while her eyes were still fixed on the opposite wall, "I am sorry, doctors, but I felt that I was obliged to put you in the right picture of our muddled situation. To do that, I should start briefing you distinctly the sequence of events right from the beginning of 1980s. That was when the fighting of the Mujahideen against the red army intensified. At that time, as my uncle explained to me that the Mujahedeen groups, including my uncle's had joined an accord under the banner of The Islamic Front for the Liberation of Afghanistan. The front was a kind of a pact based on the common objectives of the participating groups in fighting the invaders.

The fighting groups used to exchange information and their fighting used to take place according to a continuous consultation and planning. In the meantime, it was reported that the brutality of the red army had been intensified. By mid-1985, half of Afghanistan's population had been displaced. They were scattered across the countries of the neighbouring borders, namely Pakistan and Iran. My uncle clarified to me that by that time our fighting groups had received incredible number casualties.

To face that grave situation, my uncle had ordered his loyalists to build up two medical lounges to accommodate the wounded. He aimed to give the injured worriers a resting place and to receive some initial first aid and some urgent treatments before they could be transferred to hospitals in Pakistan.

He also told me that, 'Some medical personnel with their medical equipment used to come to our settlement and offered their services in accordance with the Islamic Front Agreement. But by August 1996, the Islamic Accord started to crack down, and Arabs and their aliens of the orphans of the border's schools started gathering under the name of Taliban supported by an influx of volunteers of the tribes' men from the Pashtuns tribes' land. All joined forces and started to take over the fighting groups, one by one. That had initiated a classic recipe for a typical civil war and marked the beginning of the globalisation of the Afghanistan conflict.'

Then my uncle added that more than thirty-three Muslim countries, mainly from the gulf region started sending hundreds and thousands of volunteers to the border area of Pakistan to join what they used to call the Islamic Jihad in

Afghanistan. Consequently, as my uncle explained, Afghanistan's fate was no longer in the hands of the Afghanistan's people. I was rather impressed by my uncle's knowledge when he told me that historically, a global pan-Muslim organisation founded by a religious teacher in the late 1920 in Egypt as a charity raising group had mushroomed all over the Islamic world with countless violent clusters of clandestine organisations that were working to impose their version of fanatic Islam wherever they could, under the name of Muslims' Brotherhood.

All these gelatinous octopus-like; organisations found in the war in Afghanistan as their golden opportunity to implement their rigid Islamic ideology by setting up an Islamic Emirate. My uncle explained that the advocators of that ideology of the oil-rich Arabian Gulf region planned to extend their influence in the area much earlier than the Soviet invasion. Taking advantage of the poverty and the backwardness of the people in the area, the leaders of the Arabian Gulf utilised the financial windfall they received out of the energy crisis of 1973 that was resulted by the Arab Israeli conflict. They reach out to our neighbouring country of Pakistan by donating large amounts of money to individuals and some governmental institutions. That gained them some serious influence over the country.

In the meantime, they embarked on several impressive projects that were badly needed in the country, such as bridges, mosques, and road paving, that connected the settlements across the country. Even they constructed a town and marked it with their names and religious mottos.

My uncle believed that, inevitably, the messy presence of the Arabs, or the 'Arab Afghan' as they were called, had created within them a conflict that prevailed all over the country.

One of the most dominating figures of the 'Arab Afghan' was an organiser known as Abu Abdulla Azzam. He was the founder of the House of Services in the border city of Peshawar. The House was a bureau or an establishment that used to hold lists of names of the Mujahideen of the Arab Afghan groups who were accommodated in that house. Besides the Mujahideen names, the lists used to contain their training progress, skills, and military ranks. The lists also organised the distribution of weapons, combat apparatus and medical needs among the fighters related to the organisation, the House of Services.

On the other end of the equation of the 'Arab Afghan' grouping, there was another character known as, Usama bin Laden. He was very rich manipulating character. He stood out with his rigid vision regarding the prospect of the Islamic

Emirate of Afghanistan. Bin Laden thought that the rising power of military Islam was undefeatable. As it had defeated the red army, it would be able to fight and defeat another superpower, the Western power, to extend the principles of Islam all over the world. This vision contradicted Azzam's personal vision, who believed that they should take the emerging power of Islam to sort out serious political injustice in the Middle East. However, that disagreement didn't come to the surface. That was to say, only a few high ranks of Islamist Mujahideen were aware of it.

My uncle then told me with some astonishment that, in 1989, in the heat of that conflict Azzam, together with his two sons were killed in Peshawar by a powerful landmine that exploded under their car while they were on their way to a mosque for Friday prayers.

Of course, rumours circulated that Bin Laden was behind the murder of Azzam. Bin Laden denied the accusation publicly through an Arabic media outlet. As you might have noticed, doctors, the two characters controlling the scene, had settled their differences in a gang-style despite their common objectives, which were to promote their version of Islam Salafi Islam. At any rate, the murder of Azzam at that time gave Bin Laden a free hand over all those on the battlefield."

Sister Nashmeea stopped talking for a few seconds, then quizzed me with a very direct question: "Doctor Kameela, please you shouldn't be bashful if you didn't know the answer. Did you know the meaning of Salafi?" When Sister Nashmeea noticed I was puzzled and stared at Ashu for help, she smiled and said, "Don't you worry, doctor, I was only testing your Arabic." Then Sister Nashmeea added, "As it happened, it was evident that we had exchanged the Soviet invaders by groups of worriers known as the Arab Afghans. We had no options but to learn some of their terminologies."

Ashu thought that Sister Nashmeea had put me in an awkward situation. She cracked a short laugher and put her right hand up, pretending that she knew the meaning of Salafi. "Fine, doctor Ashu, surprise us with your knowledge!"

Sister Nashmeea dropped her comment with a wicked smile while her eyes were still fixed on me. Ashu looked unsure about what to say. She mumbled a few confused words and started looking at me for assistance. I felt I had to come up with something even if I wasn't sure. To help Ashu out of her embarrassment. I directed my eyes at Sister Nashmeea and said in a low voice, "I think Sister, the meaning of Salafi was a fanatic."

Sister Nashmeea smiled and said, "Not a bad guessing doctor; I knew you would come with something creditable. I am only telling you some fact about our recent history to explain our present reality. Salafi was a word of Arabic root. Its precise meaning was an ancestor; that was to say, a Salafi was a Muslim who belonged to a sect that confined their conduct, practice, and lifestyle to become identical to the life of the ancestors Muslims, namely the prophet of Islam and his companions. That was to say, our societies should adhere to the same rules and traditions of those early Muslims who lived more than fourteen centuries ago.

For that purpose, they built up huge, isolated compounds at the western borders of the Pakistan very close to the Pakistani borders, and named them the madrasas, meaning in Arabic the schools. But those schools were not like other schools. Those who attended the compounds of madrasas had multiplied in a very short time. The buildings accommodated thousands of orphans who were driven to those asylums by the severity of the conflicts. They took refuge in those border compounds in complete isolation from the outside world and were lectured daily by Salafi fanatics, who were so-called Guides.

The camps of those madrasas were confined to male societies. They were taught or rather dictated by those self-appointed teachers. Most of them were of Pashtun's origin, and they were hardly literate. They were uncultured, self-proclaimed teachers whose knowledge of Islam was completely distorted. Hence, those so-called students, Taliban, in the Pashto language, were brainwashed and converted into no more than misinformed savages. They did not learn any craft, and they did not approach any field of knowledge or science. Therefore, they were easily conscripted by the one-eyed militia leader who appeared from nowhere by the late stage of the civil war, that was inflamed among the fighting groups in the wake of the withdrawal of the Soviet troops from Afghanistan between 1988 and 1989.

The fall of the Marxist government in Kabul on 15th August of the year 1992 enabled Taliban militant entering Kabul without noticeable resistance. However, till then, Taliban were not in control of the entire country. The powerful forces of the Hazara sect in the north was still representing a huge challenge to their advances."

When Sister Nashmeea reached that stage of her briefing, I remembered very well how Sheika Shahnaz came to London searching for a bride for her son Akrum Siraj-al Deen Safi, and the way she presented him to the Afghan community by insisting that he was a madrasas graduate giving the impression that he was highly educated!

Sister Nashmeea noticed my distracted inattention, but that confusion did not last more than a few seconds. Sooner, Sister Nashmeea noticed that I was giving her my full attention again. She smiled and resumed her briefing by saying, "At that time, my uncle told me that it was the start of the formation of the alliance of three fanatic evolving groups. The Taliban of the camps, the Arab Afghans, and the Pashtuns tribes. All have one peculiar social attitude toward women. They strongly believed that their disrespect for women was derived from their religious doctrine. Women would play no part in their society.

Girls from the age of eight can't venture to the street unless they were in the company of an adult male related to their own families. In addition, women were not allowed to go to schools, were not allowed to hold a public job and should always be covered all over with a traditional garment known as a burqa. The burqa would cover the woman all over, allowing her a few netted inches, a sort of window in front of her eyes so that she would see her way around. At the top of their attitude toward women, they believed that the tv, the music, football, high heels and make-up, video machines, tape recorders, computers, Christmas cards and so many things that had become part of human lives were all forbidden according to their Sharia, Law of Islam.

Compared with those groundless rules, my uncle was fairly educated and knowledgeable Mullah. He believed in moderate Islam. He often used to repeat a well-known verse from the Koran that made it very clear by calling for there should be no compulsion in religion. Islam, in short, my uncle believed that should be incorporated into the constitution of the country. That was to say, it should be implemented to organise the affairs of Muslims regarding marriages, divorcés, legal debates, and other court rulings.

Otherwise, people should be left to their faith; and would enjoy their civil rights on equal stand, away from the pressure of the clergymen. When my uncle would remember the crackdown of the Islamic Front under the pressure of the Arab Afghan and their Taliban's alliance, my uncle used to pull a deep sigh and repeat, uttering one sentence: 'Very bleak. The future of our country looked very bleak.'"

Suddenly, there was an explosion followed by gun shootings. The sounds were coming from the right side, from behind the bungalow. Then it was followed by repeated separated gunfire. Sister Nashmeea stayed calm, but Ashu jumped from her chair and went under the table. I was only mystified and stared inquisitively at Sister Nashmeea. Sister Nashmeea ignored my questioning eyes; she bent her head under the table and said firmly, "Doctor, please don't worry, it was a training session for some new Mujahideen trainees at the slope of the hill, just behind us. I was informed about it yesterday, but I forgot to tell you."

Then she smiled and said, "I apologise for your shock, Doctor Ashu." Ashu was back on her chair; looking in all directions, embarrassed with visibly shaky hands. Sister Nashmeea reached for an empty mug on the table; she filled it with water and handed it to Ashu, requesting her to drink some; so that she might calm down. After three to four minutes, everything in our getting-together looked back to normal.

Sister Nashmeea adjusted her seat, gave both of us fleeting look and said, "What I was telling you, doctors, was rather important. That explains some episodes of your mission and the phase we were in. I found it important to explain that Azzam's assassination had a drastic impact on the conflict and made so drastic changes in the flow of events. First, the whole command and power shifted to the hands of Bin Laden. He rounded up all the names of the recruits of the Service House and organised them according to their ages and skills in his laptop. And second, he planned that list to be his own base or al-Qaida in Arabic for recruiting and implementing his future distorted religious and political agenda.

While all those concerned were oblivious to notice the dubious intentions of Bin Laden, my uncle was very apprehensive and unhappy about his intentions. In addition to his military early control of the border province of Kandahar, Bin Laden used his wealth to negotiate arms deals with the supporting powers, including some western governments. In August 1986, after bin Laden agreed to pay the transport cost of weapons shipments, the supporting countries intensified their arms flow to his segment of the fighters. The shipments included Stinger anti-aircraft missiles. That put an end to the superiority of Soviet airpower on the battlefields and directly contributed to the final withdrawal of the Soviet troops from Afghanistan on the fifteenth of February 1989.

At that stage, Bin Laden assumed that his group of Islamists fighters had defeated an established superpower. Bin Laden started to believe that his version of Islam if stimulated, would be a giant unbeatable power. Hence, my uncle realised that Bin Laden was planning to set up an Islamic Emirate in Afghanistan that would take us into a conflict with the entire world.

Motivated by those alarming thoughts, my uncle decided to build up our local medical centre. At the peak of the war, my uncle arranged to finance a building of a strategic structure at the foot of the hill that separated our settlement from the tribes' land. The building was surrounded by a high fence and watched over by armed men twenty-four hours a day. It contained two huge medical wards, each with twenty beds and five mobile stretchers.

In addition, it included a complex of four independent rooms above the halls of the building completely separated from the medical wards and supplied with suitable furniture for use by the potential medical staff. Plus, there was a separate flight steps, away from the wards that led to well-furnished two bedrooms for staff who would stay overnight in the medical complex. We had six hastily trained male nurses who used to provide the injured fighters with the necessary first aid. In addition, we arranged to smuggle the seriously hurt fighters through the gangway to a designated hospital in Islamabad.

After the supply of the Stinger anti-aircraft missiles to the fighters in Kandahar, as my uncle used to explained that the characteristics of that era had changed. He told me that we received fewer or almost no casualties from the battlefields. On the other hand, most of the medical supplies we used to receive from the hub of the Islamic Front have been reduced to very little or near to nothing.

The Islamic front, as a political-military and resistant entity, had been frozen and replaced by a new vicious alliance between Bin Laden and the Salafi thugs who used to be led by the one-eyed Mullah, who was earlier no more than leader of a small group that was hardly participated in the fighting against the Soviet army. That was the time when my uncle started seeking medical help; first from Islamabad and then from international organisations.

Your organisation doctors thankfully acknowledged our request, but after years of waiting. You might be aware doctors, as one of the British politician put it, one week in politics is a very long time. Wars and politics have been interacting in our land continuously and for a long time."

Her Ashu jumped the gun and said, "Thatcher, Margret Thatcher, who coined that phrase." I had to shut Ashu up nicely by telling her not to talk nonsense.

Sister Nashmeea smiled broadly and said, "Doctor Kameela, I think you love to disagree with your friend Doctor Ashu."

"No, Sister Nashmeea, but if you would quote Ashu from Shakespeare and ask her to relate the quote to somebody, she would say without hesitation,

Margret Thatcher. It happened that I knew it was Harold Wilson, a previous British prime minister who had coined that saying."

We all laughed, including Ashu, who repeated, "Admiration, admiration I admire lady Thatcher." After that funny little split, Sister Nashmeea continued her briefing about the history of the armed conflict in her country. Again, she sounded confident, linking the past events with the present. Ashu raised her right hand, intercepting Sister Nashmeea. She appeared as if she had a serious question.

When Sister Nashmeea paid Ashu her full attention, Ashu asked curiously, "But excuse me, Sister Nashmeea, how did you use to get your information? Well, I meant what was your position in the hierarchy of your uncle's group?"

It was obvious from her facial expression that Sister Nashmeea was so pleased with Ashu's question. She confirmed proudly; that whenever she was around, she would function as an informal consultant for her uncle, who had reliable informers inside, almost every fighting group, as well as reliable ones in some governmental offices; in both Afghanistan and Pakistan.

"According to my uncle's sources, the war of attrition that was wedged by the Islamic Front against the red army and the communist government in Kabul took so many turns. From 1997 onward, with the help of the Pakistani Inter-Service Intelligence, the borders of the Pakistani province of Peshawar and its capital city Peshawar itself, became a training camp to prepare international recruits for fighting the Soviet troops in Afghanistan. Since then, it became obvious that the problem of Afghanistan, whether we liked it or not; had become a globalised issue."

At that stage of Sister Nashmeea's briefing, I felt rather baffled; several questions started buzzing in my head. However, I thought I shouldn't interpret the chain of Sister Nashmeea's thoughts.

The three of us exchanged eye contact. Sister Nashmeea was trying to evaluate the impact of her rather detailed briefing on us, and Ashu and I were trying to understand a meaningful picture of that muddled situation in Afghanistan. Hence, she went silent for a few seconds and said, "Let me explain something, doctors. All my knowledge of people and events were gathered from my uncle's experience."

Then Sister Nashmeea cleared her throat and said, "I would like to shed some more light on the personality of my uncle. First, I would strongly believe that my uncle was a principled character at the centre of confusing events. My uncle got his early education at a religious school. Still, he achieved good general knowledge through his private readings and travelling and his continuous meetings with officials and dignitaries."

Altogether, from what she had already said, Sister Nashmeea was proud to emphasise that her uncle Mullah Abdul Rahman was very modest in his life, and religious views.

She also explained that the Mullah participated in the fighting against the red army by a well-organised military unit that carried his name. It was an active participant among the other fighting groups under the pact of the Islamic Front.

From that point in history, again Sister Nashmeea moved to the present. She said, "However doctors, due to the messy armed conflict, my uncle decided to act independently, keeping his contacts with powerful centres in Islamabad to secure the safety of our enclave. In the meantime, he used his diplomatic skill to avoid clashing with the emerging alliance and their savage militants.

When my uncle instructed me to cut my nursing course in the UK and come back to our hamlet, he was hoping to supply the medical complex with all that it would need of equipment and the necessary staff to convert it into a high-standard medical hub, aiming to serve our community and beyond. Circumstances changed, and that hope had gone astray.

We have been cleaning and refurbishing the compound since your arrival at our settlement. Tomorrow morning, after breakfast, we will arrange to move you there. At the compound would be two decent bedrooms, one for each of you, plus a well-served cafeteria where you could relax and have food. The medical compound contained pharmacy-like storage with boxes of packs of medicine donated by groups, organisations, and individuals in the past. A lot of that medicine, such as medical bandages, painkiller tablets, and other things that don't require refrigeration, could still be valuable.

In contrast, heaps of other types could had been expired. That would be your task tomorrow. It might take you a few days to sort those boxes out. When you would state that the job was fulfilled, I would arrange for you to meet my uncle who insisted on thanking you personally and supply you with a formal certificate endorsed by his signature and his formal stamp to present to your organisation as a recognition of your kind participating in our undertaking."

Once again, I felt alerted about Jameela's case. When Sister Nashmeea stood up to wish as good night, she looked relaxed, more than usual. I was unsure if I glanced a smile on her face, but Ashu later thought that was my imagination.

Sister Nashmeea was getting close to completing our mission, but the task still needed to start for me. Once Sister Nashmeea left the bungalow, I rushed to close the gate behind her and came back to stand in the middle of the room. Ashu was rather surprised by my fast movement. She was still glued to her chair, staring at me curiously, waiting for me to say something. I felt a bit numb. I was looking at Ashu silently in the eye. Ashu kept quiet. She kept her eyes fixed in my direction without uttering a word.

# Chapter Six

Our breakfast today had passed very fast. Sister Nashmeea left the breakfast table and went close to the door gazing at the vast horizon expecting something or somebody to show up. Ashu was still munching her last piece of bread that she dipped in her favourite golden colour, natural organic honey. I stood up silent in the middle of the room, shifting my eyes between Sister Nashmeea and amiga Ashu. I was occupied with my thoughts, trying to determine the number of days and nights we had lived in this bungalow or rather, this confinement. Two days ago, Ashu claimed, we had been living here either six or seven days. The problem was I didn't trust her sense of time, just as I couldn't rely on my own. Oh well, two or three days would not make much difference.

Things were changing and I would better gather my courage and refine my strategy regarding my ultimate hope, finding out the whereabouts of my sister Jameela. My thoughts were interrupted or shuttered when Sister Nashmeea suddenly looked back and said, "Have you packed your suitcases, doctors?"

I responded with a vague smile and told Sister Nashmeea, that there wasn't much to pack; a few garments and a pair of shoes we stuck on top of everything. "Good, we better be prepared. They could be here at any minute."

Sister Nashmeea was right. A few minutes passed when I started to hear a kind of roaring in the distance. I looked at Ashu and asked, "Do you hear that noise?"

Ashu pulled an old handkerchief from the edge of the dining table. She wiped her lips and said, "Helicopter. A helicopter ride, that would be an experience." I told her to shut up and asked to be serious.

A few minutes later, a roaring of a converted military vehicle came closer. It arrived from nowhere, crept slowly and parked next to the bungalow's gate. With a gesture from Sister Nashmeea, we went out to the vehicle carrying our packages on our shoulders. I examined the vehicle with curious eyes. The front of the vehicle looked like a heavy-duty lorry, while the body was like a normal van. It was painted all over with a camouflage of green-yellowish colour. It had one big door at the back that was left open to the right.

While the vehicle's engine was still running, Sister Nashmeea looked back at the inside of the bungalow to ensure that nothing was left behind. She noticed that we both had put on our headscarves already. So, she didn't need to alert us this time. She entered the bungalow, followed by the little man with the white turban. She whispered to him a few words in Dari. Without hesitation, the little man picked up our small suitcases, one in each hand and brought them close to the back of the vehicle.

While Ashu and I stood nearby watching, the little man reached with the upper part of his body to the inside opened back door of the vehicle and pulled out a wooden step that was no more than six feet high. He suspended the top of the steps and fixed it to a horizontal bar behind the back of the vehicle. Then he flattened its end, which looked like a mini platform on the floor. He shook the steps a couple of times to make sure that they were firm in place.

Then he picked up the nearest suitcase with both hands, which was Ashu's. Then he climbed up the steps and pushed the suitcase too far inside the back of the vehicle. Then he stepped down and stared at Sister Nashmeea as if he was seeking her approval to do the job. With a gesture from Sister Nashmeea's hand, he picked up my suitcase this time and like Ashu's suitcase, he pushed it as far as he could inside the back of the vehicle. The little man stepped aside waiting for further instructions.

Then the drama started when Sister Nashmeea climbed up the back of the vehicle and extend her arms to hold Ashu just under her arms, while I was supporting her from behind, pushing her up the steps, enabling her to climb into the back of the vehicle.

Sister Nashmeea got inside the vehicle facing us with her arms wide open. Ashu came forward reluctantly moving her eyes between me and Sister Nashmeea. Putting one step forward and one step backwards. Ashu got close to the back of the vehicle. I came from behind and encircled her waist with my arms. I was almost carrying her entire body. When I pushed her forward up the steps. Sister Nashmeea held her under her arms and repeated, "We're almost there; push doctor push."

*PZZZ. ZIT. Zit.* The sound of clothes that was torn off. "No problem, Sister, part of Ashu's rim, the side I stitched up before, had been ruptured. It happened before. I hope it will be reparable."

Sister Nashmeea managed to suppress her laughter by tightening her lips and looking away while lifting the end of Ashu's robe slightly up and pushing Ashu steadily inside the vehicle. After I climbed inside the vehicle too, we were all inside. There were three seats inside the vehicle covered with red plastic material, two fixed to each side of the floorboard. Ashu and I occupied the seat on the right side of the vehicle while Sister Nashmeea was struggling to collect the steps from the hands of the little man and pushed them further to the bottom of the vehicle. After controlling the steps, she took the bottom seat at the right corner.

Once the little man shut the back door of the vehicle firmly, he slapped it twice by his hand, demonstrating to the driver that the vehicle was ready to move. When the driver accelerated the engine, I thought it would be impossible for us to hear each other anymore. The vehicle moved slowly to the left, creeping on a bumpy road. Sister Nashmeea and I both looked with sympathy at Ashu while she was reaching to the tail of her overall robe assessing the damage and feeling sorry for herself.

After the vehicle gathered some speed, the engine got less noisy than before. Sister Nashmeea moved a bit forward in Ashu's direction. Then she curved her right hand close to Ashu's right ear and shouted, "Don't you worry, doctor when we would get to the compound centre, you would be free to move with your top and jeans on between the cafeteria and your bedroom through a private corridor."

Ashu responded with a vague smile, and I thought she tried to say, "Thank you, Sister."

Sister Nashmeea said, "Once we entered the building you should hand me your robe so I could use it to measure a new one for you." Ashu looked back at Sister Nashmeea, put her right hand on her heart and said bashfully, but rather loudly, "Thank you Sister, I would rather arrange to mend it. It was of a sentimental value."

"Of course, doctor," Sister Nashmeea took it as a joke, but I was not sure whether Ashu had meant what she said. After twenty minutes of a bumpy ride, and it seemed that we had arrived at the place, the vehicle jerked for a few seconds and stopped completely.

Sister Nashmeea bent backwards and pulled the wooden steps from the far back of the vehicle and pushed them forward close to the door. Suddenly the door was opened, and the little man appeared, putting both hands up, holding the steps and going on trying manoeuvring them around. Eventually, he managed to interlock the top end of the steps to the metal bar by the opening of the back of the vehicle and fixed it, based on the floor.

Sister Nashmeea put both her hands on the vehicle's floor and crawled backwards till her feet touched the steps. Then she got to the floor. She stood close by and whispered some words to the little man who I thought went close to the driver's cabin. The little man pulled out his walkie-talkie, took a few steps away from the vehicle, commanded some words through his wireless instrument and left the scene.

Sister Nashmeea asked me to put Ashu in front of me and squat facing the back of the vehicle, holding her from under her armpits and push her gently till her feet would touch the steps. That was a job. At last, Ashu was on the floor smiling and holding the end of the ripped-off damaged robe. It wasn't that hard for me to descend. It was as easy as dangling my legs backwards to touch the step by my feet and get to the floor. Huge cypress trees on my left next to a small hill almost covered with a strange kind of shrubby land. At the bottom of the hill from the left, I could see a thick plantation of sunflowers.

My attraction to my new surrounding lasted for a few seconds, and then I shifted my full attention to Sister Nashmeea. Sister Nashmeea returns my look with a smile and said, "Don't you worry doctor, we were waiting for the young girls to help doctor Ashu up the stairs."

I smiled back at Sister Nashmeea and took another look at our new surroundings again. It was rather a strange atmosphere. The sun was at the top of the sky, but it was not very bright. It was dull and hazy across the horizon. I couldn't determine whether it was a mist or a cloud of dust that masked the sun.

Oh well, I would better stay calm, awaiting what was coming. I would say four to five minutes passed before I could see the same two teenage girls who used to serve us our food at the bungalow in their overall black uniforms moving steadily in our direction. I was baffled to see them approaching from nowhere. It looked as if they had raised from somewhere inside the sunflower's plantation.

As usual, they stood up in front of us courteously, lowering their heads twice putting their right hands on their hearts, and stood straight in readiness. Sister Nashmeea asked them to hold the split tail of Ashu's robe up behind her and follow her moves. I had no option but to go behind them. Sister Nashmeea strolled along the edge of the sunflower's plantation. Ashu was walking behind her, and the young girls were lifting the end of Ashu's black robe and walking watchfully behind her. I was at the end of that small line.

From my pitiful position, I was watching that mini parade with absolute astonishment. The sight was exceedingly symbolic. That sad black procession painted a very realistic picture for the theme of my topic, a tragic wedding.

Sister Nashmeea looked back a few times to make sure that everything was in order till we got to a square-like gap in the middle of the thick line of the sunflowers hedging plants. We were in front of a relatively high building with a huge mahogany wooden gate. Two guys with traditional local costumes wearing blue turbans were standing at each side of the gate, holding long guns along their right sides. When they saw us approaching, they lifted their guns and gave us a military salute. Sister Nashmeea stopped walking, stood firm and returned the salute with a movement of her right hand. I was impressed to see that unusual performance.

Sister Nashmeea led us to an opening of a corridor on the right side of the building. I could see two metal doors on the side of the building along that corridor. Sister Nashmeea pulled a key from a thread hanging to her neck and opened the first door. I looked curiously to see that the metal door was opened at a staircase. Sister Nashmeea started climbing the stairs, and Ashu, with her supporting girls followed, so I did. On the top of the stairs, was a wide patio with two doors five to six meters apart.

Sister Nashmeea stood in front of the first door and said, "That room would be doctor Ashu's bedroom, and the next one would be doctor Kameela's bedroom." Then she appointed to the opposite end of the patio and said, "And at that end was the other stairs that would lead to the private cafeteria where your food and tea would be served. You could go down there with only your tops and jeans. No one would bather you. Nobody would be there except the girls serving you and me. By the way, your suitcases were already in your rooms. Do not ask me how they got there, we had fused for us a practical system. That was the way we survived the brutality of our enemies."

We all entered Ashu's room. The two young girls bow slightly as they always did, with their right hands on their hearts and rushed outside the room.

Sister Nashmeea examined the room and asked Ashu to take off her damaged robe. Ashu started waveringly taking off her overall black robe and repeating, "I wouldn't worry Sister; it would be easily rectifiable." Sister Nashmeea explained that she needed the robe for measurement, "We have heaps of them in the store." Ashu folded her robe and handed it to Sister Nashmeea, who put it under her arm. Sister Nashmeea handed the key to Ashu and suggested to us to go and have a look at my designated room.

I said smiling, "That was a nice privilege, but I would miss Ashu's whistling while asleep." Sister Nashmeea cracked short laughter and said, "I wouldn't worry doctor Kameela; your friend would be only next door, we might ask her to put up the volume." We both followed Sister Nashmeea to the adjacent room. "Wow, so clean, so tidy, and I loved the light blue colour of the bed's cover."

In no time, Sister Nashmeea handed me the key to my room and asked me to take off my overall black robe and hang it in a small wardrobe near the side corner. "Now doctor, we had a long day. Let all of us move to the cafeteria to give ourselves a treat."

Following Sister Nashmeea's steps, we all moved to the other side of the patio from corner to corner to another staircase. We took the stairs to the ground floor to found ourselves in front of a cute cafeteria. Four well-organised dining tables and only one side window opened on the sunflower's plantation. Sister Nashmeea smiled and said, "You would be surprised doctors to see menus on the tables. You would choose the food you like."

Sister Nashmeea Ashu and I spent most of the afternoon in the cafeteria. It was rather a strange feeling to move from the confinement of the bungalow to a much wider space. Sister Nashmeea was happy to see us more relaxed and more confident. I decided that we should stick to a formal approach and keep my most pressing issue, Jameela's case for a later stage. We talked about so many things: the music, life in the UK, the Afghan committees in Europe, and even discussed arranged and forced marriages.

I was impressed by Sister Nashmeea's moderate views about life and religion. She did not stay long in the UK but her moderate views about life enabled her to learn a lot. There were two matters decisively covered in our conversation. First, was the task of sorting out the many packs of medicines in the store, and the second was how to secure a connection with our organisation that arranged our trip from London. Sister Nashmeea promised to facilitate our first task. "Willingly, doctors, I would do my best to help."

As for the other issue, Sister Nashmeea explained that she would take the matter up with her uncle, who would defiantly secure a contact as soon as possible. However, Sister Nashmeea suggested that today we should take a break, and the following day; after breakfast, she would take us to the store to arrange sorting out the medicines' bundles. Sister Nashmeea looked at her watch, excused herself as usual by saying, "See you tomorrow, doctors." And left the cafeteria through the back door.

The large side window of the cafeteria overlooked an opened side of the sunflower plantation, and the twilight composed a very nice green-orange picturesque view. Ashu looked busy sipping her chicken soap and staring at me occasionally as if she was trying to read my mind. After a few minutes, I noticed that Ashu pushed the soup ball aside and started yawning, covering her mouth with her right palm.

I gave Ashu a kind look and said, "Alright, Ashu I am going to bed and there, I could stay struggling with my thoughts as much as I like. Now, there would be no Ashu, whistling and interruptions."

Ashu got the joke; she smiled broadly and said, "Admit it, admit it you would miss me dearly."

"I would, Ashu, but I would be much more comfortable."

It had taken me no more than fifteen minutes to put on my pyjamas and relax my head on my pillow to hear a light knowing on my door. I jumped from my bed and went close to the door. Before I would say anything, the voice came low but clear. "Don't worry, it was me, Ashu. Please Kameela, open the door."

I opened the door to see Ashu still in her jeans, but she looked frightened. I put my hand on her shoulder and asked her gently, "What was wrong?" She didn't say a word. Instead, she took my hand and led me to inside her room, close to the side of the large window. She appointed straight at the view underneath and said, "Look."

"Look what?"

"What could you see?"

"What could I see Ashu? Trees. All I could see were trees."

Ashu was a bit irritated. She took one step backwards and said, "Kameela, you are not blind. What was there on the floor?"

I heaved a short sigh and grumbled in a low voice, "Graves, Ashu. It seemed they had used this part of the orchard as a graveyard."

Ashu shifted her eyes in my direction and gave me a serious look, repeating the word graveyard and added, "Yes, Kameela, and as it happened, that it was me to sleep in a room that was overlooking a graveyard. No, Kameela, I was not going to sleep in this room. I am not going to sleep over dead people."

I put on some courage and explained in a kind tune, "Listen to me seriously amiga, after all those years today you surprised me. I never thought you would be possibly scared of dead people who were buried under piles of earth. I would be more scared of those who were alive than those who were dead."

I realised there was no way to convince Ashu that the dead people under her window would do her no harm. She was more relaxed when I suggested that she could sleep in the room that was allocated for me instead of her room on one condition; that was she would never approach or look through the room's window.

Because I wouldn't know what she would discover. Eventually, the drama was over. Here I was in a new bed again, staring at the ceiling and started thinking about Jameela, thinking, and remembering the days, the months and the years we lived together sharing that humble room in Hounslow Central. Listening discretely to our favourite music or exchanging some mild jokes about my mother's amusing concept. My father used to tease her occasionally. I remembered very well when one Friday evening, Jameela and I were sitting thumbing our school notebooks when my father asked my mother about the distance to the new herbal shop she just discovered in the area and never stopped talking about it.

She picked up her mind and looked away at the window and said, "Not very far, say it is from her to the shrine of Sheik Yousef."

My father laughed loudly and asked her, "Sheik who?" Then my father looked in our direction and said, "Did you know, daughters, after all those years in Hounslow Central, your mother never mentally left the tribes' land. The shrine she mentioned was less than a half-mile away from where we used to live on the tribes' land."

My mother realised immediately that she was thousands of miles away. And as if nothing was wrong, she reaped her answer by saying, "Oh dear husband, I meant it was one bus stop away."

Tonight, I was in a new room, not the room initially allocated for me by Sister Nashmeea; I called it in my heart Ashu's room. There was no difference between my bed and Ashu's bed. The difference was in the colours of the sheets only. However, my mattress was not on the floor anymore. It was on a real bed. And that was enough justification to go through my usual sleepless habit for a few hours of debating before I passed out.

My mind was wandering from corner to corner and from land to land. Tonight, my obsession was the tribes' land. The magnet that used to pull my family decades back was mainly by my mother's fixed concept. I love my mother, though, I believed most people do, except that my mother was in the wrong place at the wrong time. She was simple. A very simple middle-aged lady, to the point that I would take her as naïve, and her naivety had cost us dearly. All our family members played their parts in the enslavement of my sister Jameela, even my uncle, the verbal defender of women's rights didn't stand strong against that tragic wedding. It took me a while to work his reason out.

Most likely he dreamt that through that new family connection, he might have access to his feudal estate that he left behind after the fall of the Marxist government. At any rate, my mother played a major part in Jameela's tragedy. My mother lived almost three decades of her life in west London, but mentally she never left the tribes' land and kept thinking that the tribes' land was the centre of the world. While turning myself from left to right and right to left, my thought took me back to Hounslow Central, to the same room, I used to share with my sister, Jameela.

It was mid-April of 1978. Six months after Jameela's departure, I was staring at Jameela's empty bed early in the morning. I was facing the same hazy window, leaning on the same slightly wiggly table that I used to share with my sister Jameela before she was wadded, or I should say enslaved to the tribes' land. I didn't remember how many hours I stayed there in my dream while my mind started wondering as far as the tribes' land.

In that state, it came to my mind that my mother named my sister Jameela and me Kameela. We were both born in the same terraced house in the middle of Hounslow Central, west of London.

However, my mother, who was fond of her tribe's land and its prehistoric culture insisted, as my father explained that our names should sound musically rhymed. Both names have meanings in the Farsi and Dari the dialect of the inhabitants of the tribes' land. Jameela meant pretty and Kameela meant perfect. Hence when my mother used to call me from the kitchen, which was, almost her permanent place in the house, shouting my name, Jameela would tease me by whispering, "Yes, perfect! You hope."

All that I can say when my mother used to call Jameela was that meant pretty, I used to compliment Jameela by saying, "Yes, I agree." Because Jameela was pretty. She was two years and a few months older than me. We looked almost a perfect twin in everything except in appearance. We liked the same music; we love the same type of spicy food, and we sang the same songs whenever we have the chance and even, we would mimic the performance of the music.

Jameela was slim and tall with beautiful shiny brown eyes. Her long chestnut hair reflected shiny weaves covering her shoulders, and her face reflected a vibrant, brownish-tanned skin; completed with such a lovely smile. I was shorter and chubby with black hair and typical light skin. Nothing in me was that attractive to anyone except my mother who thought the world of me.

My mother was a very quiet, introverted, but helpful lady. Though she had been living in west London for such a long time, she struggled to speak English. Mentally she was still shaped by her childhood life and early experience of the tribe's land. She was easily satisfied as she performed her ablutions and prayers to God five times a day. She believed that Allah was almightily sitting in heaven with his extensive book recording peoples' good and bad deeds and would plan their destinies accordingly.

She also believed that whatever we faced was scheduled by God and planned beforehand as our destiny or our 'Kismet', a word of Arabic root that means designated fate. According to my mother, marriage was a Kismet, just like birth and death. According to my mother's concept, Allah had planned everything for us in his book, so whatever we try to reroute it, the order of Allah will prevail in the end.

Did I sleep that night? Yes, I probably did for a few hours. My mother, her sayings, her beliefs, and her methodologies would constitute an endless subject. Whenever she occurred in my mind, my thoughts about her might continue for hours, and sometimes get mixed with my complicated dreams. This time was no different. I realised it was early morning when I heard Sister Nashmeea tapping lightly on the door and repeating rather clearly, "Doctor Ashu." I jumped from my bed, went close to the door, and answered in a low voice, "It was me, Kameela, not Ashu."

Then I opened the door a little to see the astonishment on Sister Nashmeea's face. I was right; I found Sister Nashmeea standing with wide-open eyes and mouth. Before I said anything, she said, "Don't worry doctor; please take your time. Would you please talk to doctor Ashu and let her know that I will be waiting for you at the cafeteria."

I responded with appreciation, "No problem, Sister, we will be with you as soon as possible."

# Chapter Seven

Early morning, Ashu and I took the stairs down to the cafeteria. We were much more relaxed this time. We wore our t-shirts and jeans, putting on our headscarves just in case. As Sister Nashmeea always did. We found her there, occupying her usual chair at the dining table. We wished her a good morning, and she stood up courteously and asked us to sit down. I had noticed that she was exceptionally relaxed. She reached down to the table in front of her, packed up two half-written pages and handed them kindly; one to Ashu and one to me. I was surprised to see that Sister Nashmeea had scribbled for us in English two handwritten menus. The menus contained much more variety of food than what we used to receive on the wooden cart. After quick glance on the menus, Ashu and I exchanged pleasurable smiles and thanked Sister Nashmeea for her efforts.

In this elegant new approach, we felt that we were treated like privileged guests. So, it was not suitable to use the word order. Therefore, I asked for tea and one local pastry that attracted my attention. Ashu asked for a small jar of her favourite organic honey and two free rang build eggs. Sister Nashmeea pulled a black pen from her side pouch and ticked the items we requested. She looked back at one of the familiar young girls behind the counter.

The girl came and stood in front of our table without saying a word. She bowed her head twice with her right hand on her heart. Then, she collected the marked menus from Sister Nashmeea and went back behind the cafeteria's counter.

When the tray arrived with the requested food, Sister Nashmeea smiled and said, "I think that doctor Ashu would stick to the same food as long as she was here with us." The phrase, if she was here with us, alerted me like an alarm bell. Sister Nashmeea, with her noticeable physiognomy, did not miss my obvious reaction. The phrase that Sister Nashmeea had dropped casually reminded me that we were getting close to the end of our mission or might be the way I had read it. Ashu gave me an empty look, avoiding showing any noticeable emotion. I felt it was time to move toward our major issue, the Jameela case.

Although I was not relaxed, I gathered my courage, looked Sister Nashmeea in the eye, and said, "Sister please, you ought to forgive us. We had a kind of serious confession to make. Yes, Sister, it was true that we had volunteered to serve in our homeland, which we considered the idea was a very noble one, still, on the back of all that, there was another very important problem that worried us enormously. You might think, Sister that what troubled us was no more than a personal matter, but it happened that you had the experience. You have noticed that our people of the communities in the civilised world suffered traditionally from split personality. And that kind of attitude might cause a lot of injustice, particularly toward powerless women."

After that emotional assertion, I stared at Sister Nashmeea to find that she had supported her chin with both hands and pinned her elbows to the table in front of her. Her mouth was open, and her eyes were fixed on my eyes. I felt I had to come to the point and cut a long story short.

So, I whispered with obvious passion, "It was my sister Jameela, Sister Nashmeea. Jameela was wedded or enslaved to the tribe's land by the deviation of arranged marriage. Jameela, my sister was taken away from my world in a wicked arrangement like a sudden death. When a dear person passed away, all those who loved that person would reconcile themselves to the fact that the missing person had gone forever. But when a dear person would be taken away and trapped at a certain spot of the world that you couldn't reach, the pain of that missing feeling would develop into physical pain."

I was talking while my eyes were fixed on Sister Nashmeea's face. My vision got blared because unwillingly, they got full of tears. Hence, I was unable to read Sister Nashmeea's reaction to my story. Alternatively, I directed my attention to Ashu to find her in a rather strange mode. She placed her forehead flat on the table in front of her and tangled her both arms above her head.

In a swift movement, Sister Nashmeea adjusted her position, reached for a clean white handkerchief that she pulled from her right pouch and handed it to me suggesting drying up my tearful eyes. I thanked Sister Nashmeea with my rattled voice and rubbed my eyes gently with her handkerchief. Then I could see Sister Nashmeea's sad serious face more clearly. In a genuine reaction to what I just said, Sister Nashmeea said in a very confirmed tone, "I fully understand your concern, doctor. I would like to assure you that my uncle's contact net fully penetrated the family structures of the tribe's land. That was necessitated by the imminent danger of the civil war engulfed our societies for almost the last three years. I would promise you that I would arrange with my uncle to use whatever that in our power to reach out to your sister Jameela and sort out what we could of her dilemma."

After five seconds of silence, Sister Nashmeea directed her attention to Ashu who looked as if she was frozen over the table. Sister Nashmeea gently put her right hand over Ashu's head and whispered emotionally, "Come on, doctor, everything would be alright."

Then she told me directly and in clearly in firm language, "Listen, doctor, let us be methodical in our approach to this critical sensitive case. First, I knew that families of the tribe's land gathered into social groups, so if you could provide me with some names of people or clans involved in Jameela's case, I assured you that would be more than enough guidance to reach Jameela's whereabouts. Once we got to that stage, we would know what to do next. And as an advocator of women's rights, the other point, doctor Kameela, which would be equally important, I would find it deeply disturbing to learn that such women's rights violations would still occur in that civilised part of the world."

At that time, Ashu had lifted her head and looked at me with very cloudy red eyes, and muttered in a shrill voice, "Come on Kameela, I believed you had researched that problem in our community deep enough to the point that you could inscribe it in a book."

Both Sister Nashmeea and Ashu fixed their eyes on me. I had no option but to pull myself together and remind Sister Nashmeea about her experience with our community in Coventry. I cleared my throat and said gently, "To some extent Sister there were a lot of similarities between our communities in Britain and that you witnessed in Coventry. Most of our people historically were unplugged, against their will from a simple tribe's societies and planted in an entirely different world. Of course, their integration in the new land would depend on two factors; there would be the new generations of those who were born in the new world. Those would have no problem integrating into the modern society.

However, if one or both of their parents would continue to adhere to their past, their offspring would have no option but to lead a double standard in their lives. People like my mother, who was born, brought up and got married in the tribe's land, would find it very hard to understand the values of her new environment. My mother believed that any performance in life that didn't go with the traditions of the tribe's land was a dreadful act, and it would be against the will of Allah. Heresies, religious myths and gossip were her social life. In addition, our communities didn't live in one area of London. Part of it lived in Hounslow Central, others lived in Acton, and some in Harrow.

Middle-aged ladies like my mother would pass their stories and the rumours that they would go around over the phone. More than that they had shopping times where they would move in groups from one grocery shop to another, exchanging gossip and fake news. My father was a different character altogether. When my mother returned from her shopping trips with a ridiculous story, my father would laugh it off. He would spend a few hours a day in my uncle's corner shop and now and then, he would attend some religious and social occasions without getting deeply involved with any formal organisers. He was moderate in his attitude towards his past tribe's culture, though he used to respect some common traditions.

For this reason, he disagreed with most of my uncle's lifestyle, but he would never consider him an infidel. My uncle, Siraj Khan was five years younger than my father. Therefore, my uncle used to stick to the traditions of respecting the older. He used to visit us, in the company of his wife Samia Khanum, almost every fortnight. My mother did not like Samia Khanum, because she believed that Samia Khanum was an arrogant woman. She would always put on her golden garnishes with or without appropriate occasions.

My mother did not like my uncle either because of his leftist non-religious ideology and she believed that he was the one who persuaded my father to abandon his farming land and move with her to Kabul. That was after the Marxist government took over, convincing my father that he would get a better-paid job. Nevertheless, my mother tolerated my uncle and his wife most of the times because she admitted that my uncle rescued her life and my father's life by smuggling them abroad when he discovered that the Marxist government was about to arrest my father, accusing him of being a reactionary element and not in harmony with the people's revolutionary regime.

By the same token, my uncle managed to obtain documents issued by those who claimed power after the fall of the Marxist regime, sentencing him to death and accusing him of supporting the communist regime. As a result, both my father and my uncle ended up as political refugees in the same country, the UK, except that my uncle somehow managed to leave with the farmers union budget that was deposited with him by the Marxist government."

I stopped talking for a few seconds and threw investigative looks at Sister Nashmeea and Ashu. I found that Sister Nashmeea fixed her elbows on the table again and supported her chin with both hands. Her lips were slightly opened, and she looked like she was all ears. On the other hand, Ashu looked a bit bored and half asleep, as if she had no interest in my tell. Ashu reacted to my look by adjusting her seat and grumbled softly, "Oh, come on, Kameela, get on with it, touch on the core of the problem, so that Sister Nashmeea would know how to tackle it."

Sister Nashmeea leaned back on her chair and whispered with excitement, "No, please doctors, that background was very important to me; it would give me an insight about the whole issue." Then she looked at me and said, "Please doctor, continue with your story down to the finest details that led to that tragic arrangement."

Sister Nashmeea's comment encouraged me to elaborate further on my tale. One minute later Sister Nashmeea looked back in the direction of the cafeteria and yelled, "Suroor."

A girl from inside replied, "Yes Sister."

Sister Nashmeea looked around and yelled back, "Pot of tea without sugar please and three mugs with a ball of sugar cubes." That was the first time it happened that I knew the name of one of the two girls who were serving us since we had arrived in that strange land. I couldn't help but ask Sister Nashmeea, "I knew Sister that 'Suroor' in Dari language would mean happiness, so Which one of the two girls was called Suroor?"

Sister Nashmeea with a very broad smile replied, "They were both happiness. They were my recruits and in my training."

That tea break gave me a good rest and helped me a great deal to pick up my thoughts again. A few minutes later, while Ashu still sipping the last drops of her tea repeated softly, "I was sorry. To take such a long time, I liked my tea cold."

Sister Nashmeea ignored Ashu's remarks and started looking at me with questioning eyes. I resumed my briefing by saying, "You could see, Sister that in addition to the circulating rumours among the community that my mother used to bring back from her shopping trips, we had our uncle, who was considered a dignitary member of our community." His information was different from my mother's, but putting the two together, we usually achieved full insight into community affairs.

"My uncle was a bookworm, but his wide education, in general, was hunted by leftist ideology. On the other hand, my father's readings were confined to Islamic history. One issue that could sometimes bring them closer was my father's admiration for a school of thought that occurred at the early stages of Islam known as Mutazila. The term meant the isolationists. A group of Muslims isolated themselves from the mainstream of Islam and called for reason over transmission.

My father and my uncle usually would start their conversation with an amicable discussion, revising their memories and exchanging some information regarding the community. But in no time that conversation would develop into a heated argument. My mother would hardly ever participate in their conversation, except when my uncle would refer to the power of nature and the impact of the economy on societies. Then my mother would pull her headscarf over her eyes and recite under her breath a certain chapter from the Koran, 'I seek refuge to Allah almighty and seek his protection.' Then she would go back to her nature, serving her visitors tea and homemade cake.

However, my uncle usually conceded that my father was right. It was an inherited tradition in our culture that called for the withdrawal of the younger from the disagreement regardless of the outcome of the argument.

Jameela and I got used to that periodical visit of my uncle, usually in the company of his wife. As a matter of courtesy, we would stay around for a while, sitting silently on the corner sofa, listening to my father's welcoming and greeting words to my uncle. However, once the debate between my father and my uncle entered its serious stage and my mother would start refuging to her God almighty, Jameela and I would wish everybody a good night and would refuge to our bedroom.

Our house was rather small. Sometimes, we would hear some words or fragmented sentences of their typical talk in the hall. It would be no time for homework. Alternatively, we would pick up our cassette player from under the table and share through our earbuds listening to one of Abba concerts, or any other tape of pup music that Ashu had smuggled for us from her brother's shop."

Sister Nashmeea smiled and interrupted me respectfully, "But excuse me, doctor, what you told us was very interesting. First, you and Jameela somehow managed to create your privacy in that unhealthy atmosphere. While the family's seniors were arguing their heads off, you enjoyed your favourite music. What astonished me in those meetings among your family members was how you kept yourselves away from their useless affairs."

"Sure Sister," I replayed promptly. I was pleased with Sister Nashmeea's comment that gave me a chance to elaborate on some aspects of our connections within the community.

I looked Sister Nashmeea in the eye and said, "My father would always criticise those people he met in the mosque during his Friday prayers, and how some of them would never donate a penny for the charity of the Mullah, the character who cared about the community all the time.

Sister, no one in the community knew the full name of that Mullah, who was in his eighties. He lived in a house in London somewhere near an area called Willesden Junction. The Mullah's house was his residence. In addition, it was used to contain a large praying area and a small reading place with shelves organised with books, most of them were old references. Community members would gather in the Mullah's house on religious occasions like Eid al-Fitr and Eid al-Adha. My uncle would always mention his generous donations to the Mullah's house, and he was always proud of his civilised attitude as a women's rights advocator, his permanent example in the conversation was his attitude toward his wife.

He would say, sometimes in a very low voice, that his wife was a barren lady, but as a matter of respect, he never thought of marrying another woman. But whenever he would come to this point of his conversation, my mother would face the wall to hide a cynical smile. Once my uncle and his wife would leave our house, my mother would give my father a funny look and declarer that every member of the community knew that the cause of your brother having no children was because of his deficiency, except him. My father would acknowledge my mother's comment by giving her a serious look, but he would brush it away whispering his usual phrase, 'male pride.'

In that family atmosphere, Sister, there was something unusual started to occur. Neither Jameela nor I thought that their whispering and low-profile debating had anything to do with us.

However, by the second week of August of that year, 1995, Ashu and I got our final exam results, while Jameela was still waiting for her exam results. All the same, Jameela was celebrating with us our great achievements. I wouldn't bother you, Sister with the details of our education system, but both of us had achieved highly recognised marks; Jameela was happy for us, but she used to tease us by saying wait till you see my marks, they would lead straight to the gate of Hammersmith Medical College. The three of us arranged some cassettes for dancing music waiting for the day when we have the house free for us so we would dance our heads off.

But that was a frustrating time for us as my mother gave up her long shopping trips. She was always on the phone, and all her shopping was local and fast. My uncle's visits to our family had become more frequent, and they were no more confined to Fridays. Some noticeable fact that when my uncle was started to visit us on his own without of his wife. In the meantime, Jameela and I had noticed that there was a lot of whispering between our parents. From that strange atmosphere, Jameela and I had concluded that there was a conspiracy around. The thought of a conspiracy as such didn't bother us, but whenever there was a conspiracy there would be a victim. Jameela and I didn't dare to ask any of my parents about what was going on.

Hence, we decided to meet Ashu in private to find out some facts about the mysterious events that occupied our family and how they resonated in the community in general?

When I had the chance to phone Ashu, her mother came on the phone. She greeted me with kind words, but she was sorry to tell me that Ashu was not well, and she was in bed. She added that nothing to worry about, it was just a common cold. Then she promised to let her know that I had phoned as soon as she would be awake. Jameela and I had almost a week of uncertainty trying to guess what was happening. During those few days, I had a lot of teasing from Jameela. She used to change the wording of Abba's song Fernando and made it sound like, there is something in the air Kameela.

Eventually, the time came to meet Ashu in the coffee shop near the underground station. Ashu was astonished that we didn't know what was going on in the community. Ashu explained that it was well known in the community that a VIP lady, Sheika Shahnaz Khanum had been in London for the last two weeks. The lady Khanum, as she was called by most of the community members, was in London for one specific reason.

The lady Khanum was looking for a suitable bride for her young handsome educated son Akrum Siraj-al-Deen Safi. Ashu told us that the lady Khanum used to keep a large black and white picture of her handsome son in a folder and used to flash it to the community members who visited her in her private wing in a hotel close to Heathrow airport."

Sister Nashmeea was all ears. She was listening wholeheartedly. However, at that stage, she adjusted her seat, touched my right shoulder with her right hand very lightly and said in a soft voice, "Excuse me, doctor, so sorry to interrupt you. What you were telling us was very interesting, but I would like to know, and my question would be to both of you, did anyone in your community knew that when Sheika Shahnaz was talking about her son as a Madrasa graduate, she meant he went to those isolated compounds erected along the Afghan-Pakistani borders to accommodate hundreds of the war orphans and spoon-fed them violence and fanatism?"

Before I had said any word, Ashu volunteered to say, "No Sister, before your kind briefing the other day, even Kameela and I used to take the word Madrasas by its Dari, meaning as schools."

Sister Nashmeea looked a bit sad. She picked an empty glass from the table in front of us and shouted rather loudly in the direction of the cafeteria for a jar of water. After a few sips of water, Sister Nashmeea looked more relaxed. She powered some water in another glass in front of me and said, "Have some water, doctor; I believe you need it. However, I would like to know at what stage Sheika Shahnaz tagged Jameela to be her son's bride?"

When Ashu noticed that I was still busy wetting my lips, she sat straight and directed her eyes toward Sister Nashmeea and said, "By the second week of the presence of Sheika Shahnaz in London, her name and her son's name Akrum who was a handsome and Madrasa-educated had become the talk of the town."

There, I felt I had to interfere to clarify the issue, that's why I direct my words to Sister Nashmeea and said, "Sister, I tend to believe that you know better than us about that sub-culture of the tribes' land. When a young widow decided not to marry again and she was the only child of her parents, she would inherit the entire wealth of her family, including their land. Society would grant her the title of Sheika. Which was the female version of the privileged title of Sheik, a person who was highly respected among his people."

Sister Nashmeea was nodding her head up and down as a motion demonstrating that she was in full agreement with what I was explaining. Then I resumed my telling directing my eyes to Sister Nashmeea, "Events were moving very swiftly. After two weeks, everything regarding Sheika Shahnaz mission had come to the open. A court had been hired and reception had been arranged for the Sheika along High Chiswick Road."

Ashu excused herself and said, "Sorry, Kameela. Don't forget the lavish campaign published and circulated for that reception."

"Yes, Ashu, I didn't forget that, but to my great astonishment that the campaign for the reception itself was all arranged by my uncle. Two hundred paper bags of a mix of sweets were donated by the Mullah of the community advertising that reception. On top of that, it seemed that the cost of hiring the court, as well as the advertisement cost of the reception in a grand hotel as well as the costs of the adverts in local newspapers, were all paid by my uncle. My mother was restless and excited, and she started to thumb her old copy of the Koran frequently as she believed that whatever would come randomly in front of her eyes in the holy book would be a directive from God that she should follow. It was her kind of astrology that would give her peace of mind.

Between my uncle's attitude and my mother's persuasion, my father looked powerless, and he had nothing to say. He was around but he was like a zombie. He was hardly engaged in any conversation regarding that matter. He was there all the time, but he was silent most of the times, and it was impossible to read his mind.

On Friday, the eighteenth of August of that year1995, my mother was up early that day. She piled some items from her recent shopping bags on the breakfast table. From that pile, she picked a rose colour baggy pants and a beautiful golden colour striped shirt and handed them to Jameela. Then she went through her pile of garments again and picked two identical pieces except that they were a smaller size, and the shirt was a silver colour striped and handed them to me. Then she whispered her usual short prayers and asked us in an emotional voice to go to the bedroom and try the garments.

When we came out of the bedroom, my mother received us with thrilling cries of joy. That was when my father had just arrived home after a short trip to collect an early morning delivery to the corner shop. When he glanced us, he stopped next to the door rubbing his eyes in astonishment and repeated his thanks to Allah for giving him such wonderful angels. He begged my mother to remind him to ask my uncle to take pictures of the girls when he arrived. 'Sure, they look like angels' my father commented.

Jameela and I had a lousy breakfast despite the lovely spicy mushroom omelette my mother had prepared, simply because we were too excited about our shiny traditional costumes. We spent a lot of time staring at ourselves in the large mirror in our bedroom."

Sister Nashmeea looked left and right and nicely asked, "But excuse me, doctor, were you completely unaware of what was going on around you?"

My answer came spontaneous and firm as I said, "Believe me, Sister, it was a conspiracy that was mapped by our entire family, and you might know very well Sister, whenever there would be a conspiracy, there would be a victim, and the victim of that conspiracy at that time was my sister Jameela."

When I got to that point, Ashu reached for some tissues in her pocket and dried two heavy tears were wiggling in her eyes. I tried to gather my courage and continue talking, but Sister Nashmeea put her right hand up gently requesting me to stop talking for a while. She looked back at the cafeteria and shouted at one of the Suroors to bring us a pot of tea with a ball of some cubic of sugar. Without thinking, I looked at Ashu to notice that she drew a vague smile through her tears. The tea session was a good rest for me that went for about seven minutes.

However, that break kept me away from my subject for a short while, though events of that day were moving in front of my eyes as if they had occurred yesterday. So, when I noticed Ashu had a few sips of her tea and Sister Nashmeea leaned back on her chair gazing at me in anticipation, I said, "I was sorry Sister; I couldn't overlook the tragic side of the events. Realistically, the entire outcome of that arrangement was nothing but a man-made tragedy." When I noticed that Sister Nashmeea was very keen to hear my telling, I resumed my story by saying "Then as time went by that day, just before midday, I heard my uncle's car was parking outside close to our door. He rang the door's bell once and then entered the main hall passage.

My mother welcomed him with a smile and ask him to come further. Then she suggested rather loudly to Jameela and me to come out of our bedroom for our uncle to see us. My uncle was so impressed to see us with our traditional shiny costumes. He hugged us and thanked the luck that gave him, such beautiful nieces. When my mother asked him to take us a few snaps, he explained that he left the camera with his wife in the car, but he promised my mother that he would take us a lot of snaps in the reception. When my father came out fully dressed from his bedroom, we all went to be squeezed in my uncle's car.

The journey wasn't so pleasant for me; I was the only one who was left without a seat. The smallest, and the youngest, I was hidden on the floor between my mother's and anti-Samia Khanum's legs."

Sister Nashmeea smiled, touched my head lightly and whispered with passion, "Poor Doctor Kameela, you were always the one who was sacrificed."

I smiled back and said, "Well Sister, there would be always one, and that one happened to be me. Nevertheless, Sister, the court was not too far. Give and take, it was forty-five minutes trip, and my uncle found a side road parking close to the court. We entered the court in three groups. My father and my uncle went through the huge wooden gate first, followed by my mother and Samia Khanum, and then it was Jameela and me.

I was amazed to see that the organisers had managed to layout about ten parallel lines of chairs across the length of the court. The first horizontal row close to the stage was reserved for us my father and his family. Shahnaz Khanum was sitting on the stage, and behind her was a large black and white portrait of a handsome guy in the traditional distinguished Afghan costume.

That was the first time I saw the famous Shahnaz Khanum in person. I stared at her with amazement for more than five minutes. She looked like a middle-aged woman with a slim figure. She was moderately dressed in a silky traditional Afghan costume with a black headscarf dropped loose around her shoulders. But what attracted my attention were her wide shiny brown eyes and the two dark crescent shape under them. Her eyes looked like a wild eagle's eyes. Staring at them would hypnotise you and control you unwillingly.

I estimated that over one hundred to one hundred twenty people in the court that came from different parts of the city. The crowd was noisy and poorly organised, but they all went relatively quiet when my uncle took over the stage. He welcomed Sheika Shahnaz eloquently with a nice short speech calling her the symbol of our culture and the pride of our great past and present. Sheika saluted him from her seat several times. When my uncle finished his speech, he returned to his chare between my father and his wife. Whispering had occurred between my uncle and my father, but I couldn't guess what that whispering was all about. My mother pretended to be so calm, but I could tell by a short glimpse at her in the corner of my eye that she was rather anxious."

Sister Nashmeea raised her right arm a little and said, "But excuse me, doctor, where was Ashu during all that social drama?"

Before I could say anything, Ashu brought her head forward and said, "No, Sister, my family was of a different attitude. They used to think that living in the past would distort our present. Therefore, we had heard of that gathering but we decided not to attend it."

While Sister Nashmeea was listening keenly to Doctor Ashu, one of the Suroors put her head out of the bottom barrier of the cafeteria and spoke out gently but firmly telling Sister Nashmeea that there was an urgent message for her, Sister Nashmeea stood up slothfully. She looked at her watch and said, "I was so sorry, doctors. It was nearly five o'clock in the evening, I could stay whatever it would take, listening to that great insight of events narrated by Doctor Kameela in such a way that made me feel as if those events had happened yesterday. I did not think I would be able to come back to you today, but I would try to come tomorrow as early as possible and devote the whole day to you."

When Sister Nashmeea wished us a good night and left through the cafeteria's back door, Ashu rubbed her hands and said, "Kameela, you were wonderful. don't think any professional writer could tell Jameela's story any better. It is a perfect presentation of her tragic wedding."

# Chapter Eight

After the end of yesterday's session, I discovered that recalling the events of the painful past might stimulate the same chronic pain they caused. But I finally dared to get rid of the heavy load of my heart, after all that hesitation finally I got the courage to involve Sister Nashmeea with Jameela's problem. Jameela's was the predicament that caused me countless sleepless nights over the years. My night yesterday had passed rather mixed up between unclear dreams and nightmares.

However, Ashu's voice next to my bedroom door in the morning calling my name brought me back to reality. Just before ten that morning Ashu and I went down to the cafeteria to have our usual breakfast and wait for Sister Nashmeea to turn up. To my surprise, Sister Nashmeea was already there, occupying her usual seat and sipping her breakfast tea.

After exchanging the morning greeting, Sister Nashmeea stood up smiling and invited us to sit down and said, "The breakfast menu today included the spicy mushroom omelette, I believed it was one of Doctor Ashu's favourite dishes. I have an urgent commitment that will not take long of my time. I would invite you to enjoy your breakfast and hopefully, I will be back with you within one hour. Then we would have the whole day for ourselves."

Sister Nashmeea left us in a hurry through the cafeteria's back door. Minutes after the disappearance of Sister Nashmeea one of the Suroors came up from behind the counter of the cafeteria, one hand on her heart, showing the usual courtesy gesture. She handed each of us a handwritten menu of the day. Sister Nashmeea made a mistake when she mentioned that the mushroom omelette was Ashu's favourite dish. It was me who used to ask for the spicy mushroom omelette, while Ashu was happy to ask for her favourite natural honey and bread and the pot of tea with a ball of cubical sugar.

While I was busy crunching my food, suddenly, Ashu stopped eating and put on a serious face and said, "Kameela, please, for heaven's sake, be very accurate when you would bring up names of people and places. Especially when you recall events of Jameela's story because I believed Sister Nashmeea would use that information in her investigation to find out as what had happened to Jameela in the tribes' land."

My response to Ashu's remarks was imminent, "I went back to my lousy notes number of times. I made sure that the names of those involved were correct, but I didn't find much information about the places."

Ashu said, "I believed that the tribes in the tribes' land were known by their clans, not by names of their people."

While we were in variety of debates, Sister Nashmeea appeared from behind the counter of the cafeteria. She was gasping as if she was short of breath. Ashu and I stood up welcoming her and wishing her safe arrival. She called Suroor for a pot of tea with a ball of cubical sugar. Before the arrival of the tea, we all sat at the table. Sister Nashmeea apologised for being a bit late, "I didn't like to leave you waiting for long. We had a big task in front of us. Please Doctor Kameela, would you take us back to our important subject and tell us how things developed during and after that reception."

I was pleased to see that, Sister Nashmeea was keen to fellow Jameela's quandary.

I took a sip of my tea and started by saying, "Yes Sister, five minutes after my uncle finished his speech, he noticed that ineptitude had prevailed among the crowd. Hence, he climbed the stage again. He took on the microphone and announced loudly that Sheika was kind enough to give us plenty of her precious time, and it was time to move forward. Then he invited the families to come up in line to greet the Sheika before they would leave the court. Sheika Shahnaz leaned back on her chair and extended her right arm, supported by the chair's arm.

Ladies went up to the stage and greeted the respectable Sheika by touching her hand very softly. Some went further as they kissed her hand before leaving the stage. Sheika Shahnaz looked honoured and happy with that show. Fifteen minutes passed when the stage become less crowded, my mother stood up and signalled to Jameela and me to follow her. Naturally, Jameela was first behind my mother, but Sheika Shahnaz greeting to us was different from her greetings to the others.

When Jameela touched her hand, Sheika Shahnaz pulled her left hand and put it on top of Jameela's hand, and she wouldn't let her go for a while. From my position, I could see that Sheik's eyes opened very wide scrutinising Jameela from top to toes and from toes to top. Until then, it didn't occur to my mind that the whole purpose of that reception was to give Sheika Shahnaz the chance to choose a bride for her son. The whole matters became clear to me when we got home, and all those telephone calls started congratulating my mother and wished her all the best. That was to say, Sheika Shahnaz had chosen my sister Jameela to be the bride for her son. While my mother received the news with ultimate happiness, my father didn't show any obvious reaction.

I was shocked to the core by that news. I didn't know how to react. All I had in my mind then was that Jameela would be taken away, too far away. You could imagine Sister when suddenly I felt I was on the verge of losing my friend, my company, and the twin of my soul. Whenever I tried to think of a way to express my objection to that unwelcoming disaster, I would lose my thoughts. I remembered my mother's favourite slogan; a good girl would never say no to her parents. Hence, I felt numb and powerless. I tried to put the matter to Jameela, but every time I tried to talk to her, I found her absent-minded. She looked like a lamb being led to the slaughter, unaware of what would happen to her.

From the reception of Friday to the following Thursday, many preparations took place. My mother had a strong faith in what she called Henna's night. I would wonder Sister if that herbal dye that used to shade the hands and the feet of the bride-to-be before the wedding day was still popular around here?"

Sister Nashmeea glanced at her right palm with a mocking smile and said, "Yes, they believed that the prophet of Islam (peace upon him) used to dye his beard with Henna. I didn't know how authentic that story was, but you would know doctors, when villagers believed a story, there would be no way to take it out of their minds. That proved to me that a civilised environment would not change them a bit till new generations would take the lead. Therefore, the Henna was a blessing to be used as body decorations on the occasions of marriage."

I resumed my telling by confirming what Sister Nashmeea had just explained. With an excited tone. I repeated after her, "Yes Sister. Hence my mother thought that Henna's night, as she called it was the most important event in the wedding preparation. My mother had a few stories about her life. She repeated them whenever we were sitting together, and story number one was Henna's night in her wedding memory. However, that Thursday evening, our house started to receive number of ladies, some on their own and some with their teenage daughters. While my father had stayed away and spent the evening with my uncle, Ashu and I stood in the corner of the lobby staring at the faces of those who gathered in our house with absolute amazement.

Sometimes we looked at the crowd, and sometimes at each other. Ashu asked me, and I asked her in return; 'Who were those people?' Wherefrom did they come? 'Who invited that middle-aged lady who looked like she had Henna expertise?'

Ashu and I felt completely isolated. Hence, we took refuge to my bedroom. A few minutes later, we heard a kind of rhythm associated with vocal chanting. We went out to look; we saw some ladies playing on their hand drums and forming a dance circle around Jameela's chair. I didn't know why, but I was so embarrassed to see my mother had moved within that dancing circle that was formed around my frozen sister. My mother could hardly move with her heavyweight, but she was lifting the ends of her headscarf up and down following the drumming rhythm. Ashu and I stood there for a short while watching that mockery scene till Ashu whispered to me to go to my bedroom again. When we went inside, Ashu lazed down on Jameela's bed, while I sat on my bed, waiting to hear an end to that comedy.

Gradually. The noise was dying down. I could hear our house door open and shut, and cars were moving away from our neighbourhood. I estimate that just after midnight, Jameela came into our bedroom. Her hands and feet were banded by black garments to prevent her fresh Henna from staining her bed. Jameela looked exhausted. It was no time to say anything. Jameela and Ashu slept in our bedroom while I went out and slept on the sofa that night. Yes, my sister, that night looked very strange. My mind was completely blank.

I couldn't think about anything. Questions piled in my head. Jameela, the twin of my soul was on the verge of being taken away from me. What would I do after her departure? am I going to see her again? It might be yes, but where and when. I didn't know whether I had slept or just passed out that night. The noise of my mother's early morning activities preparing our breakfast brought me back to reality. After half an hour my mother started to urge us to have breakfast and be ready and take Jameela, God willing, to her happy trip.

An hour later, we had a phone call. My mother answered the call to tell us that it was our uncle called. He told her he had hired a ten-seat limousine to take us all to Sheika Shahnaz wing in her hotel near the airport. Once my mother heard the vehicle's horn, she took Jameela's hand close to her chest and signalled to all of us, including my father who arrived earlier, to follow her outside to the limousine.

It was a short distance between our house and the Sheik's wing in a hotel close to platform four of Heathrow airport. However, and despite Ashu's presence I was completely absent-minded along that journey. The only thing I remembered was my uncle's request to have a look at Jameela's passport just to check its validity. My mother told him that Jameela's passport was less than one year old. She got it last April when she joined a school trip to the continent. When they decided to move to the airport, Ashu and I stood aside and asked my father's permission to bid Jameela and everybody their farewell and go home.

My father did not ask why as Jameela came forward and we gave her a passionate hug. In the taxi that we had taken to go home, Ashu and I were silent, we did not utter a word. Once I was at home, I went to our bedroom to throw myself on Jameela's bed and started sobbing continually. Ashu was next to me on the top of my bed, and I could hear her non-stop whimpering that shook me to the core.

Our sobbing spell lasted for about an hour, but when we had enough. We pulled ourselves together and took a conscious oath. I put my right hand on the nearby table and asked Ashu put her right-hand above mine and repeated after me. 'We would work very hard at school. We would earn a degree in medicine. We would seek an international charity organisation to help us to serve in the tribes' land. That would be the legitimate way to reach Jameela and find out the reality of her life.'"

Sister Nashmeea glanced at her watch and said, "Great doctors, my admiration. I am glad to tell you that you were close to your target. Just get me the right names involved and I will arrange with my uncle to scrutinise the matter fully. It was getting late, and you must be hungry. I suggest I wish you a good night now, and leave you to order your dinner, and I look forward to meeting you tomorrow to continue our conversation."

Once Sister Nashmeea left through the back door of the cafeteria, one of the Suroors approached us with a new handwritten menu.

# Chapter Nine

I went to bed last night with mixed feelings. On one hand I was hopeful believing Sister Nashmeea's promise that she would help us to reach out to my sister Jameela. On the other hand, I had a lot of worries regarding the mystery that might evolve out of that unpredicted encounter. However, as usual, my suffering of insomnia yesterday continued and once more, late in the morning Ashu called me to wake up. She stayed waiting next to my door for five minutes till I was ready to get out. When we went down to the cafeteria, one of the Suroors came along and greeted us with the usual curtsy and put in front of us two handwritten menus and a fresh pot of tea.

Instead of looking at the menus, Ashu and I started looking at each other. It was rather unusual to get to the cafeteria that late in the morning to find that Sister Nashmeea was not there yet.

Ashu noticed that I was watching the cafeteria bar most of the times, hoping that Sister Nashmeea would pop out. Ashu touched my right shoulder lightly and said, "Listen, Kameela, I know you were anxious to meet Sister Nashmeea. Me too, but we should both know that Sister Nashmeea was a very busy lady. She was kind enough and had given us a lot of her time. When we meet her next time, I will suggest to her to allocate to us the job of sorting out the packages of medicines in the store. That would keep us busy while doing something useful. In the meantime, that would give Sister Nashmeea an adequate time to investigate the whereabouts of Jameela."

I took Ashu's hand gently off my shoulder, and I kissed it with passion and said, "You know Ashu, believe me, sometimes I feel I would be useless without you." Ashu reacted humbly with appreciation by saying, "Come on Kameela, we were a perfect team."

It passed 11 am, and there was no sign of Sister Nashmeea. I tried to control my anxiety to please Ashu who advised me to calm down. Minutes later we heard Sister Nashmeea's voice coming from inside the cafeteria. Ashu and I fixed our eyes in the direction of the cafeteria. I was so relieved to see Sister Nashmeea coming out from behind the cafeteria's bar.

We both stood up and answered her morning greeting. Sister Nashmeea joined our table and immediately she said, "I have some good news for you doctors. I had a very important meeting with my uncle this morning. You would like to know that the topic of my discussion with my uncle was Jameela's plight. When I mentioned the names of Sheika Shahnaz and her son Akrum Siraj-al Deen Safi, my uncle combed his beard with his fingers and said that the Shahnaz family was well-known among the families of the tribes' landlords. He said there were only three feudal landowners on the tribes' land and Sheika Shahnaz was one of them. Accordingly, my uncle promised to instruct our clandestine informers to give him a detailed report about the lady, her son and Jameela's situation. Let us hope for some good news."

When Sister Nashmeea finished her sentence, I felt numb and went silent. But Ashu dared to say, "Thank you very much, Sister. You had been open-handed with us. We will never forget your kind effort."

Sister Nashmeea had blushed a bit and repeated, "Don't mention it doctor, I was only affirming my principles. That was my task. I am here to defend the victims of backward societies. Now doctors, please forgive me, but I was curious to hear your heroic plan. The plan that got you here and how did you achieve the help of that low-profile international medic organisation. I am baffled. Please enlighten me about your heroic adventure with its fine steps forward from A to Z."

After a short silence, I said, "Well Sister. Although the plight of Jameela was nagging me night and day, realistically, our story started in early April 1990. That day in London, spring was showing earlier than usual. The days were getting longer and warmer. It was Friday afternoon when Ashu and I finished our lab session at Hammersmith Medical Centre quite early that day. It was sunny and fresh and instead of taking the bus, we decided to walk it to Hammersmith Station. The station's area was very busy, and the yellow daffodils flowers scattered in bunches over the street's isles; reflected their yellow spring colour in all directions. The scene was inviting, and Ashu and I decided to relax at a corner café near the station."

However, it was human nature, I believe that when we relax and unwind for a while, some thoughts would find their way to our heads and embitter our respite. Thus, that pleasant spot reminded me of Jameela, and I wished her presence to share our pleasant atmosphere. It was difficult to explain my feelings. I was missing my sister Jameela so much. I missed her so much that I started to feel as explained before, her missing was nagging me just like physical pain. I was sinking in my thoughts while Ashu went to the bar to collect our coffees.

When Ashu returned to our table, she noticed my tears still flickering in my eyes despite my efforts to hide them. She knew the cause of my depression immediately. She didn't say anything for a while and waited until I dried my tears up and calmed down. She asked me kindly if there was any news from Jameela?

"No, Ashu; not for the last three years." Ashu reacted by pulling a deep sigh and reminded me that once, we thought we could do something about Jameela's fate. Even we could arrange a trip to the tribes' land and meet Jameela and find out first-hand what troubled her and prevented her from communicating with her family. Then we were in the final year of our medical studies. In a few weeks, we would be graduated and formally; we would be called doctors. Ashu took a deep breath, adjusted her seat, and asked, "Don't you think that after our graduation we would be more capable of accomplishing our hope regarding Jameela?" Yes Ashu, "that would be more possible."

We both went silent for a few minutes. Then I reminded Ashu that I wished it was as simple as that. Then I gathered my thoughts and said, "Yes, Ashu," I suppose we can utilise our profession to start our move. But first; we need a formal cover from an established global organisation that would agree to accept us as members of its institute and then they could introduce us formally to the authorities wherever border crossing would be required. That would not be possible without proof of practical service in the medical field for at least two years.

At that point, Ashu went silent, and her eyes started shifting from one corner to another. Then she looked me straight and said, "You would never know; by then, we could have received some news from Jameela."

No sooner after she had finished her sentence that she realised that I disagreed with what she said. She did not wait for my comment. She got my disagreement from the way I shook my head. I knew very well from the few letters; we had received from Jameela during the last seven years, that there was nothing in her life that she would tell us about. All what she was trying to do was to give us peace of mind "All that she said in those letters that she was well."

On that bright spring day, Sister, I had a strange feeling. A feeling of courage and determination. Simply because that was the first time Ashu and I discussed Jameela's issue quite seriously.

Since then, Jameela's problem became our topic whenever we met and had time to talk. Time passed very fast. And we had been over two years in the medical field. One of the hard conditions that would enable us to apply for voluntary service abroad through a charity organisation was achieved. One day Ashu surprised me when she told me that she had written to several global charity organisations that provide medical aid for troubled parts of the world. Though five of them, as she told me, so far had answered negatively.

Fundamentally, they stated very clearly that they would not give us the option to choose the country we intended to serve. If I forgot, I would never forget that Friday evening when Ashu and I met in the cafeteria of Hammersmith Faculty. Ashu looked as if she was in obvious disappointment. She first said, "Kameela, I am sorry to disappoint you, but no news-bad news."

We were performing two different shifts that afternoon and had to travel home separately. By eight-thirty that evening, back home, I was sitting for the tasty dinner my mother had already prepared for me. My mother was astonished to see me staring at the food without touching it. I had no appetite to eat. Simply because I couldn't stop thinking about the setback of our applications to get the support of a global organisation that would make it possible for us to execute our plan.

For me, that setback was too hard to digest. To avoid my mother's curiosity and usual worries, I pulled my plait from the dinner table and took it to my bedroom. But no sooner than I settled there, than my mother's voice came whispering and firm: "Kameela darling, Ashu was on the phone."

It was rather unusual for Ashu to phone us after nine o'clock in the evening. It occurred to me that there was something important had taken place. While getting close to the phone, I had butterflies in my stomach. Here came Ashu's voice through the wire, "Good news, amiga."

Ashu sometimes used a Spanish expression for a friend whenever she was cheerful, an expression she picked up during her latest summer holiday with her family in Majorca. "Tell me please."

Ashu came back with an excited voice. "An organisation called Ready Doctors for Overseas Volunteering and Raising Donations came with a positive response." She explained that the organisation had offered that we might choose the country where we intend to serve and they would extend their support and guidance, but that would be subject to an arranged interview. "Ashu, my wonderful amiga, this was an opportunity that we should never miss."

Ashu and I agreed to meet the following day at 10 am near Hounslow Central tube station and I begged Ashu not to forget the letter of the organisation so that we could print a few copies, just in case. I was over-excited, but I managed to sneak my dinner into the fridge without my mother noticing, so it would be my early breakfast the following day.

My sleep was interrupted by funny dreams that night, but by nine-thirty that Sunday morning, I was standing up on my own near the station. When Ashu appeared tumbling while walking and weaving the letter in her right hand, I felt my heart leaping for joy. Remembering it was Sunday and no shop would be opened before eleven am, we stood up near the corner of the station and read the letter together more than once, without interruption.

Ashu suggested that she knew the people who run a coffee shop at the beginning of the next side road and believed that they would serve us anyway. She was right. There I was more relaxed and read the letter once more. There was no address at the head of the letter. But there was a PO box number, the same PO box Ashu used to correspond with the organisation. In addition, there was a telephone number at the top of the letter followed by three extensions. One for donations, one for enquiries and one for volunteers.

Before we separated that afternoon, we made sure that each of us had two copies of the original letter. Ashu suggested jokingly that we should get more copies of the letter, frame the original one and hang it on the wall of her bedroom. We decided to phone the organisation on Monday; the first opportunity we would have the chance. Here came Monday. Without preparation, at about fifteen pasts one in the afternoon, during our lunch break, we both reached the public phones at the cafeteria of Hammersmith medical faculty.

Each of us carried a copy of the organisation's letter. What did we find? tow telephones were out of order, and the only working one was occupied by one of the cleaners who seemed to be enjoying her argument with someone on the other end of the line. We stood nearby staring at each other waiting for the cleaner lady to finish her call.

I whispered to Ashu, "Have you heard of Murphy's law?"

"No, Kameela I never heard of it."

"Do not worry, Ashu, I will explain it to you one day." Heavy ten minutes passed and the lady on the phone ignored our frustration or pretended that she never noticed us. Eventually, I gathered my courage, moved close to the lady, and politely asked her to hurry up with her call as we had an important call to make. She finished her call but not before another three minutes. I held the telephone with shaky hands and Ashu stood next to me with some extra coins in her hand; just in case we needed more time for our call. Once my call was answered, I was relieved. A calm lady's voice came on the line. First, she announced the name of the organisation and then she asked how she could help me. I asked for extension 3.

She came with a very firm answer, "Do not worry about the extension, just give me the reference number of your application as we stated in our letter."

I reached to Ashu's copy and read: AK 500-5. The lady on the line said, "Just let me confirm few points. Your application was a joint application, is that correct?"

"Yes madam," I answered.

"Fine," she said, and added, "In two weeks' time you would receive a letter from us with an application form for you to fill. By receiving your application, we would arrange for your first interview." Then she asked if our address was still the same.

"Yes, madam it was."

"That was okay then." The lady on the phone confirmed that they would arrange for our first interview as soon as they received our completed application. I thanked her very much and closed the line, and immediately I jump to Ashu and gave her a very warm hug. Since that day and for a fortnight our hourly subject was the anticipated letter from the organisation. It was the end of the second week after our daring phone call when Ashu called me to tell me that the waited letter had arrived by late Saturday post. We both rushed to our usual meeting point near the station.

Ashu looked unhappy regarding the contents of the letter. "I think they came with some hard conditions." Ashu grumbled and handed me the letter which was signed by the Secretary-General of the organisation. I read it very carefully. The signatory requested us to write a joint essay in which we would explain our connection to the terrain we were going to serve and if we might speak the language of the people there, and if other motivations had encouraged us to volunteer with our service. The organisation should receive that essay at least five days before the 30 August, the day of our interview.

The secretary added that in attending the interview, we should not forget to bring copies of our graduation certificates and our passports that should be valid for over six months. I gave the letter back to Ashu and asked her disagreeably to show me any hard condition in that letter.

I explained to her that originally, we were both from that part of the world, plus I speak the language of the people, if not perfect but reasonably enough to communicate, and you understand that language though you did not speak it. On top of that, we have family connections as my sister Jameela, even though she was there because of arranged marriage but, she lived there. Ashu uttered a few unclear words, and then she agreed with me, "Oh Kameela, I wished I had your confidence."

The letter came with a self-address returning envelope to the UK branch of the organisation. We were asked in the letter to print our names on the bottom of the form and put our signatures next to them as a confirmation of our consent and send the letter together with the requested essay back to the organisation. We did not wait for two weeks. Systematically, on the spot we took the letter to the corner shop and made four copies: two for Ashu and two for me. It was an act of anxiety, just in case. We rushed home holding the original letter with fresh copies like a valuable treasure.

Back home, I pulled a small notebook from my shelf, sat on the same table I used to share with Jameela and started thumbing through it to refresh my memory regarding places and families' names in the tribes' land. I added what I considered to be substantial information to be listed in the required essay. I left the table when I finished the designated essay requested by the organisation. My mother had noticed that I was over-occupied. Important to mention that Ashu and I had previously agreed that we should put our parents' minds at peace by preparing a reasonable story that would justify our absence. We agreed that we could tell them we were advancing our carrier by serving abroad.

For example, if I would tell my mother where precisely we were going, she would die out of worries and anxiety. So, we agreed to claim to our parents that our mission was to north Africa, namely Egypt. That abroad could be anywhere except the tribes' land. So, when the question was raised with me; the answer was ready: "Yes mother, Ashu and I preparing for a short overseas service. It would be necessary to advance our carrier."

My mother had accepted the fake news; or let me say she took it with a pinch of salt. Without any hesitation, I handed the essay I drafted to Ashu the following day and requested her to give it a second reading and adjust or even change what she might believe was necessary. Ashu was very pleased with my draft. We sat down and revised it together one more time and we agreed on some minor adjustments.

Eventually, we reached what we had called the final version, which had come to one full page and a half. That was by the following Monday afternoon when we folded it together with the application form, we sealed them in the self-addressed envelope, and we felt a great relief after we had posted the sealed envelope as recorded delivery.

Now we had to face the heavy waiting time for a response. Two weeks passed and we were waiting to hear from the organisation. However, suddenly, something drastic had happened. It was Monday afternoon when I received a message from the reception of the faculty telling me to contact home as soon as possible. I excused myself to my superiors and rushed to the telephone downstairs. My mother answered the phone, but she was not her normal self. From her fragmented sentences, I understood that my father had collapsed while she was watching him digging around an old plant in our back garden.

My mother kept repeating it was her fault because she was the one who requested him to move that plant to another location. I asked her kindly to stop blaming herself and tell me about my father; and where he was now. She said that she had contacted my uncle, who came soon and arranged for an ambulance and moved my father to a close-by private hospital. My uncle was a man who was full of contradictions. He would advocate social justice and women's rights, but once the subject changed, he would revert to traditions and religion, his version of religion. He was a socialist and a feudalist at the same time. His general education was different from my father's. He was brought up in the city; therefore, he had proper schooling; up to the intermediate level.

While my father went to a basic religious school in the tribe's land, where they would teach reading and writing and traditional Islamic theology. My father and my uncle never fully agreed on one single topic. Usually, they would start their conversation amicably. But that would not last long. One disagreeable word in the conversation and my father would show a sort of irritation. Hence my uncle would change the subject and calm my father down.

My uncle was the one who would condescend, following deeply rooted traditions, as he was younger than my father. My mother and my uncle's wife would hardly ever participate in their everlasting debate or what they would call their continuous arguments. My father had little interest in controversial social issues, and he described himself as moderately conservative. At the same time, my uncle who would think he was a man of a progressive mind and a women's rights advocator, participated in persuading Jameela to accept her arranged marriage. Maybe he was hoping to realise his long-waited dream, reaching out to his confiscated land by warlords ruling the tribes' land after the fall of the communist government.

When my mother phoned my uncle that afternoon and told him that my father was not well, he left everything behind, attended to my father within ten minutes, and arranged for an ambulance to get him to the nearest private hospital. When I arrived home, my uncle had just come from the hospital. He explained to me the condition of my father. I immediately concluded that my father had suffered a mini stroke. Considering my uncle's speed in getting him to the hospital, I knew that he would recover quickly. However, I could not guess how long that would take. In the evening, my uncle drove us; my mother Ashu and me to the hospital where my father was resting.

When my father saw us around his bed, he smiled and told us with some difficulty that he was okay. His doctor told us that he was okay, and his condition would improve within two weeks. Maybe in three weeks, he could go home. My uncle drove us back home. Once we got home, my mother toddled to her bedroom, generating some heavy sighs. Ashu and I waited for her till she had gone upstairs. Then we waited for a few seconds at the bottom of the stairs, and then we went to my bedroom where Ashu used to occupy Jameela's bed whenever she was late to go home. Ashu stretched out on the bed while I was sitting next to our working table. With my head between my hands.

I reminded Ashu about my usual saying, "Life is ironic." How much we used to be anxious to receive an appointment from the organisation to proceed with our plan, now I would like their invitation letter to not arrive quickly. I did not think we would go ahead with our move before my father would be back in perfect health.

Ashu nodded her head, agreeing with me. Then I reminded her that I told her; sometimes ago, one day I would explain to her the phrase "Murphy's law." She sat in her bed and begged me to elaborate further.

I told her, that it was exactly what we are facing here today. We had set up a plan that would be almost perfect; ninety-nine possibilities were thought of, except for the one per cent negative possibility that could occur from nowhere. For example, whoever thought that my father would fall ill close to the day we were ready to start our precious trip? That was the meaning of the term Murphy's law. Ashu nodded her head again agreeing with what I had explained.

At any rate, a month had passed without hearing a word from the organisation. Luckily my father was back home, and his condition was significantly improved. Though he was using a walking stick, he could talk again with some difficulties, and he eat with the help of my mother or a nurse. With the help of a physiotherapist, he was regaining his health very rapidly. My uncle used to visit him every second day when he was in the hospital and the day, he arranged to discharge him and brought him home, he paid the cost of his three weeks in the hospital.

It was Friday afternoon when my uncle brought my father home, He was a bit weak, but his movement and his speech have drastically improved. My mother was very pleased, and Ashu and I went back to our 'conspiracy', Ashu and I then agreed there would be no concern left regarding my father's health, and it was time to contact the organisation to find out if there was any progress in our case. Ashu suggested that the people of the organisation so far had been serious and cooperative, so we should wait for their decision rather than pushing them into a hasty act. It sounded logical, and after all, what options did we have?

A few days later, Friday evening 23 July 1993 Ashu phoned me with obvious excitement in her voice to tell me that the long-waited letter had arrived. In that letter, the organisation specified that they had successfully negotiated with our employers by explaining that we were getting involved in an overseas humanitarian duty. Therefore, they were requested to disengage us from our daily duties at the faculty as soon as possible. The letter went further to tell us that we should attend to our faculty to finalise some papers works and to agree on a date for the disengagement of our duties.

The letter added that our final meeting will take place on Tuesday, 30 August 1994, at 1.30 in sky court, in High Sky hotel in the vicinity of Heathrow airport while our planned journey had been designed for Wednesday, 15 September 1994. I read the letter more than once. I was so excited that I hardly slept that night.

By Friday, 13 August, we both finalised our assigned duties at the Medical Faculty and by midday, we went up to the third floor to shake hands with our supervisors and thank them for their kind support. Once we finished these formalities, we zoomed out of the faculty to the main road. It was sunny and warm, and I surprised Ashu by waving down a taxi. That was so sudden that I even did not give Ashu the chance to question our direction.

I whispered the address to the driver ensuring Ashu didn't hear the address. When the taxi stopped ten minutes later in front of the Persian restaurant at Fulham High Street, Ashu realised I was treating her by inviting her to her favourite dish, the well-known Persian kebab. Apart from that little celebration, we got very busy preparing for our interview. We worked jointly to perfect our required essay. In the meantime, I started gathering some further information regarding the route and the targeted terrain of our intended mission.

I concluded that Jameela had been trapped in isolated land that offered no communication with the rest of the world. In addition, I discovered some facts I would never have reached by probing into my parent's tales and memories. I learnt that in that part of the world and beyond what was known as the district of 'Maywand' close to a stretch of land that included several provinces in the far southeast of Afghanistan and west of Pakistan known as the Pashtuns' belt.

The inhabitants of those provinces were overwhelmingly ethnic Pashtuns. Then I went further in my research to conclude that the Pashtuns' tribal society consists of several tribes that speak the Pashto and or the Dari languages. They followed a very restricted traditional code of tribal conduct. The bottom of that geographical belt was composed of a semi-parallelogram bordering Pakistan from the east and Iran from the far west.

This was the part of Afghanistan where my parents and associates had initiated their moves to the rest of the world, forced by the political conflicts that gripped the country since it had realised its independence from Britain in 1919. All that I had come across in my research which sometimes looked like fiction tale that we were going to face as an actual reality during our intended journey. Yes, the time had come.

Tomorrow was Monday, the 30 August 1994 and we had to be prepared for the interview that would decide the fate of our plan. That day was special in our lives. I met Ashu in the afternoon, and she brought with her the items we intended to present in our meeting, including the required essay. Ashu stayed with me the whole day, and then she decided that we should spend the night together so that she would calm me down. Ashu, as usual, occupied Jameela's bed and went into a deep sleep. I could figure out from her low tune whistling nose habitually would play whenever she would go into a deep sleep. After I had wished Ashu; sweet dreams, I tried desperately to sleep. That night, I was twisting and turning left and right in my bed, unable to sleep.

Sister Nashmeea was listening to me with great interest, and I was pleased to be able to recall the events of those days so clearly and efficiently. I suddenly felt as if Sister Nashmeea had lost track of my story. I was talking with my eyes fixed on Sister Nashmeea's direction. When I stopped talking for a second, Sister Nashmeea nudged me to have look at Ashu on my left. I was shocked to see Ashu flat on her face on the table with her arms hanging on her sides. I lifted Ashu's head gently and asked her if she was alright?

"No, Ashu answered, I had a terrible headache," Sister Nashmeea called one of the Suroors and asked her to sit next to Ashu and massage her head for a while and asked me to go with her to the medicine store to get some tablets for Ashu. We went through the back door of the cafeteria, which was opened in a corridor. In the corridor were three metal doors. One on the opposite wall and one on each side of the aisle. Sister Nashmeea pulled a metal key from her pouch and opened the left door. Sister Nashmeea climbed a few steps into the room, and I went behind her.

Although there was a large side window on the top of the back wall, the room was rather dark and smelled of medicines. In the middle of the room, there were piles of carton boxes. Sister Nashmeea picked a small size box and opened it using the metal key in her hand. She picked three packs of Aspro from the box and asked me to have a look to see if they were still valid. "Yes, Sister, they were valid for another six months."

Sister Nashmeea and I went back to the cafeteria the same way we came to find Ashu relaxing in her chair. When Sister Nashmeea noticed that Ashu's health was improving, she said, "I believe we had enough for today, doctors; I would suggest that you both go upstairs and have a very good rest tonight, and I would try to be with you tomorrow as early as possible."

Sister Nashmeea opened one of the packs and peeled two tablets. Back in the cafeteria, she handed them to Ashu with one hand and a glass of water in the other, before she vanished through the back door of the cafeteria.

# Chapter Ten

When Sister Nashmeea left the cafeteria, wishing us a good night and wished Ashu a good health, I took Ashu's hand and helped her climb the stairs. We strolled till we got to her room. Then I helped her to take her shoes off and supported her to lie down in her bed without changing her clothes. Then I sat next to her on the edge of her bed and touched her forehead with my right hand to ensure that her temperature was normal. She put her hand on my hand and said with a light smile, "Do not worry, Kameela. I don't think I had a temperature, and my headache was no longer severe. Please, Kameela, go and light that little lantern in the corner; I cannot stand the darkness." I pulled myself and went to that small corner table where that little old lantern was. I used several matchsticks to light that lantern without success. It used to burn for a few seconds and then it went off.

Eventually, Ashu lifted her head and told me to stop trying. She told me that most likely that her lantern had run out of gasoline. "But why Ashu, whey the gasoline did not last you longer?"

Ashu smiled and said, "You asked me why? Simple, because I used to leave it burning the whole night." Then she went on saying, "Kameela. Although you have given me your room which was not directly overlooking the graveyard, you should forgive me for leaving my lantern burning the whole night. I fear darkness."

Well, what should I do? I took Ashu's lantern to my room, brought my lantern to her room, and lit it.

Ashu and I were in one room again. Hence, we would never stop chatting. We had so many issues to discuss, and so many things to talk about. Once again, we revised how I presented Jameela's case to Sister Nashmeea. Ashu told me once again that she was very impressed by my clarity regarding the sequence of events and my ability to win Sister Nashmeea's heart and genuine support. "Sure, I said, please Ashu, you should remind me to ask Sister Nashmeea to report to our charity organisation in London and inform them that we were okay, and everything was in order."

Ashu agreed with me, but she added that, "We were at the beginning of the fourth week of our mission and that was not too long, taking into consideration that we had a three-month assignment."

However, my penalty that night was to creep to my bed in the darkness. And struggle silently to get some sleep if I could. The night passed, but slightly different from my usual nights. I could not find a clear explanation for my relaxed feeling. Possibly I was able to have a few hours of deep sleep. As a result, for the first time on our trip got up before Ashu.

Therefore, immediately after I had dressed up and put myself in order, I went close to the door of Ashu's bedroom, called her name, and reminded her that we had to be ready to meet Sister Nashmeea who promised to come early that day. Ashu did not hide her surprise that I was up before her. Her voice came back rattling as she repeated, "Oh my God, you shocked me, Kameela. Please give me a few minutes to be ready."

Then, we went downstairs to the cafeteria. We were astonished to see Sister Nashmeea was already there. She had taken her seat in the cafeteria, wiggling her teapot to make sure that it had brewed properly.

When we got close to Sister Nashmeea, Ashu lifted her right hand and repeated her morning greeting, so I did. With a broad smile, Sister Nashmeea stood up and gave Ashu a warm hug and said, "How nice to see you in excellent health dear doctor. Please take your seats, doctors and request your breakfast first." Then she added, "In the meantime, we should resume our yesterday's subject. I was dying to hear from Doctor Kameela about her first meeting face-to-face with the organisation's executives that arranged your assignment."

The breakfast was a secondary issue for me that morning. Ashu went straight to her honey jar and had a few dips of the brown bread while I went straight to some pieces of homemade cake placed on a plate on the table by one of the Suroors. The cake tasted delicious sustained by a few sips of warm tea. Once I was satisfied, I took a glance at Sister Nashmeea to find her was staring at me waiting for me to resume my telling regarding the instructions and recommendations we received from the humanitarian organisation before our trip.

However, before I said anything, Sister Nashmeea said, "You knew doctor, you told us, yesterday that you both went to bed that Sunday prepared to go the following day to the office of the charity organisation with your documents. I would tend to think it was the very interview that had put you on the truck of your plan."

I cleared my throat and said, "Yes, Sister, as I explained in our yesterday's meeting that Ashu and I were over-excited to receive that long-waited invitation."

The night before, we double-checked everything we would take to the interview before we went to bed.

Ashu occupied Jameela's bed and it didn't take her long to start the usual barely heard whistling. Which meant that she was in a deep sleep already. Great, but what about me? It seemed something unusual had happened to me that night. I felt much more relaxed than before. I woke up the following morning to my mother's voice whispering next to the door calling us for breakfast. I looked at Ashu to find her sitting in the bed sheltered by a faint green morning light coming from behind her through the old green curtains.

"It was 8 o'clock, Kameela," she said in a very low voice, and she started getting dressed. We moved to the small hall and sat around the breakfast table. I had very little appetite, but I had to take a few bites of cheese on toasted bread just to please my mother. Most likely because I was so nervous about the coming interview. To my surprise, Ashu was enjoying her breakfast as usual. She was much calmer and more composed than me.

Time passed very quickly, and by 12.30 we rushed out aiming to Hounslow Central underground station. We quickly managed to hire a cab to sky court, in the High Sky hotel near Heathrow airport. Upon our arrival at the hotel, we met a formally dressed guy. Once we mentioned to him the name of the court, he guided us to the gate of that court. Though we were ten minutes early for our appointment, a watchful person was waiting for us at the court's door. The minute Ashu uttered the symbolic code word that was given to us earlier, our receiving official opened the court's gate and invited us in.

The first thing I observed inside the court room was a long mahogany table, surrounded by nicely arranged red leather chairs, occupying the middle of the court. At the far-right corner of the court room were another small table with four greenish colour chairs. Our lead appointed to us to take our seats on the wall side of the long mahogany table. Five minutes later, a door at the bottom of the court was wide open and a tall bearded dignified gentleman emerged, followed by a middle-aged pleasant-looking lady. Both moved slowly and stood in front of us across the large mahogany table. Ashu and I stood up silently as a sign of respect.

With a gesture from the gentleman hand, the gentleman indicated to us kindly to sit down. He introduced himself as Doctor Shashi, the managing director of the U K branch of the organisation, and then he introduced the lady next to him as Lady Nazeema, the chief administrator of the branch. Then he started his speech by greeting us and wishing us a great afternoon. He welcomed us to the family of Ready Doctors for Overseas Volunteering and Raising Donations organisation. Ashu thanked him in our name and promised him that we would be up to the expectation of the organisation.

The lady moved closer, collected our passports and the file of our essay from Ashu, and vanished into the back door of the court. Dr Shashi apologised for the interruption and resumed his briefing by glancing from time to time at a printed leaflet in his hand. I opened the pad in front of me and started taking some notes. I felt at ease as Dr Shashi's calming voice and charming confidence prevailed in the court. So did Ashu.

However, I was impressed when Dr Shashi went on to say, "We should always remember, doctors that we belonged to a humanitarian organisation, and we would voluntarily offer our medical aids and assistant to those who needed it regardless of their colour, religion, or their ethnic group."

After a short review of the history of the organisation and its international humanitarian activities, Dr Shashi paused for a few seconds and gave us a direct look with a soft smile tinted his oval face and said, "In the name of our organisation, I would like to express our gratefulness to you for coming forward for this undertaking. I would like to state some facts regarding the inhabitants of the land you aim to serve. I might touch upon some historical events, but please do not take what I'm going to elucidate as a lecture on history, that would not be my intention. You are going to deal with people. Some of them were hard to understand, especially when you considered their beliefs and their understanding of religion. But please remember that you would be there to help them, not change them."

Ashu and I took a brief look at each other, and we both moved our heads down and up twice, a sign of agreeing with Dr Shashi statement. Then Dr Shashi pulled a slid box from the side of the table and reached for a warped map. He unfolded it and hung it up to a side pole fixed to the edge of the mahogany table.

After a brief absence of Lady Nazeema through the small back door of the court, the back door was slightly opened, and Lady Nazeema emerged out again.

The lady was holding two brown envelopes and a standard 12-inch red plastic ruler. She apologised again for the interruption. She handed the ruler to Dr Shashi and handed the envelopes to Ashu, saying, "Hi doctors, here are your passports, check them, please. In the second envelope, you would find an amount of two hundred dollars. That amount would be some petty cash that you might need, just in case, as we were told that all your expenses would be covered locally. You would notice that we had converted one hundred dollars of the amount into five dollars notes because you would not find bureau de change if you might need to break the big notes while you were away from the airport."

And then she pulled a chair near the other end of the mahogany table and sat there quietly gazing at the map that was hugged by Dr Shashi. I examined the map very carefully. It looked familiar. It is like the one my mother used to keep hanging on the wall of her bedroom. I was the map of Afghanistan, a part of this copy of the map was given a green shade along the Afghan-Pakistani borders and another shade with brown colour along the west of the country on the Iranian border. Dr Shashi appointed the ruler at the map, encircling it around the middle on the map and said, "You see doctors? That beautiful country was always influenced by the politics of its neighbours."

Then he elaborated further, explaining that "Historically that country was a British colony until 1919. Since then, several coups de' estate and countercoups de' estate had taken place up till 1978 when a leftist/communist group took over the government. They embarked on an ambitious land reform program that put their regime into gigantic trouble. That obliged them to call for the Soviet troops in their alliance for help. In 1978, the red army invaded Afghanistan.

Under the banner that classified the communists as atheists, the immediate reaction came from three local centres. The first active centre was set up by the formation of the Assembly of Islamic Clerics, a fundamentalist political front that had enormous influence over some important officials among the formal establishment in neighbouring Pakistan." Then, he went on to explain.

"Here, in that green shaded area along the Pakistani Afghan borders where all kind of military activities used to take place.

It was the tribes' land, the very area we were meant to serve. It was never a peaceful terrain. It was relatively complicated by its very religious and social nature. However, that was our task. We were not to choose easy spots to serve.

That would undermine our very existence. We meant to outreach those who would need our help. That is the meaning of the charity in our field. In the meantime, in our move, we had two issues we considered them to be of top concern; the safety of our volunteers; and the benefit of the people that we were aiming to serve.

Hence, I would like to put you in the picture of the country you would serve. I would be very short and very specific, and you could take some notes if you would like. But please be careful. Do not take these notes with you, they were for your revision before your departure, in case, that your notes would fall in the hands of the wrong people who could consider them suspicious or insulting."

Then he explained the nature of the conflicts in the area or the terrain we aimed to reach. At that stage, I realised that Dr Shashi was getting to a new phase of his lecture. In his description of the ongoing conflict in Afghanistan, he mentioned some facts I had come across through my private research about the country.

I know for example, the nature of the conflict among the groups of the Mujahideen that followed the withdrawal of the Soviet Union's army. And the six or seven militia groups were fighting the Soviet Union troops, were now engaged in a bloody conflict within themselves. However, one fanatic group known as Taliban had emerged as the most brutal and powerful among the rest.

We thought we better rely on Dr Shashi's briefing, who explained that it looked like so far, the group had been unable to extend their control over the entire country. Then Dr Shashi went further and said, "Our latest information revealed that the fanatic militia was facing a vicious resistance from the division of Ahmad Shah, the leader of the Hazara sect that controlled the North-East province of the country. Mind you, for several reasons, The Pakistan Inter-Service Intelligence would always have a great influence on all warlords and other local leaders. Therefore, we arranged with the Pakistani authority to get you to the area through a very safe enclave under the control of a moderate wise leader in full communication with the Pakistani authority."

Suddenly Lady's Nazeema pager that was attached to her ballet started making a signal. She pulled it up and scrutinised its message. She rushed to the back door of the court and stayed there for a few minutes before she came out. Dr Shashi speculated that Lady Nazeema received a message, requesting her to call their representative at Heathrow airport. Then he said, "It was most likely regarding the air tickets for your trip."

"Yes, Sister he was right." A few minutes later Lady Nazeema came out from the back room with a smile on her face, and said, "Great news, doctors, that would save you another appointment; I had been just told by our representative at Heathrow airport that your air tickets had been dispatched to us half an hour ago. Therefore, I would expect them to be with us soon." She was right.

A couple of minutes later, there was a knocking on the court's gate. Lady Nazeema went to the gate and made a narrow opening in a slide window on the left side of the gate. Somebody handed her through that opening a medium-size white envelope. She returned to her chair and started thumbing through the envelope's contents.

Ashu and I waited silently so was Dr Shashi, till Lady Nazeema lifted her head and said, "Good, very good. They got you two return business class tickets, open for six months. We would suggest to you to book your trip a week ahead, preferably you would choose a weekday and keep us informed. Please, you would make sure to report to British Airways at the indicated terminal four hours before the take-off." Then she stood up and handed the white envelope to Ashu, repeating: "Happy journey and safe return."

Then Lady Nazeema added, "Would you please let us know the day of your departure, and upon your arrival put on your white coats and stay close to British Airways deck so that our staff there would recognise you."

Then I went on to say, "Well Sister Nashmeea everything went according to plan except Ashu's lantern that had run out of fuel yesterday." Then I bent down and picked up Ashu's lantern from under the table and put it in front of Sister Nashmeea. Ashu looked slightly embarrassed, but Sister Nashmeea laughed her head off.

While one of the Suroors took the lantern away to fill it with gasoline, Sister Nashmeea stood up and said, "Thank you very much, doctors. Despite some early difficulties, you had executed your part of the plan perfectly. Now the ball was in my court. I would like to tell you that my uncle's people in the tribes' land had already started their investigations regarding the whereabouts of Jameela. My uncle told me that he was informed that she was alive and well and they planned to communicate with her soon."

When Sister Nashmeea wished us a goodnight, I felt anxious and shaky and kept repeating her last few words as if I was in a dream. I woke up when Suroor brought back Ashu's lantern and put it in front of me on the table. I picked up the lantern while Sister Nashmeea smiling and wishing us a good night.

# Chapter Eleven

When Sister Nashmeea left the cafeteria, I felt. Confused and I went sinking into my own thoughts. My tongue had become stiff. My vision went blurred.

My eyes were fixed on Ashu but, I was not seeing her. I was neither seeing nor hearing anything around me for at least five minutes. That lasted till Ashu shouted my name and wiggled my chin gently. When I heard Ashu calling me rather loudly, I regained my senses slowly and gradually.

It seemed that one of the Suroors had heard Ashu calling my name. She came outside the cafeteria and stood behind us without saying a word. Ashu looked back at her and said, "Sorry dear, there was no problem, it was Doctor Kameela who had got depressed and went into an unconscious fit for a few minutes."

By then I was completely up and about. I gathered my courage, looked back at the young girl, and requested her to serve us a fresh pot of tea. Suroor smiled and said, "With pleasure, doctor, with a small ball of some cubic sugar."

I believed Ashu had realised that it would take me a while to go back to my normal self. The news of Jameela that was revealed by Sister Nashmeea as I tried to envision had shaken me to the core. However, Ashu's presence around was a calming factor. Once the young girl placed the pot of tea on our table, Ashu filled my mug with tea and put it in front of me. Sipping our tea kept us busy for a while. We didn't talk much. Half an hour passed before Ashu asked me if I was okay to go upstairs. "Yes Ashu, I would be fine enough to move, but please you should not leave me on my own. Stay with me in my room for a while."

I looked back in the direction of the cafeteria and thanked Suroor for her kind attention. Then we moved slowly upstairs. I watched my steps carefully while Ashu supported me from behind. When we got to my room, I threw myself on the top of the bed, while Ashu took her seat on the edge of my bed facing me directly with a sympathetic look. All I remembered then was Ashu's affectionate face that evening before I had closed my eyes. It seemed I was mentally exhausted. I had no idea when and how Ashu had left my room. That physical state gave me a long heavy sleep.

When Ashu knocked on my door the following morning, I noticed a ray of light strongly shining through the window. I assumed then that the time was at least nine o'clock in the morning.

"Give me a few minutes. Please Ashu, I need a few minutes to wash my face, brush my teeth and change my socks."

In response to my request, Ashu's voice came very soft, "No, problem amiga, take your time. I will be waiting here for you."

When I went out, I found Ashu a bit apprehensive. She came closer and said, while giving me a passionate hug, "Great amiga, you looked perfect." I couldn't say anything. I just tried, with some difficulties, to smile. Then we went downstairs to the cafeteria. We got busy taking our usual breakfast, a process, which lasted for about half an hour. But when one hour passed without any sign of Sister Nashmeea, I got rather nervous.

Ashu noticed my anxiety. She tried to calm me down. She looked me right in the eye and said, "Listen to me, Kameela. You should appreciate that Sister Nashmeea had given us a lot of her time, and we should appreciate the fact that she was a very busy lady. You have noticed that she was one of the decision-makers among the local authority. We should be grateful that she had given us all that attention, but I believe her time could be beyond her control."

I stared back at Ashu and said, "I didn't fully understand what you just had said. Did you mean that Sister Nashmeea had no control over her time?"

Ashu smiled and answered me quickly, "Listen to me, thick head. Supposing that Sister Nashmeea had entered an important meeting and that meeting lasted much longer than she expected; what she would do?"

At that stage, I suggested that we should talk to one of the Suroors and request her to contact Sister Nashmeea for an authority to take us to the medicine's store to start sorting out the mixed packets and categorise them according to their medical values and validity. By that, we would make use of our waiting time and give our mission a reasonable justification.

Ashu's reaction to my suggestion was very clear, "I would fully agree with you amiga, you should initiate the move."

I looked back in the direction of the cafeteria and raised my voice slightly calling Ms Suroor to attend to us for a few seconds. It didn't take more than a few seconds to see one of the Suroors standing in front of us with her usual smile and courtesy greetings. Ashu excused herself and asked Suroor if it was possible to contact Sister Nashmeea today! "No, doctor except in an emergency."

Then Suroor added, "But if you would tell me doctors about your need, I might be able to answer it."

Ashu stood up and said, "Thanks. It was not a big deal. We wanted to know if it was possible to get Sister Nashmeea's permission to do some work in the medicine store."

Suroor smiled and said, "But you have that permission already doctors. Sister Nashmeea told us you could attend the medicine store anytime you like. I had the key to the store. You would follow me to take you there. But please doctors, leave the store door open, and knock for me on the back door of the cafeteria when you would finish the job."

The medicine store was a bit damp and dark. There was only one little lookout on the top of the back wall of the store. It was obvious that it would be hard to stay in that atmosphere for a long time.

However, the task was easy. We were requested to sort out the packets of drugs according to their use and validity. First, we isolated all boxes that contained tubes of plasma and synthetic feeders and any other drug that we thought it would expire without being kept in a refrigerator. We piled them on one side. Then we opened the small boxes and examined the packets inside. We put any pack that passed its lifetime in one of the large empty boxes. We got involved in the job without realising the passing of the time till Ashu suddenly looked at her watch and said, "Oh dear Kameela. Do you have the time? It was nearly four o'clock in the afternoon. That meant that we had been here for almost five hours."

My reaction to Ashu's comment was spontaneous, "Oh well, we got over seventy per cent of the job. Let us call it a day. I don't think that Sister Nashmeea would show up today. Let us go to the cafeteria and eat something before we refuge to our rooms."

As requested by our smart hostess, Suroor, we left the medicine store door open.

Once we knocked lightly on the back door of the cafeteria, the two Suroors came out. One went to lock up the door of the store and the other welcomed us in with new handwritten menus in her hand. In the meantime, I had the chance to examine both yang ladies closely trying to find out if there was any physical distinguishing between the two. No way, they looked like an identical twin. We reached out to the dining table and a new evening had started. We had taken our diner in a hurry as if that long absence of Sister Nashmeea for the first time that day impacted our mood. We both went up to my room.

I got busy changing my clothing, while Ashu took her seat at the edge of my bed. I stretched myself on the top of the bed and asked Ashu whether she had read any developments regarding Jameela's case in Sister Nashmeea's absence today? Ashu adjusted her sitting direction to face me and said, "Listen Kameela, do not read too much in the one-day absence of Sister Nashmeea. It could be that she was not well or might she be obliged to go some were. Surely, we would hear from her soon."

"Yes, Ashu. I hope soon. God help me to control my thoughts till that soon would be here." We spent over two hours debating and discussing without reaching any conclusion. I was still awake when Ashu decided that we had enough of each other. She had gone to her bedroom, and I was left again to my mental struggle. As usual, I couldn't guess how long time had passed before I had passed out.

All that I remember, at a certain time of my struggle to sleep, I felt as if the walls of my room had disappeared. I found myself bare feet in Rocky Mountains land. In front of me in the horizon were seven high cloudy mountains. The highest mountain was the one in the middle and was shaded by a thick dark cloud. While I was staring curiously at the top of that mountain, the cloud opened on a balcony like cave. On the edge of the cave, I could see Jameela waving to me with her headscarf and shouting, "Kameela, you should stay where you were. Don't move, I was coming, I was coming."

It occurred to me that Jameela was going to jump from that cave. Hence, I shouted from the top of my head, "Don't, Jameela don't."

When I heard the knocking on my door with Ashu's voice asking me if I was okay, spontaneously I jumped away from my bed and moved out of my nightmare.

I opened my door for Ashu. She tried to calm me down by offering her understanding and sincere empathy. It was nearly five o'clock in the morning and the only way to pass the next few hours till nine o'clock when the cafeteria would be opened was to try to sleep again. Ashu could have gone back to bed, but for me it wasn't as easy as that.

I kept rolling left and right in my bed till I noticed the morning light was apparent through the window, and it was getting close to nine o'clock. I arranged myself and went close to Ashu's bedroom and knocked lightly on her door. Ashu responded to my knocking in a lazy voice, "Yes Kameela, I would be with you in a few minutes."

Once we had taken our seats in the cafeteria, one of the Suroors attended to us with the usual greeting and the familiar smile, and two handwritten menus. However, before we had selected what to eat for breakfast, Suroor excused herself and said, "Doctors, I had a message from Sister Nashmeea. Our lady would like you to know that she would be with you about midday, and she requested you to wait for her in the cafeteria."

Great news, but did I have an appetite.? No, instead of selecting my food, I started looking at Ashu. I did not notice any reaction on Ashu's face She was as calm as ever. She urged me to stay calm and wait for Sister Nashmeea's news.

Between nipping some food and taking a few sips of tea, a few hours had passed. That waiting time was heavy, slow, and tedious, but it passed. When Sister Nashmeea appeared from behind the cafeteria's bar, we both got excited and stood up greeting and welcoming her with courtesy.

After a few seconds Sister Nashmeea settled in her seat and one of the Suroors came with a fresh pot of tea, and a tray of homemade cake. Before touching anything, Sister Nashmeea looked at me and said, "Malaise! I had heard that you had been exposed to a mild malaise doctor."

"Yes Sister, it was anxiety, worries and lack of sleep I suppose."

Sister Nashmeea adjusted her seat and said, "Please doctor, rest assured that with the help of my uncle, I would do everything within my capacity to sort out Jameela's issue. I would like to explain a few things to you. Since the day you informed me of your concern regarding Jameela's whereabouts and her destiny, my uncle alerted all his informers in the tribes' land and asked them to research for her and find out the latest news of the widow Sheika Shahnaz, her son Akrum and the Safi family in general. That would be the best lead to Jameela.

The family of the Safi clan used to live close to the town of Delaram, which was not far from the suburb of the tribes' land, within the west-north province of Nimruz. Fortunately, that province was adjacent to our terrain, and we had some relatives among the habitants of that area.

Consequently, we enjoyed a full access to that area. Historically, after the departure of the red army, my uncle instructed a group of his loyal supporters to convert one of his military camps into a rehabilitation centre. The objectives of that centre were to promote the moderate concept of Islam and to help those ladies who lost their family's providers or their dear ones in those aimless interior battles.

Conversely, when the Taliban savages swept over the area, they destroyed everything in their way. They stopped the program of the centre by sacking all the ladies who used to run it. My uncle wisely avoided clashing with them. Instead, he instructed his followers to keep a low profile and wait for a change of circumstances. The centre used to be managed mainly by two ladies, who graduated from my uncle's Islamic centre that he used to run under the slogan of the well-known Koranic verses: 'There should be no compulsion in religion.' And 'You should never kill the soul that God forbid you to kill.'

After a while, the Taliban had suffered a setback, because of the fierce resistance that they faced from many fighting groups in the county, particularly the mobile military division of the Hazard sect under the command of Ahmad Shah who controlled the northeast province of the country. My uncle grabbed this opportunity and reactivated the rehabilitation centre on the borders of the tribes' land.

My task was to provide the centre with my uncle's lecturers in the form of headlines with summaries of my uncle's ideas about the moderate and anti-violent Islam. The ladies who used to run the centre would study the headlines and elaborate on explaining their meaning to the attendees. Hence, intellectual seminars and useful discussions were used to prevail among the lecturers and the attendees of the centre.

Five young ladies used to attend the classes. All went into hiding when the Taliban swept the area. We managed to get four of them back and arranged for them to resume their daily presence in the centre. We still trying to contact the fifth one without success. When I heard that Jameela, had crept back close to our settlement where we had set up the rehabilitation centre after the murder of her so-called husband by a land mine in a battle with the Hazards, I urged the attendants of the centre to sway Jameela to joining the centre, particularly when I learnt that Sheika Shahnaz had passed away. In my second short visit last week, I was pleased to tell you that Jameela was there sitting silently in the corner, fully covered by her blue burqa."

When Sister Nashmeea stated that she had met Jameela already, I felt a shiver in my spine. I couldn't help staying silent. I apologised to Sister Nashmeea and interrupted her without hesitation by saying, "But please Sister, I think you would know how much I was longing to meeting Jameela, I wondered why you didn't take me with you to meet my sister."

Sister Nashmeea put on a serious face and said, "I was sorry, Doctor Kameela, but I didn't want to expose you to undue disappointment. Jameela had been, for a long time, under the wrong teaching of the meaning and the true spirit of Islam. The years she spent under the control of the Taliban-Pashtuns culture had changed her drastically. She was completely brainwashed. She was the only one among the others sitting in the classroom of the rehabilitation centre, with her burqa on. Hence, I could not see her facial expressions.

Nevertheless, I asked her whether she had any children, though I knew that Akrum who was meant to be her husband was castrated by an herbal specialist who prescribed him the wrong herb, believing that he was strengthening his manly power. Regardless of that fact, the Taliban continued to consider Jameela as the widow of Akrum Safi. In my early short visits to the rehabilitation centre a week ago I was pleased to see Jameela was among the attendants of the centre.

After half an hour of discussion in that class regarding some verses of the Koran that instruct Muslims to be kind to their parents, I asked Jameel if she was in contact with her parents. She said, no, not for a while. When I asked her, how long was 'a while?' She uncovered her eyes and gave me a very serious look. After one minute of silence, she managed to mumble that she did not know. Then she added might be four years.

At that stage, I dared to ask her whether she had known that her attitude toward her parents was not compatible with the teaching of Islam. She told me that she was away serving the Mujahideen in a military camp, and it was impossible for her to meet somebody who can take her letter abroad. I asked her would she hug and kiss members of her family if they would surprise her with a visit? Her answer was no because that would be Haram, or illegal in Islam. You see Doctor Kameela; from that dialogue I had concluded that it would be premature at this stage to take you to meet Jameela.

However, the good news was that Jameela's outlook toward fanatic Islam was changing. On my second visit, I asked Jameela why she was clinging to her burqa? She told me that she did that according to compulsive Fatwa, religious advisory. In that connection, I passed Jameela one of my uncle's written lectures that explained the real meaning of Fatwa and who had the right to issue it, and the difference between a genuine and a false Fatwa. I spent most of yesterday talking and discussing with the ladies in the centre the real values of Islam and the meaning of Fatea.

By the end of the day, we all agreed that the burqa was no more than a false Fatwa, and hair covering in Islam was a social tradition, not a religious practice. To my ultimate happiness, I had heard today from one of the attendants of the centre before I came to you that Jameela had attended the centre without her burqa. You see doctors. Please be patient.

All of us might sometime next week, God willing, would be meeting to celebrate your reunion with Jameela."

When Sister Nashmeea stopped talking, I touched my forehead with my right hand and looked Ashu in the eye trying to make sure that what I just heard was real and not a dream.

Then news came like music to my ears, when Sister Nashmeea said, "I would suggest you spend tomorrow in the medicine store to finish up the job you started. But please before you get to the store leave your passports with Suroor. That would enable my uncle to photocopy them and prepare a letter to your charity organisation in London expressing our gratitude for your service in our settlement. My uncle intended shortly to visit Islamabad to sort out a few issues including arranging some documents for Jameela in case she did not keep her British passport anymore."

Ashu spoke for both of us when she said, "Sister Nashmeea, we did not have the words to thank you. It was our good luck to meet you in this troubled part of the world. We had just one request left. That was you would provide us with an easy contact where we could reach you from any part of the world. Believe me Sister, we would never forget your help and your kindness. By uniting us with Jameela, we would be three sisters again, but by knowing you we would consider ourselves as four sisters whether you were close or far away."

Sister Nashmeea smiled broadly and said, "Sure I would provide you with Aunt Shabnam's address and telephone number in Islamabad. A letter or a telephone message might take a while to reach me, but it would reach me anyway."

Then Sister Nashmeea wished us a nice afternoon and said, "I would be away for two or three days. Take it easy, doctors, and remember that you had plenty of time before you would call it a day."

Sister Nashmeea left us that day, but the great hope of being reunited with Jameela was the greatest promise of that day.

# Chapter Twelve

On her way out yesterday afternoon, Sister Nashmeea didn't forget to repeat to us that she would be busy for a few days. She asked us not to worry if she wouldn't turn up to see us for two to three days. However, worries become my second nature. Ashu was holding firm, and she looked much calmer and more realistic than me. She was not less concerned than me about Jameela's fate, but that was her calm nature, and my anxious character. Though I would assume that Jameela was safe, and it was just a matter of days before we would be together, but what would be next? Most of the times, I would debate silently. But when I reached that point of my silent deliberation, I would direct my question to Ashu, "Yes indeed, what would be next?"

Ashu reversed my question to me and added, "That would depend on so many things."

I didn't like Ashu's answer and my reaction was rather unkind. I looked back at Ashu and said, "What were those so many things? First, after the death of so-called her husband, Jameela was naturally disconnected from the Safi family. On the other hand, she had fallen off with the gangs of Taliban So what would be holding her in that strange land?"

Then, Ashu softened her voice and said, "Listen Kameela, I didn't say it was impossible to extract Jameela from that miserable situation, but I meant that might require some planning. For example, we wouldn't know whether she kept her old passport, and how to arrange for an alternative document if she didn't?"

That sounded logical. However, once we finish our traditional breakfast. Ashu took the initiative. Without asking my opinion, she looked back at the cafeteria and requested Suroor to take us to the medicine store. In less than a minute, Suroor appeared in front of us with her usual greetings and courtesy performance. Suroor didn't forget to remind us once more to leave the door of the store open, and to knock on the back door of the cafeteria to alert her when we finished.

The work in the medicine store was rather tedious and time-consuming but it was the best way to pass those a few days waiting for Sister Nashmeea to bring us Jameela's news. Ashu was taking her job seriously and she was working silently non-stoop. I was doing the same, but now and then I would say something just to explore Ashu's opinion regarding some thought that would occur to me. Still, Ashu's comments on my thoughts were much wiser than mine.

For example, when I said, "What do you think Ashu, say if Sister Nashmeea would manage to sort out Jameela's issue? Would we be able to take her with us in the same flight on our way home?"

Ashu would drop whatever was in her hand and said, "Kameela, were you serious? First, even if Jameela would be ready to leave with us, and she did not find her British passport, it would take at least three months to supply her with a replacement document."

Then Ashu asked me seriously, "However, what we would do after we finish sorting out those silly packs? Should we stay like a burden on our host without thinking of doing something useful? Be sensible, Kameela and think logically, please."

I couldn't find short, straight answers to Ashu's questions. Again, Ashu was more realistic than me. I could be on the peak of my emotion and overwhelmed by my thoughts, but simple logic would be too far from my thinking.

My silence lasted for a few minutes. Then I stopped working and asked Ashu again, "Do you think that Sister Nashmeea would take us to meet Jameela after those a few days?"

Ashu without hesitation, said, "No, Kameela, I believe that when Sister Nashmeea would feel that Jameela was no more under the curse of fanatic Taliban teaching, she would bring her to us rather than she would take us to her. Logic Kameela didn't you see it that way?"

"Yes, Ashu. You have a very clear mind. I would think by the end of tomorrow, we would declare the end of the store's job but, what would be next?"

Ashu adjusted the box that she was using as a seat and said, "Well we would leave it to Sister Nashmeea to decide our next move."

I found Ashu's comment rather provoking. I could not hide my disagreement with what she said. Hence, I reacted spontaneously, "Excuse me! What did you mean by our next move? What was left for us but to take Jameela and proceed in our journey to London?"

Ashu disagreed with me, but she cut the argument short by saying, "I am sorry Kameela, but I didn't think the issue was as simple as that."

Then, to close that pointless disagreement, Ashu looked around and said, "Did you know Kameela, I would think that we better slowdown in sorting out the medicine packs? Not much work left for us. We might need a few hours tomorrow and everything would be done. What would keep us busy after tomorrow?"

At that point, I wanted to show Ashu a bit of smart thinking. First, I went quiet till I was sure that Ashu was giving me her attention. I looked at her and, asked, "What would be the problem if we finished the job tomorrow? I would suggest that by the end of the working day, we would ask Suroor to provide us with a sweeper and an old bucket to use for clearing the litter from the store. Then we would organise the boxes around the store as neatly as possible. What would you say to that, Ashu?"

Ashu smiled and said, "I would say that you were thinking rather clearly."

Intentionally, we had decided to stop working early that day just to leave some of the job left for tomorrow.

As soon as Ashu knocked lightly on the back door of the cafeteria, one of the Suroors opened it with the usual courtesy and a pleasant smile. A few seconds after we had taken our seats around the dining table. Suroor came with the familiar wooden try and the colourful teapot and newly handwritten manus. Our dining feast did not last for more than half an hour. Then we both settled upstairs in my room. We were sitting on the edge of my bed when Ashu said that she was tired and stated jokingly that I shouldn't expect longish chatting from her that night. Regardless of what Ashu had said I knew how to involve her in a longish conversation.

Once she went silent for a few seconds, I gathered my thoughts and asked, "But listen, Ashu, supposing Jameela had lost her expired British passport, how could we prove her identity?"

Ashu smiled and said, "I would think that was a good question, Kameela. It would be obvious that they would use your passport's information and take your written declaration under an oath that Jameela was your sister, and she would share with you the same usual names, including your family name."

I had thought about that before, but I liked hearing it from Ashu because of my worrying nature. Oh well, I managed to stretch the conversation with Ashu for a few long hours. When I noticed that she started yawning continuously, I excused her and told her that it was time for her to go to her bed, assuming that, as I knew Ashu, she would have no problem to sleep. What about me. I went through sleepless hours with some settled differences from the nights before. My dreams changed into messy ones. Travelling, flying wedding parties, but when Ashu woke me up in the morning I couldn't remember any of my last night's dreams. Ashu from behind the door asked me jokingly if I were ready to go downstairs, or if she would go back to bed for another while?

I pulled myself from the bed and told Ashu not to be silly. I asked her to give me a few minutes to be ready.

On the dining table, we found that our new manus was already there. Ashu lifted a menu, and appointed at a certain item, and asked me if I would know that dish. After I looked it up on my menu, I smiled and said, "Definitely. It was one of my mother's favourite dishes. It was a mixture of goat's yoghurt and dates juice. In Dari was called Khurma juice."

Ashu was happy with my explanation and decided to try it and asked Suroor to bring us a small ball of that dish among other things we usually requested for breakfast. When our breakfast was ready Ashu hesitantly dipped her teaspoon in that strange dish. When she put it in her mouth, she felt sick. She put her spoon aside and looked at me with complaining eyes repeating, "For heaven's sake, Kameela, why didn't you warn me?"

I could not help but suppress my laughter, and said, "I am sorry amiga, I wouldn't tell you anything before you would try it."

When we asked Suroor to take us to the medicine store Suroor did not need to tell us anything as we already knew the rules.

As we expected, within two hours and a half, the job was finished. Every single pack was checked, marked, and put aside.

The bad news was Ashu didn't feel well. I noticed that she was looking pale and covering her forehead with her right hand. When I asked her if she was alright, she said that she had a terrible headache. I picked a valid pack of Aspro from one of the piles of the packs that were in front of us and said, "Listen Doctor Ashu, let us get to the cafeteria where you could eat something first, and then you should take two tablets of Aspro with a full glass of water."

She examined the back and said, "Yes Doctor Kameela, I wouldn't know what to do without you."

In the cafeteria, one Suroor went to lock the store and one Suroor came to us with two nicely hand-scripted menus. Ashu told her that we do not need much food that evening, it might be just a pot of tea and a few pieces of homemade cake. While Suroor was still around, I requested her to find us a sweeper and an old medium-size pocket to use for the trash after cleaning the store tomorrow. Suroor's response was as pleasant as usual, "Sure doctor, no problem at all."

We did not stay long that afternoon in the cafeteria and for a change, I went with Ashu to her room. Ashu put on her striped pyjama and flung herself on the top of the bed. I sat on the edge of her bed and put my right palm on her forehead for a few seconds to deduct if there was a sign of temperature. There was no sign of complication, and five minutes later, the light whistling of Ashu's nose had started. For me, that was a definite indication that Ashu was asleep already. I moved very slowly out of Ashu's room trying to avoid making any disturbance.

On my own again trying to convince myself that we were close, very close to seeing Jameela. I passed out dreaming of Jameela and her blue burqa and if it was possible to keep it as a souvenir that would remind us of the suffering time. Luckily, I passed the night with a variety of confusing dreams without nightmares.

When I woke up and saw the light covering the room, I felt somehow pleased with myself. That could be caused by the feeling that we were getting closer to seeing Sister Nashmeea again, and God willing with Jameela by her side. It could be no more than wishful thinking, but that thought motivated me to be ready for the coming day. I moved slowly close to Ashu's door and asked her if she was ready to go downstairs.

Ashu came out laughing. I was a bit puzzled and asked her, "What was funny?"

Ashu controlled her laughter and said, "Did you know Kameela what psychology could do? Out of your confusion yesterday you had picked expired two packets of Aspro for me. You didn't check their expire date properly and I did not check either except that they worked like magic." We both laughed, and I suggested that she should keep them as a souvenir.

In the cafeteria, at the dining table, there were the usual menus. But on the right corner of the table, there was a sweeper. Ashu picked up the sweeper and said, "Wow Kameela, it looked like an artwork," I took the sweeper from Ashu and examined it thoroughly. First, it was brand new and had never been used. Second, I found out it was weaved by different colours of palm-trees leaves and arranged in such a way that they form a nice embellishment.

Our breakfast today did not take long because we were both anxious to finish the job in the store. After half an hour at the dining table, Ashu picked up the sweeper and stood up and called Suroor. When Suroor noticed that the sweeper was in Ashu's hand, she got the message. She just mentioned that the pocket for the trash that we requested was already there in the store.

Then she directed us swiftly to the store. In the store, I started to move the boxes we had already marked as 'G' (good) to one side of the store, and Ashu was sweeping behind me. Within one hour and a half, the store looked clean and very well-organised. We took a final checking for a couple of minutes and then decided to move out to the cafeteria. Ashu looked back and asked me if we should take the sweeper with us. I did not say much, I just looked at her and said, "Don't be silly, just leave it next to the boxes."

When we got to the cafeteria, it was a bit too early for dinner. Just the same, Suroor came with her two handwritten manus and a pot of tea. Before she was leaving, I requested her to bring us a pencil and a blank sheet of paper. Ashu was looking at me with astonishment, but she understood my purpose when I put the paper in front of me and said, "Now Ashu before we would forget, how many boxes were there in the store?"

Ashu squeezed her forehead and said, "Wait, let me visualise in my head the area of the store. Five rows of ten, that would be fifty boxes, plus five isolated ones. That would make a total of fifty-five, boxes, correct? Out of that lot, we isolated seventeen good ones, correct?"

I applauded Ashu and said, "Wonderful, at last, we would know what to put in our report to Sister Nashmeea."

Ashu looked left and right as if she wanted to make sure that no one else, apart from me would hear what she was going to suggest and went on saying. "Do you think that we should suggest to Sister Nashmeea to add to her final report that we were helping to rescue a British young lady who was trapped in the tribes' land throughout a disastrous arranged marriage?"

Impulsively, my answer was no, "No Ashu, that would give the impression that our volunteering to serve around here, was motivated by a personal matter. Don't you think that might discredit our mission?"

Ashu agreed with me, but that was not the end of our debate. There was always something to think about, and something to talk about. Time passed so fast. It was getting dark, and it was time to climb to our rooms. There was no news that day from Sister Nashmeea. Oh well, no big deal, I thought by then we got used to disappointments now and then. I did not forget to ask Ashu to hand me the sheet on which I drafted the report.

Before we moved upstairs, Ashu made it clear that she was sleepy, and that she would go straight to bed, so I should not expect her to keep my company for a while.

Once I was in my bedroom I sat on my bed and took my time to redraft the report in organized meaningful shape.

My night was peaceful. No panic, no nightmares except the annoying voice of Ashu in the morning, telling me that it was time to move, and it is late already.

When I eventually emerged from my bedroom, I surprised Ashu with A neat copy of the report I scrambled the day before. Ashu took a fast look at the report, and without hesitation, she dated it and put her signature next to my signature on the bottom page of the report.

# Chapter Thirteen

After we had reached the cafeteria, I was astonished to see that Sister Nashmeea was already there. She was smiling and, staring at her mug of tea. When she saw us, she stood up and gave us the usual morning greetings. On one hand, I was pleased to see Sister Nashmeea again, but on the other hand, I was disappointed to see her again without Jameela. Oh well, I hoped to see Jameela sitting there with Sister Nashmeea waiting for us, but there was no sign of our missing sister. However, since Jameela was wedded to the unknown, disappointment had become a permeant feature of my life.

So, there were no change for the time being. After we had taken our seats around the dining table, leaving Sister Nashmeea occupying the middle chair, I handed her our report regarding the medicine store. She expressed her thanks and appreciation and confirmed that her uncle would be very pleased to receive it. Then Sister Nashmeea said that she had some wonderful news for us, "Doctors first you should have your breakfast and then you would listen to my story."

Ashu moved her chair a bit forward and said, "Please Sister, if you wouldn't mind, tell us the news while we were having our breakfast. Having our breakfast would not prevent us from listing. You might appreciate that we were very anxious to know what had happened during the last long three days." Sister Nashmeea responded positively. She cleared her throat and said, "Sure doctors, choose your foods from the menus and let Suroor do the rest."

When Sister Nashmeea called Suroor, who came quickly moving smartly carrying a wooden tray with a pot of tea on top together with a few mugs. We both appointed at some of the items on the menu and Suroor took the handwritten menus and left with her usual courtesy and familiar smile. Sister Nashmeea reached to the mugs on the tray and put one in front of me and one in front of Ashu. After Suroor came back with our food, it was obvious that we were keener to listen to Sister Nashmeea than willing to eat. Sister Nashmeea felt our anxiety.

She looked at me first and then she looked at Ashu for a few seconds before she shifted her eyes again in my direction, and said, "Doctors, you would be glad to know that I had spent most of the last three days with Jameela. By special arrangement, I managed to suspend the usual program of the rehabilitation centre and sat it up for private meetings between Jameela and myself for continues three days. I would be glad to tell you that on the third day and gradually during our discussion, I started to notice that Jameela was almost back to normal. She gave me a full description of the past events of her life. She told me that she was mentally absent on the day of her wedding.

She said that she even didn't dare to ask her parents about their intention of what was happening. She told me that on one hand, she was flattered that she had attracted the attention of the Sheika Shahnaz out of all that crowd of girls. But on the other hand, she was worried that she was being pushed by her parents into the unknown. Yet, she explained that she used to convince herself that her parents wouldn't do her any harm. She also said that she used to think that her parents would know what was good for her. She told me that of course, she was thinking about her studies and her educational future, but under those circumstances, all that was pushed aside of her mind. She told me, that yes, it was a hard experience, but it was mitigated by the love and the kindness of Sheika Shahnaz. She went on to explain to me that at Heathrow airport, they passed the official desk without difficulties. Sheika Shahnaz told her in advance that she should stay silent and leave the talking to her. She told me that the only few words she had to utter to the man behind the desk, were her full name and address while the official was examining her passport. But when he asked her the reason for her trip to Islamabad, she told me that she stared at him silently. After a few seconds of silence, Sheika Shahnaz rushed to say, 'Visiting, visiting her sick aunt.' The official was satisfied with the Sheik's answer, and he stamped their passports wishing them a safe journey."

When Sister Nashmeea reached that part of Jameela's story, the expressions of her face had drastically changed. She looked somewhat sad. She shifted her eyes between Ashu and me and said, "What was going on in your civilised country doctors? And what kind of guidance did that official at Heathrow airport had received to pass a young lady in in the company of an old woman travelling to that part of the world without further questioning? I am seriously baffled."

I was embarrassed and found it was difficult to comment. But Ashu gathered her courage and said, "I agree with you Sister. Mind you that was not the only lope hole in the system that exposed women in the UK to imminent risk. I should think that this issue should be brought to the public attention by an organised campaign."

Ashu's comment gave me a hell of confidence. I looked Sister Nashmeea in the eye and said, "Promise you Sister. That campaign would be our next move when we get home, and I hope Jameela, who was a victim of that messy practice would play a major part in that campaign."

Sister Nashmeea smiled and said, "What we knew already some facts about women's oppression all over the world, and we knew already that it was just the tip of the ice burg. We needed to stand together to change that injustice."

Ashu and I nodded our heads agreeing with what Sister Nashmeea had said, but when I gave Sister Nashmeea a curious look, she realised that I was keen to hear the rest of her exploration regarding the facts of Jameela's life while exiled in the tribes' land.

Hence, Sister Nashmeea adjusted her seat and said, "From what I heard from Jameela about the sequence of events she had gone through in the tribes' land had given me a great lesson about the capability and the endurance of women in general. But the story took so many aspects. Jameela told me that Sheika Shahnaz had shown her a lot of kindness and attention during the eight hours flight between London and Islamabad. Upon arrival at Islamabad airport, she said they were received by two ladies in official uniforms. They took them with their luggage to a VIP room, outside the building of the airport.

There was a minibus waiting for them. Jameela told me that she couldn't work out the directions of their move. Four hours or could be less in the run, she told me that everything they passed looked rather strange to her eyes. The landscape, the trees and the entire surroundings didn't look familiar at all. She told me that suddenly, she found herself together with Sheika Shahnaz in what she thought to be the tribes' land. Then Jameela described the residence of Sheika Shahnaz. She told me that the house of the Sheika was a castle-like.

A high fence of red bricks, with one huge gate that was opened for us by armed guards. Inside, Sheika Shahnaz as she recalled, led her to a nice building inside the fence and in the right corner of that building, the Sheika led her into a private room repeating, 'That would be your bedroom, my daughter.'

Jameela remembered that she looked around the room and astonished to see everything from furniture to decorations were rosy and shiny. She told me that she could not work out if she was seeing that the decoration of the room was a work of silk or satin. Then about midday Sheika Shahnaz told her to have a rest, and she would come to take her to the celebrating room. She informed me that the Sheika used to call her daughter, while she called the Sheika, aunty. Then Jameela explained to me that Sheika Shahnaz did not forget to tell her that all the clothes in those two wardrobes in the room were her property, and she could choose any dress to put on for the evening party.

Then Jameela told me, when Sheika Shahnaz left her in the room, she sat on the edge of the bed and put her head between her hands and sobbed cautiously. She told me, at that stage, she felt as if she was a queen in a jail. At that moment she had a great desire to go back home to Hounslow Central her natural habitat where she could hug her sister Kameela and her friend Ashu. That would be her burning wish at that moment."

Sister Nashmeea went silent for one minute, then she apologised for being so vivid in telling Jameela's story as she received it from her mouth, and added that she had to be realistic in conveying the facts. She called Suroor to bring us a fresh pot of tea. Then she waited for us to settle down and relax.

After serving the tea, Sister Nashmeea said, "Listen, doctors, if you would keep reacting with this kind of high emotion, we would not touch the facts."

By this comment, Sister Nashmeea achieved our silence and full attention. Hence, she resumed her talking and said, "As Jameela explained to me that she had overslept on the top of that bed till the evening when she started to hear clapping and some sort of chanting associated with the sound of hand drums. She elaborated that she did not wait long to see Sheika Shahnaz on her doorstep. She noticed then that the Sheika was carrying a silver colour ewer with a similar colour wide vessel decorated all around with supplications of good wishes.

Jameela then told me that Sheika asked her to stand next to the bed and the Sheika poured some water from the ewer into her palms and asked her to wash her face, disposing of the excess water in the silver vessel. Then Jameela went on telling me that the Sheika opened one of the wardrobes and pulled a fresh velvety white towel and went on drying her fac. As she put it then she felt as if she was a powerless baby in the hands of the Sheika. Jameela then told me that Sheika Shahnaz told her to go through the clothes' collection in the wardrobes and select a nice bright dress for the evening party.

Jameela explained to me that after the Sheika left the room, she went through the so many dresses in the wardrobes. She was very impressed to see all those varieties of nice dresses with their beautiful flowery patrons. She confessed that the dress she liked most did not fit her figure right. It was too wide for her west. But as she explained there were plenty of dresses to choose from, and she kept trying one dress after another, till she settled for one she liked, and it fitted her figure neatly. Then while she was watching herself in the wardrobe's mirror, Sheika came back.

This time she entered the room carrying a silver tray again, except that the tray this time was full of pieces of jewellery and gold and the Sheika started decorating her with jewelleries, while repeating that was her dowry. And then as Jameela told me that Sheika Shahnaz held her right hand and opened the door shouting glorify the prophet of Allah.

Then Jameela told me that she was astonished to see seven or eight young girls were waiting nearby echoing all together in one voice the Sheik's prayers. Then, doctors, you might be keen to know that Jameela gave me a vivid description of the procession that was prepared for her in one of the master rooms of the house. She was seated on a highchair in the middle of the room, while some girls were holding flaming candles, and the others were chanting and clapping around her. She explained that she was hoping to see the end of that show soon, but the party went on for a few hours.

Then Jameela told me that she was taken to the dining room which was furnished with matrices and pillows. Then Jameela gave me a full description of those parties and feasts that were repeated for her every evening for three consecutive days. Jameela then explained to me that when the peak of the events calmed down, she started asking herself the natural question, where was Akrum, her expected husband?

She explained; when they wedded her, they told her that she was going to marry a guy called Akrum. But she was too shy upon arrival in the tribes' land to ask about the whereabouts of her supposed husband. She kept wondering and asking herself that essential question. In her new life in the tribes' land, she told me that She didn't have to kook, and she didn't have to clean either. Two of Sheika Shahnaz housekeepers were put at her service. A few days passed when Seika Shahnaz noticed her frustration. One evening, Sheika Shahnaz asked her to come closer and whispered in her ear that Akrum, her husband would be her next Friday.

Jameela confessed that she was too shy to ask the Sheika how many days were left for next Friday. But eventually that Friday had arrived and there was Akrum arrived too. Jameela told me that she was astonished to see Akrum did not look like the guy she had seen in photograph that Sheika promoted in London. He looked exhausted, dusty, and armed to the teeth. She expressed her disappointment to me by stating; oh, well that was my kismat, destiny as her mother used to say. She elaborated by explaining to me that, although her new family made her feel that she was very special, she was no more than one member of the family and friends who surrounded Akrum welcoming him that evening.

When the guests departed, Akrum went away to wash for a short while and then he came back putting on a buggy white galabia (a night shirt). However, she explained that a new dilemma was discovered after they went to bed. Akrum was unable to function as a man, and out of his frustration, he started cursing that herbal guy who prescribed to him that blend of mysterious weeds claiming that the herb would increase his sexual power. That preparation had a side effect that had halted his manhood. She said that Sheika Shahnaz advised him to consult another herbal guy to reverse his condition, but he was too scared to try that, he started to seek the help of those who believed have the powers of amulets and religious prayers.

That did not help either. His two weeks leave at home had passed very fast, and he had to go back to his militia unit that was fighting the Hazards in the far northeast of the country. One day before his departure, he had chosen to tell the Sheika that according to his military rules, he had to take his wife with him to serve in the front. Jameela remembered very well the sad face of Sheika Shahnaz when she heard that news from Akrum. She looked at me and then she looked at him and asked him firmly whether he had to report his marriage to his fighting group.

Jameela told me that at that moment, Akrum put on a very grim face and told his mother that the news of his marriage would leak to the commanders of his unit, and they would shoot him after a mockery trial if they would discover that he had failed to report his marriage to the commander of his military division. Jameela then told me that when Sheika Shahnaz heard what Akrum had said, she shivered, put her right hand on his head and told him to avoid that risk by all means. She told him reluctantly that he can take her with him if he would promise to take care of her, protect her and keep her away from all dangers. Jameela told me at that moment, Akrum nodded his head agreeing with his mother's conditions.

However, Jameela explained to me that she did not take Arum's promises seriously. Jameela went further to tell me that their destination was a battlefront and who could protect anyone in that burning hell?"

Sister Nashmeea noticed that Ashu and I got too emotionally involved in the story of Jameela's experience. So, she had decided to give us a break. She called Suroor to serve us a fresh pot of tea and the traditional homemade cake. The tea break lasted for ten to fifteen minutes. We did not say anything during the tea break, Sister Nashmeea noticed that Ashu and I, despite the painful details of Jameela's story, we heard we had a burning desire to hear Jameela's experience in the fitting zone as she described it to her.

However, Sister Nashmeea went silent for a few seconds as if she was trying to weigh up our readiness to hear the awful details. Then she shifted her eyes between us and said, "Please doctors I am reluctant to tell you what Jameela had told me about her experience in that part of the tribes' land, because that experience was tragic, miserable, and painful. I was worried that it would cause you some emotional harm."

Before I was ready to react, Ashu brought her chair forward and said, "Promise you Sister, it was a sad story altogether from A to Z, but it would be very important for us to scrutinise all the miserable facts of the story. That would help us in our future campaign against that type of social injustice. Sister, you would know that every a few days, even in civilised countries like the UK, a young girl like Jameela would be pulled out of her school, her friends' company, her natural environment and sent away to a place that was incompatible with her education, culture, and her human nature.

Those crimes, Sister, now and then would pass unnoticed. Even in our civilised parts of the world, another Jameela would be wedded to hell against her will. So please Sister, we might never have the chance to know what had happened to Jameela because of that tragic wedding unless you reveal to us that you had heard from Jameela herself."

Sister Nashmeea nodded her head three times agreeing with what Ashu had said, I was satisfied with Ashu's explanation, and I did not have anything to add to her statement.

# Chapter Fourteen

Sister Nashmeea left us yesterday in suspense. Ashu and I went looking silently at each other without uttering a word. When one of the Suroor came around and asked if we needed any service, Ashu glanced at me first, and then she thanked Suroor for her kindness. Without saying anything we both left the cafeteria in the direction of the stairs. Silently again each went to her room mentally shattered. As usual I thought Ashu would has no problem to sleep it off. Not me. In my bed, I repeated in my head what I heard of Jameela's story. When Ashu called me in the morning I could not recall how and what time I slept. I was exhausted but anxious to meet Sister Nashmeea again to give us more details about Jameela's ordeal in the tribes' land.

Down in the cafeteria, before getting the usual pot of tea, Sister Nashmeea appeared from behind the counter. Though she repeated her usual greetings and tried to put on a pleasant face, it was obvious that she looked weary and not her usual self. Yes, we had our tea, and we nipped some food, but that all was a secondary issue. We hardly settled around the table when Ashu looked at Sister Nashmeea and begged her firmly, "Please Sister, Jameela's life in the camp. That part of her story would be an essential component of our future campaign."

Sister Nashmeea adjusted her chair backwards and forward and said, "Well, then let me repeat to you what Jameela had told me in that connection. Jameela explained to me that when the time had come, she was left with no option but to join Akrum on his journey from the settlement in the tribes' land to the battlefront at the Hazara tribe's borders. First, she had to put on her blue burqa and wait for one of the maids to arrange for her a small pack of some clothes and other light niceties. When the pack was ready, with one of the maid's helps she lifted it and placed it on her head and stood silent next to Akrum.

After a few minutes, Sheika Shahnaz came out of her room repeating invocations to Allah to protect her and Akrum from all evils. Jameela told me that after Sheika had kissed them goodbye, they walked out of the house while

Sheika was following them with her eyes with an obvious concern. She told me she followed Akrum walking behind him to the north end of the settlement. There, they encountered two guys in the company of two ladies wearing the burqa waiting at a certain corner of the hamlet's border. She told me that Akrum went close to the men, while Jameela systematically went close to the ladies. They were composed of two groups and each group stayed ten metres apart. Then Jameela explained that the ladies didn't talk to each other. But about half an hour later, one lady whispered asking her if she had been to the fighting zone before? Her answer was no, and that was the end of that conversation.

An hour passed when two military vans had arrived and stopped close to their gatherings. The driver of the first van signalled by his hand to the men to climb up the back of the first van, while the ladies waited till a lady in a black burqa came out from the back of the second van. The lady greeted them with the Islamic traditional greeting, salaam alaykum, but she was not keen to know if they answered her greetings.

Then the lady urged them to climb up to the back of the van and helped those who carried packages or containers of water to reach up to the back of the vehicle. Then Jameela explained to me that the back of the van contained three seats. Two long ones along each side of the van, and one small seat that linked between the two long seats at the bottom of the van. The commanding lady occupied the left corner of the bottom seat of the van and showed them a kind of authority. She produced an old file from under her seat and started writing down their particulars, namely their names and their husband's names, and the part of the settlement they lived. That did not take long, and they all went in boring silence again.

After two hours in the move over rough land, she told me that suddenly the convoy came to a halt. After five minutes, the commanding lady opened the back of their van and went on watching along the left side of the vehicle. Then Jameela told me that after a short while they started to hear a man, most likely he was the driver of the first van, shouting in his walky-talky some fragmented sentences. She explained that he was shouting in Dari dialect repeating one phrase, give me direction. Then Jameela elaborated to tell me that after half an hour of that standstill, the commanding lady started to produce some sounds of indignation. Then the commanding lady moved to the backdoor of the van and went out for a short while.

When she came back, Jameela explained that she told them that the route they were taking would lead them to an unelaborated spot, and that would have exposed them to an imminent danger. Hence, Jameela told me that their commanding lady told them that they were waiting for instructions to change direction to be on the safe side. Then Jameela explained that none of the ladies in the van had said anything. Eventually, she noticed that the convoy diverted its direction by about thirty-degree to the east. Then they resumed their travelling. The women in that van had expressed a sigh of relief. Jameela then explained that after three hours in the move again their convoy had stopped for the second time. Then their commanding lady opened the back door of the van and descended without any explanation.

After five minutes she came back and asked us to come out of the van. At that time, Jameela told me that she felt very stiff and had an urgent need to urinate. Then she looked around to find that they were close to a mini oasis. There was a small pond and a small bunch of trees near the end of that pond. She went behind the trees and relieved herself discreetly. Later, the commanding woman guided them to a sheltered part of the pond away from the sight of the men. There, they had the chance to undo the tops of their burqa and splashed some water on their faces.

However, as Jameela told me that the luxury of that break did not last long. After twenty minutes or so, the commanding lady shepherd them back to the van and their small caravan resumed its rough creeping on that rough land. Jameela estimated that it was after five hours in the move they started to hear sporadic shootings. Now and then they used to hear some bombardments, but she couldn't work it out as what kind of weapon was in action.

After a few minutes, their van came to halt. Then a few seconds later, the commanding woman moved forward holding her file under her arm. In a swift move, she opened the back door of the van and signalled to the ladies in the van to follow her. Jameela told me then she looked around to see a huge primitive military camp surrounded by armed men and contained hundreds of scattered tents, some large and some small but all were covered by camouflage garments.

Akrum and his companion including the driver of the other van were led by a gunman and entered the camp through a certain gap in the fence. Then Jameela told me that together with the other ladies were received by two commanding middle-aged ladies. They accompanied the commanding woman who escorted them through their journey. Jameela told me then one of the new commanding ladies approached her and told her to follow her through another gap in the fence of the camp. There she noticed that the camp was divided into two sections, separated by a high fence of rocks. The new commanding lady took her to the left section of the fence and stopped next to a very miserable-looking small tent.

There, the woman pulled a dirty small piece of paper from her pocket and rudely handed it to her. Then the commanding lady asked her if she could read the number that was on that paper. Then Jameela told me that she told her new commander that yes, she could hardly see the number, but it was one hundred and thirty-six. Then Jameela explained that when she told her the number, she looked at her with a grim face and told her to memorise that number. Then she told her that the number would be their permanent tent's number and Akrum her husband would have it as well.

Then Jameela explained that before the commanding woman told her to enter the tent, she explained to her that the tent which was marked by a green garment would be her permanent home, where she could meet her husband only when there would be no alert in the camp. Jameela told me that when the commander lady left her and she crept into that tent, she had the shock of her life. The tent covered a small area. It contained a rug, two blankets and a hard longish pillow. In the right corner of the tent, there were two black cooking pots: one was small and one was a medium size containing a bronze scoop with a long handle. She added that things inside that tent were dirty and with a terrible smell."

At that stage, Sister Nashmeea couldn't control her emotion anymore. She stopped talking and reached for her mug and helped herself with some sips of water. A few seconds of silence had passed before Sister Nashmeea picked up her breath again and said, "You might know doctors that Jameela who used to live in such a quiet comfortable environment had to go through all that unbearable tough misery. Jameela was a victim of fanatic reactionary society, and you had done so far everything possible to stand against the injustice that was forced on her. I would full-heartedly applaud you doctors for your courage and commitment. However, what would cause me sleepless nights was to think that how many other young ladies like Jameela in our world had their lives been wasted elsewhere without recognition?"

I wanted to say something, but I felt that my tongue was fixed to the top of my mouth. I only kept looking left and right with a thoughtless mind. Ashu, as usual, had come to my rescue. She leaned backwards and said, "Exactly Sister, to put an end to that injustice or might be able to achieve a limitation to that kind of atrocities, I would think, with your participation, we should set up a global organisation that would campaign aggressively against all social injustice against women. That was why we thought we should keep in contact with each other after we would go back to the UK. Sister, we would make our voice heard through the press and other forms of media, such as broadcasting and public gatherings. We would reach out to members of parliament, as well as political parties and union leaders. That was why Sister, we would like to be fully aware of all the facts of the hard times Jameela had gone through because of that family's primitive arrangement."

Sister Nashmeea looked Ashu in the eye and said, "I would fully agree with your doctor, and I would promise my full support and cooperation. Let us stand together for our rights and our principles and involve others in protesting against the habitual conduct of injustice against females all over the world."

At that point, I directed my words to Sister Nashmeea and said, "You would know Sister, under the circumstances, it would be impossible for us to debrief Jameela as you did regarding her life in the military camp. The more information we would get from you in that connection the more we would know how to run our future campaign."

Sister Nashmeea adjusted her seat and said in a sad tone, "Well doctor! Did you say her life in the camp? Do you think Jameela had a life in that terrible military camp? As Jameela told me that she had to join a washing-up team or a cooking team alternatively every second week. Each team consisted of twenty to thirty ladies. When their turns would come, they were used to be called to gather early morning at a certain corded part of the camp. There would be a huge carriage full of bundles of dirty clothes arrived pulled by a motorcyclist who would disconnect it from his machine upon his arrival and would start throwing casually the bundles of the dirty clothes in front of the girls.

There would be nearby seven large barrels, a kind of cylindrical container full of boiling water, with opened tops balanced on several large bricks that allowed to set up fire underneath. The task of the girls was to continue feeding the fire with wood from nearby piles and stir up the dirty garment with thick sticks till they looked relatively clean. Jameela told me that the girls then would pick up the clothes with the same sticks and spread them out over a wooden formations away from the barrels to dry up. All that working time, whisperings or talking to each other was rustically forbidden. A supervisor woman would come now and then to the spot, to make sure that the work was in progress."

At that stage, Sister Nashmeea looked mentally tired. She stopped talking for two minutes and then she said, "I am sorry doctors to convey to you the awful experience that Jameela had gone through. I had to be very truthful, and my objective was of two folds; one was to set the record right for our future struggle in the field of women's rights. Second, to spare you digging into Jameela's story, later, the time she would try to forget and recover from her ordeal."

I nodded my head agreeing with Sister Nashmeea's explanation without saying anything, while Ashu had decided to beg Sister Nashmeea and urge her to resume the story as she had heard it from Jameela without reservation or hesitation.

Sister Nashmeea pulled a long sigh and said, "Fine doctors, the other hard labour Jameela told me that she had to go through was her mandatory participation in the cooking team of the camp. Her turn used to come every two weeks as an alternative for clothes washing. Jameela told me that the cooking procedure was more and less similar to the clothes washing, except that the barrel would be changed by huge pots to boil vegetables and a kind of rough barely flour used to be brought to them in sacks. After two hours of cooking, men would start queuing with their pots to scoop some of that soup, and to collect pieces of bread from a nearby pile of black pieces of bread scattered on an old matt.

After high noon, the men's queue would finish, and the women's queue for collecting some food would follow. Talking openly with each other in the queues was unforgivable crime. Authorised inspectors, males for the men's queue and females for the women's queue were continuously inspecting the lines. Jameela also told me that she was terrified one afternoon when a bunch of gunmen started to go around the camp gathering everybody inside around a square near the camp. They led the men to one side of the square and the women to another. After ten minutes of waiting, they brought a tall lady dressed in a blue burqa. The lady could hardly walk because her feet were tied together by a metal chain.

Two gunmen escorted her to the middle of the square and forced her to lean on her knees. One of the gunmen started reciting some Koranic verses that call for the termination of the traitorous. He said this criminal was spreading a rumour against the leader of Taliban. The second gunman put the open end of the barrel of the gun next to the lady's head. One-shot and the lady had fallen to her side. Jameela told me that she couldn't sleep that night. Every time she would close her eyes trying to sleep, the murdering of that lady would be repeated in front of her eyes.

Jameela then explained to me that her ordeal in the camp lasted for over a year till the news came that Sheika Shahnaz was very sick. Akrum pleaded to some authority in the camp to release him and Jameela for a short while to attend to his sick mother. After two weeks the chief commander of the camp agreed to release them from duty for two weeks. Jameela and Akrum were allowed to join the next caravan on the trip from the camp to the mainland of the tribes. After waiting for five days Jameela was informed by a local woman commander to be ready and wait at a certain gap of the camp's fence. At the sunset, she stood close to that designated gap as she was instructed. She told me then close to that designated gap she witnessed the familiar two military vans approaching.

The two vans stopped twenty meters apart. She could see in the distance that Akrum and two other guys getting into the far van while a woman commander guided her to, and two other women get into the nearby van. The trip back as Jameela explained was much easier than the trip of coming to the camp. She explained that during the eight hours of rough riding, she sat on the floor of the van and put her head on the seat and dozed away most of the times of the journey.

Upon arrival. She met Akrum along the isolated lane of their hose. She said that he looked very sad and very tired. She told me that Akrum hugged her, and they moved inside the outer gate of the house which they found it was wide open. One of the housekeepers received them and told them that the Sheika was in a deep sleep, and it would be better if they go to wash and have something to eat and then they would attend to Sheika when she would be awake. Then she told me that they took the chief housekeeper advice and went to wash themselves up and sleep for a few hours.

Jameela also told me that she might have slept for less than two hours to leave the bed to the main reception of the house. After a few minutes, one of the housekeepers came to her service. Her first question to the housekeeper was whether Sheika Shahnaz was awake already? She said that the housekeeper told her that the Sheika was awake, but she could hardly talk. She requested the housekeeper to take her to Sheika Shahnaz bed. She found Sheika Shahnaz was resting flat on her back and her eyes were half-open and staring at the ceiling of the room. Jameela told me that she stood up next to Sheik's head and whispered her name in a low voice.

She explained that when she repeated 'Aunty Shahnaz' as she used to call her, number of times, Sheika Shahnaz opened her eyes and moved her right hand upward in a very slow motion. Jameela lifted the Sheik's hand and kissed it emotionally. Jameela described herself then that she was overwhelmed with sadness, but she exerted an effort to hide her tears. However, Jameela after seeing the Sheika in that condition, concluded that Sheika Shahnaz would not live long. She moved to the gussets' room to find Akrum sitting there drying his tears. Jameela added that she moved with Akrum to the Sheika's room and spent sometimes whispering some prayers next to her bed.

Then they both moved to the guest's room again and had a very important conversation. She told me that she asked Akrum if the family ever had sought some medical advice for the sick lady? Akrum explained to her that he had discussed the issue with the team who used to run his mother's affairs, and he learnt from them that the nearest medical doctor was living more than five miles away in terrain outside the authority of Taliban. Then Jameela explained to me that Akrum added that his mother had an old cousin we used to call her Grandmother Hadia. And his mother trusted that lady immensely.

Hence it seemed when his mother felt very sick, she gathered all her valuables and deposited them with this well-trusted cousin. He also explained to her that Grandmother Hadia was living in a nearby settlement under the control of a virtuous mullah, known as Mullah Abdul Rahman. He went on explaining that Mulla Abdul Rahman was a man of peace and had a very different interpretation of the religion and he managed to avoid all direct conflicts with 'Taliban.' In that way he protected the residents of his settlement from their pressure. Jameela added that Akrum assured her that Mulla Abdul Rahman maintained a very good relations with the authority in Islamabad. That special relation made him a rather influential personality among the conflicting heads of the civil war in Afghanistan.

Then Jameela told me that, she realised for the first time that Akrum cared about her. She said that he told her that the one-week leave would over soon, and he would not think that he would be granted another leave to see his mother while she would still alive. Hence, he advised her to leave their settlement, and go and live under the wings of Grandmother Hadia. Two days later a militia informer came to tell Akrum to go in the evening and wait at the settlement border's spot to be collected by a passing patrol on their way to the front. Then Jameela confessed that if she would forget so many events, she would never forget that day when she went with Akrum to have a final look at his mother before his departure to the front.

On their way to the guest's room and before Akrum collected a few things of his belongings, he hugged her and advised her to plan her life without him. Jameela told me that she had collected her valuables, particularly her dowry gifts and packed them together into a small package. Then within that one week after Akrum's departure, Sheika Shahnaz had passed away. It was early morning when she was told the sad news by the chief housekeeper of the house. She explained to her explained to her that Sheika had confirmed in her verbal will that she should be buried in the family's graveyard in Grandmother Haida's land.

According to religious belief, the body of the deceased should be buried on the same day of the death. For this reason, the chief housekeeper did everything possible to hire a wooden minibus from a nearby village to carry the coffin of Sheika Shahnaz to the neighbouring settlement. Jameela took the advantage of being invited to the funeral procession. She got into the bus together with the chief housekeeper and three old ladies who used to be close friends of the deceased. She explained that the problem was the minibus had to use the only unpaved road that linked to the settlement of Grandmother Haida At the crossing point of the border between the two settlements, there was a checking point that was run by two gunmen and one middle-aged lady.

One of the gunmen came closer and took look at the passengers of the bus. When he noticed that all the passengers were females, he retreated to the checking point's stand and signalled to the woman who was standing nearby watching, to move forward to the minibus. The woman who looked like she had an authority approached us with a very grim face. She was holding a shabby notebook in her hand. She opened the front door of the bus and shouted in a rough voice asking about the person who was leading the procession? The chief housekeeper introduced herself as she was the one who was responsible for the arrangement of the procession. The checkpoint woman asked the chief maid to give her the name of the deceased and the names of the passengers and their relation to the deceased.

The chief maid went through the names of the passengers. When she came to her name, which was the last on the list. The checkpoint woman got alerted. She pushed her head forward inside the bus and asked who was Jameela Safi? Jameela told me that she was reluctantly put her right hand up. The inspecting woman gave her a nasty look and ordered her to descend out of the bus. Next to the bus, with the small pack of her belonging under her right arm, the inspecting woman ordered her to go with her behind the back of the bus away from the sight of the men at the checking point. In that sheltered corner, she asked her the name of her husband. Jameela told her that his name was Akrum. The checkpoint women demanded her full name.

The checkpoint woman noticed her hesitation. Hence, she asked her again if her husband was a Mujahid still fighting in the north front? Jameela told me that she had no option but to confirm what the checkpoint woman had stated. The checkpoint women told her then that she should be judged and controlled by the same jihad law. That was to say, she was not allowed to step outside the authority of the chief commander of Taliban. Jameela told me that hearing that statement, she felt a chill in her spine.

However, Jameela elaborated that she manged to hold herself together and told the checkpoint woman it would be only a few hours and she would be back in the settlement. She explained that the checkpoint woman gave her a suspicious look and told her to provide a proof of her intention. Jameela at that point felt some relief. She opened the package of her belongings and picked up one of the gold necklaces of her dowry and handed it to the checkpoint woman. When the checkpoint woman noticed that nobody was watching, she slipped the necklace into her pocket and ordered her to go back to the bus.

Then when they arrived at the cemetery and while the traditional burial of the Sheika body was going on, she noticed among the few people who attended the event, an old lady with a walking stick and supported in her walking by another middle-aged lady. She assumed that the old lady, most likely must be Grandmother Hadia. After they finished the burial, she went to that old lady and told her that she was Jameela, daughter-in-law of the Sheika. The old lady couldn't hear very well. She asked her to come closer and repeat what she said a bit louder.

When the old lady heard her name, she dropped her walking stick and hugged her passionately. The old lady invited her to her house. So, Jameela told me she went to the chief housekeeper of the Sheika's hose and told her that she would stay for a while with Grandmother Hadia. She believed that the chief housekeeper got the message. She gave her a suspicious look, and wished her a good luck, and moved away.

Jameela then told me that after she got to Grandmother Haida's house with the help of the old lady's housekeeper, she explained to the lady her suffering on the battle front. She said that the old lady was shocked, and repeated; no, not my daughter, you should never go back under the control of those criminals. Then the old lady asked her housekeeper to arrange a bedroom for her and feed her regularly. Then Jameela was so happy to be invited to the habituation centre and told me how lucky she was to meet me."

Sister Nashmeea then paused for a while and said, "I would be glad to tell you, doctors that my uncle was back from Islamabad where he took photocopies to your passports, in case Jameela would not be able to recover her old British passport. Therefore, my uncle would use the information on Doctor's Kameela's passport to arrange issuing a travelling document for Jameela. However, if Jameela would manage to recover her old, expired passport from Sheik's belongings, she would save us a lot of time and effort. Hence, Jameela asked me to allow her three days during which she would try to convince the grandmother to allow her to dig out her passport from Sheik's belongings. At any rate doctors, and before I wish you to have a good evening, I would love to tell you that between us and the happy news two to three days."

Sister Nashmeea left us that evening with a hell of anxiety. When I went to my room upstairs and found an extra bed in my room, I screamed, 'Ashu!'

Ashu rushed to my help and tried to revive me with some calming words and sips of water.

# Chapter Fifteen

Ashu stayed in my bedroom for more than one hour discussing and debating my endless questions. Why did Sister Nashmeea would still keeping Jameela away from us while she was no longer under the authority of Taliban? Neither I nor Ashu could provide a logical answer to this puzzling question. However, Ashu continued to say that Sister Nashmeea must have a good reason to delay our getting-together. That could be right, but I would not like to be left in suspense. Ashu and I both agreed that we should discuss this issue in our next meeting with Sister Nashmeea. "Sure Kameela. Just have some sleep right now."

That was Ashu's final advice before she had left me that night and went to her room. I agreed with Ashu, but when I went to bed the question continued to circle in my head and the stopped dialogue with Ashu changed into a silent monologue that continued till, I passed out. When Ashu woke me up in the morning, she agreed with me that we both were living in a state of vigilance. We reached down to the cafeteria hopping to see Sister Nashmeea soon. When we found that Sister Nashmeea was not there yet, we took on our seats around the dining table silently. Ashu broke our silence when she said, "Let us wait for Suroor, she could have some news from Sister Nashmeea."

After a few minutes, the smiling Suroor appeared with her usual greetings and curtsy gestures, and two fresh handwritten menus in her hand. Ashu could not wait, she took the menus from Suroor and instead of looking at the menus, she looked Suroor in the eye and asked, "Excuse me Miss Suroor, but was there any news from Sister Nashmeea?" It seemed that Suroor used to mutter a few words in English, but she would find it rather hard to hold a lengthy conversation.

Hence, Suroor struggled to say. "Yes, doctor, in her message this morning, she said that she would be here around midday."

Ashu thanked Suroor and moved her eyes in my direction and said, "Well two hours would not be too long."

We took our breakfast in slow motion just to pass the waiting time for Sister Nashmeea.

As we expected, about midday, Sister Nashmeea appeared from behind the cafeteria smiling and greeting us lively. We both stood up to receive her with our usual welcoming words and greeting gestures. Sister Nashmeea took her middle seat around the dining table, and without introduction, she shifted her eyes between us and said, "I could read your minds doctors. You might wonder why it had taken us such a long time to bring Jameela along since she was not under the Taliban's authority anymore?"

Without delay, Ashu looked at Sister Nashmeea and said, "Exactly Sister, you got it right. That was the question that gave us some sleepless nights recently. Please Sister, we would be very grateful for some explanation."

Sister Nashmeea looked left and right and leaned backwards on her chair and said, "Doctors, the whole problem was to do with our complex relationship with the Taliban. Yes, we were in no direct conflict with them, but you could say that we both were governed by a semi-treaty of truce. However, underneath the surface, there would be a deep distrust and suspicion between us. We had planted our lines of informers around them. In the meantime, we believed that they had planted some of their informers around us. The problem with them, they often would react to events in a gangster's style, not like a responsible military group.

I would wonder doctors if you heard the proverb about single hair! I would think it was a statement of an ancient Arab leader describing his attitude toward his opponents. He stated that his stand with them was connected by a single hair. When they pull, he would give, and when they give, he would pull, and in that way, he would keep the balance till he would get enough power to fight them.

I am sorry doctors to tell you that just yesterday the news came confirming that after three days of Akrum's returning to the front, his unit had suffered a vicious attack by the Hazards fighters that killed eleven fighters of that unit. It would be sad to tell you that Akrum was among those who lost their lives. According to that unexpected development, Taliban would consider Jameela as a widow of a martyred. In that case, they believed that Jameela should be confined her life to Sheika Shahnaz house for forty days of religious mourning.

Immediately, thereafter, she should resume her service on the battlefront and would be ready to marry another Mujahid, according to their terms. That was why we had adopted a low-profile policy in our approach to Jameela's issue. I am not saying that Taliban would send an assassinating squad to eliminate

Jameela while she was in our protection, but we thought there would be no need to stimulate their wild aggression.

We had already instructed the two ladies who used to attend the rehabilitation centre to deny any knowledge about Jameela's whereabout. Once she would recover her old passport from the belongings of the late Sheika who deposited them with Grandmother Hadia, my uncle would use his contact in Islamabad to work with the British consulate to issue Jameela with a valid British passport enabling her to travel home. Mind you, that arrangement would be separated from your returning flight that had been already arranged by your charity organisation."

When Sister Nashmeea stopped talking, Ashu and I started staring at each other silently till Ashu said, "All that you said Sister made perfect sense. We shouldn't have questioned your wisdom. Surly we had faith in you, but our anxiety that pushed us to ask those questions."

Sister Jameela smiled and said, "Do not worry doctors. I fully understand. The day after tomorrow, I would hope to meet Jameela with her old passport in her hand, otherwise, the hard job would start to get her a replacement document. In both cases, that would require some effort, but one job would be easier than the other. Let us now concentrate on what was due. My uncle was happy about your report, and he asked me to arrange for you a meeting with him to thank you personally for your efforts by your come to our land and for your participation in our hard life. That would require some preparations for that meeting.

It would make my uncle very happy. I would tell you later what to be ready for the meeting and you have the whole evening to rehearse the possible requirements. You knew that my uncle was a moderate devoted Muslim. He believed in the human aspect of Islam. So, he might ask you a few questions to authenticate your faith and justify his support for your assignment. I would not think that my uncle would ask you difficult questions.

For example, I wouldn't think he would ask you to perform a Muslim's prayers in front of him. That would be too hard to carry out. Most likely my uncle would ask you to narrate the Muslims' testimony of faith. I bet you both knew it. It is very simple, 'There is no God but Allah, and that Mohamed was his prophet and his messenger.' Or my uncle would ask you to recite just a short chapter from the Koran. Then you could choose a very short one like the opening or the short chapter of 'Say God is one.' Whatever you would choose. Doctors, you should not forget to open your reciting from the Koran with the phrase, 'In the Name of Allah, the Most Compassionate, Most Merciful.'"

That was a very valuable instructions from Sister Nashmeea, but Ashu looked a bit puzzled. She was looking in all directions just to express her uncertainty. To get over her embarrassment, Ashu looked at me and said, "Poor Kameela, you would have a hard task tonight."

Sister Nashmeea wished us very good luck and reminded us to wear our headscarves and overall black robes, the right-wear for meeting the Mullah, and she promised to be with us the following day early morning as the meeting with her uncle would be in or about midday. When Sister Nashmeea had left us, Ashu and I spent a few seconds staring at each other. Then we climbed the stairs up to my bedroom. There I realised that I did not have a copy of the holy Koran. Therefore, I had to rely on my good memory and tried hard to remember the daily prayers and the reciting of my parents in Hounslow Central.

Ashu and I stayed together in my room and spent more than two hours memorising, revising, and repeating some related sentences and phrases till we were satisfied that we were more than ready for the coming meeting. In the process of the exercise, on one hand Ashu proved to be a particularly good student, and on the other hand, I proved to myself to be a very good teacher. However, when Ashu started yawning repeatedly, I suggested that we had enough. Ashu excused herself and moved to her room. A few seconds later, I went to bed. Strangely enough, that night I had the least struggle to fall asleep. Either because I was extremely tired or it could be that I felt we were close to achieving the target of our mission.

I was already awake when Ashu knocked on my door telling me that it was ten o'clock in the morning. Ashu received me with a confident smile and followed me downstairs to the cafeteria, where we found that Sister Nashmeea was already there. She was sitting with her headscarf on and dressed in her overall black robe. She stood up welcoming us with her usual smile. After we exchanged the morning greeting, Sister Nashmeea moved her chair a little bit forward and said, "Doctors, today we had a menu of celebration. I was so happy that everything went as it was planned. My uncle confirmed to me in the morning that he expected us later today."

Ashu got excited and said, "Fine Sister, I thought you should test my Islamic testimony in its original Dari language."

I almost lost my temper and told Ashu to shut her mouth up and said, "Ashu please, be careful. I was glad you stated that here and not in front of the Mullah. The testimony and the holy Koran verses were written in Arabic, not in Dari."

Ashu apologised and asked, "Are they two different languages?" Sister Nashmeea smiled broadly and said, "Of course doctor, they were two different languages, but if you were insisting on mixing them up, that would be a kind of creative approach." We laughed a bit loudly in appreciation of Sister Nashmeea's sense of humour.

Between chatting, discussing, and enjoying the test of the specially prepared home cake, time had passed relatively fast. Sister Nashmeea glanced at her watch and said, "Doctors, it was nearly eleven o'clock. It would take us about forty minutes to get to my uncle's headquarters. So, now it would be just be the right time to move."

Sister Nashmeea proceeded in the direction of the back door of the cafeteria, followed directly by me, while Ashu had followed in my footsteps. We emerged through the same door we used to take to the medicine store, but that time we diverted cautiously to the right of the building. After a few minutes of walking, we found ourselves overlooking the sunflowers' field. From our position, the sunflowers' fields looked very vast. It covered a very wide area. Sister Nashmeea was leading the way till we reached some wooden steps that led to inside the sunflowers' field. Sister Nashmeea stopped for a few seconds. She looked back and said, "Be careful doctors, we were going to descend down the steps."

We found that the steps led to a narrow footpath completely shaded by the high sunflower's plants. Sister Nashmeea continued her walking along the narrow path and Ashu, and I were walking behind her. Suddenly, Sister Nashmeea looked back and said, "Please watch your feet doctors, and do not step accidentally on a grass snakes. They were not poisonous, but their bites could be very painful."

When Ashu heard what Sister Nashmeea had just said, she jumped closer to me and squeezed the back of my robe with her both hands, I laughed and said, "Do not you worry Ashu, to be bitten by a grass snake, would be the highlight of our journey,"

Ashu did not like my jock. She told me to shut my mouth up and that I shouldn't scare her any further.

By the end of that footpath, we reached an open area that looked like a small untidy square. By the bottom of that square, there was an old building. When we got closer. We could see that the building had a side wooden gate. The gate was, a large one, but on both sides of the gate stood up two gunmen with the traditional Afghan white buggy trousers and brown shirts dropping down to their knees. Their white turbans were matching the white colours of their trousers, and the guns that were resting on their shoulders looked shiny and brand new.

When Sister Nashmeea got closer, they stood in a military-style tension, and they said some words quite loudly and gave Sister Nashmeea a military salute. Then they slung their guns up their right shoulders and rushed to open the gate. Sister Nashmeea returned their salute with a movement of her right hand and entered through the gate. We followed Sister Nashmeea to find that the get was opened on a long corridor. Sister Nashmeea went inside the corridor and waited for Ashu and me to get in. After we passed the gate, Sister Nashmeea rushed to lead us down the corridor.

The guards hurried to close the gate behind us, and we proceeded slowly till we came to a wall that looked like closing our way. Sister Nashmeea took the footpath to the right along the wall, and Ashu and I proceeded behind her. On the end of the wall, we followed Sister Nashmeea to the right. Two to three meters along the wall we found ourselves in front of a modest building with an opened door. The door was opened to a room with an old furniture.

The room had no windows. Despite the few candles glowing around, it took us a few seconds to adjust our eyes to the dim light of the room. At the bottom of the room, there was a huge working desk. Behind it there was a man in his late sixties with thick grey eyebrows nearly touching the edge of his white turban.

Two piles of hardback books on his left and right sides. Sister Nashmeea stood stiff at the door. I was in her right and Ashu was in her left. Then Sister Nashmeea nodded her head three times. We both did the same and waited for Sister Nashmeea's next move. When the old man lifted his eyes in our direction, Sister Nashmeea greeted him with the usual Islamic Arabic Phrase 'Al-Salam-Alaykum.' Meaning that 'May the peace of God be upon you.' Ashu and I did the same, The Mullah leaned back on his chair and greeted us back in the same style.

Sister Nashmeea took one step forward and said, "Your reverence, I would like to introduce my doctor friends who volunteered from London in response to our applications that we sent to charity organisations to help us set up the suggested medical centre then. Unfortunately, the process of those applications took such a long time, and the situation on the ground was drastically changed.

Though they could not fulfil their dream of serving in their predecessor's homeland they had been useful in so many aspects. They sorted out our medicine store, and they put it in excellent order."

Mullah Abdul Rahman clear his throat and said, "You would know my daughter, that what had happened in our land was beyond any body's control. The most important in their act was their wonderful intention. Your friend doctors had come to help us with their skills and their knowledge. Our circumstances were too complicated to give them that chance. But Allah, almighty would reward people according to their intentions, not according to their success. I was utterly grateful for their good intention and genuine efforts, and I would present them with the best possible report of thanks and appreciation to take back to their superiors in London."

Mullah Abdul Rahman stooped talking for a few seconds, and he pulled an old notebook from the corner of his desk. He thumbed through that notebook and concentrated for a few seconds on a certain page. Without lifting his eyes, the Mullah asked if we were good Muslims? I remembered at that second the appropriate answer for such a question from my parents. Without hesitation, I said, "Thanks Allah for his blessing."

The Mulla then asked, "How many times a day do Muslims perform their prayers?" While the Mulla was looking back at his notebook. I lifted my right hand showing my five figures separated.

Ashu picked the signal and uttered, "Five." Then Mullah Abdul Rahman closed the notebook and looked in our direction. I was surprised when he said, "In the back of all that, I admired your concern regarding the fate of your mate or sister who was pushed brutally into an unjust arranged marriage in extraordinary circumstances. I had learnt recently that the lady had lost her husband in a battle over the Hazard front. Since there would be no progeny out of that marriage, plus the area, where she lived was governed by the jangle law of Taliban, the lady was legally entitled to be repatriated to her parent's place. I promised you daughters to do everything within my capacity to help that lady to go back to her parent's home. In thanking you again, I call upon my God almighty, to thrive his mercy and blessing upon you."

After Mulla Abdul Rahman went silent for two minutes, Sister Nashmeea moved half step forward and said, "God bless you, my lord, we were overwhelmed by your blessings and your kindness. Please forgive us for taking such a long time of your precious day. Please give us your permission to leave for now."

When Mullah Abdul Rahman lifted his eyes from his desk and nodded his head twice, Sister Nashmeea started to move backwards keeping her face in the Mulla's direction. We followed the same movement till we all got outside the room. Away from the sight of Mull Abdul Rahman, we went to the left along the wall. When we got close to the get of the corridor, the two gunmen who looked like they were waiting for us, gave us a military salute again and opened the get for us. Once Sister Nashmeea proceeded on the footpath, away from the headquarters of Mulla Abdul al Rahman, she looked happy and relax.

# Chapter Sixteen

Back in the cafeteria, we took our places around the dining table. When I stared at Sister Nashmeea's face I found it glowing with happiness. While Ashu looked nervous and shaky. I found it hard to read her mind. To break the silence, I started to chat with Sister Nashmeea. All my talking with Sister Nashmeea was about her uncle, Mullah Abdul Rahman. I expressed my admiration for his kindness and his profound understanding of Jameela's case. Sister's Nashmeea comment came as an appreciation for my remarks. She said, "It could be an extraordinary luck to meet a person like him around these surroundings. He was a self-made character. A self-educated with an unobstructed vision and moderate outlook on religion and life."

Sister Nashmeea thought it was a good occasion to celebrate the high afternoon with some pieces of homemade cake and a fresh pot of tea. Suroor was ready as usual to answer her request. While Sister Nashmeea and I were happily revising the success of our meeting with Mulla Abdul Rahman I noticed that Ashu looked confused. She hardly participated in our comments or conversation. She did not test the cake, and I noticed that her hand was not stable on the table.

After about half an hour of talking and discussing, Sister Nashmeea said, "You could be tired doctors. Tomorrow I would be late. Early morning, I would creep to the next terrain to meet Jameela, and if she would come with her old British passport, she would be here with us joining our dinner. Please be prepared, hopefully for the coming excitement."

Before Sister Nashmeea finished her sentence, I found myself clapping hysterically. After I calmed down, Sister Nashmeea repeated her sentence adding, "Yes, as I said, be prepared for the excitement of being reunited with Jameela or it would be one more disappointment for another passing delay." I took Sister Nashmeea's sentence with great expectation.

After Sister Nashmeea wished us a good evening and left the cafeteria through the back door, we went through a phase of silence. Then my full attention went to Ashu. I touched her right shoulder lightly and asked her if she was all right? She did not look directly at me. She continued staring at the entrance of the cafeteria. After a few seconds, she told me in a faint voice that she was tired, and she would like to go to bed. I felt obliged to agree with her wish, and we both took the stairs up to her room.

Once we were there, she threw herself on the top of the bed. I sat on the edge of her bed touching her forehead to find out if she had any temperature. Her forehead was a bit worm but not what I could call it a real temperature. After two minutes, I thought I better leave her to rest.

When I got to my bedroom. I had many thoughts started mounting in my head. Was it possible that we could meet Jameela the following day? How would Jameela react to seeing Ashu and me next to her close to the tribes' land? Would she be shocked, happy, or confused? Or the wise Sister Nashmeea would have prepared her for the surprise? While I was in that debate, I heard a scream from Ashu's room. I could not work it out what Ashu had said in her scream, but I thought that she was in a bad dream. I lifted my head from the pillow and listened carefully. Ashu went quiet, but not for a long time. Might be less than fifteen minutes and the scream occurred again. At this time, it was clear to hear what Ashu was screaming about. "Green, green."

Those were the words that Ashu was repeating loudly. When that scream occurred for the third time, I left my bed and went to the door of Ashu's room. I knocked lightly first. When I did not get any response, I pushed her bedroom's door open. I found Ashu as I left her two hours ago. She was lying down on the top of her bed, except that she had taken her shoes and black robe off. It seemed she heard me getting into her room. She lifted her head and started staring at me.

After a few seconds, I realised that she was not fully awake. She was looking at me, but I did not think she was seeing me. Suddenly, she repeated the word, "Green." I supported her from behind her shoulders with my right hand and massaged her chin lightly with my left hand, and asked her rather loudly, "Ashu. Amiga, what was green?" She opened her eyes wide and looked at me, but I thought that she was still in her nightmare.

I repeated my question, "What was green?"

Ashu moved her lips with some difficulty and uttered, "The snake, the grass snake." Eventually, I managed to wake her up. When she was fully awake, she started to look around and apologised for the trouble she caused. I got her some water to drink and explained to her that she had a green snake phobia. I reminded her that we were not in the field anymore, and she should feel safe and secure in her bedroom. Gradually, Ashu went back to her normal self and agreed with me that she had suffered a kind of phobia attack, that was much beyond her control. I advised her to change her clothes and relax in her bed for the few hours left of that night. When she put on her pyjamas and sat on her bed, I left her and returned to my bedroom hoping that she would sleep peacefully.

Back in my bed, I lost my desire to sleep again. By now I had mixed feelings. Every time I would try to sink asleep, Jameela would appear to be sitting on top of a strange hill, calling upon me to take her down and lead her the way to our home. Every time I tried to climb up that hill in my dream to get there to Jameela, I fail back into a deep valley. On the third fall, I found myself next to my bed on the floor. Good timing, I said to myself. There was enough light in the room. It was time to make a move. It took me five minutes to wash up and put myself in order. My next move was to go to Ashu's room. Though I left Ashu's door unlocked the night before, I knocked lightly and listen attentively. Ashu's voice came from inside her bedroom. "Good morning, Kameela, I was awake. Would you come in?"

When I pushed the door open, I found Ashu was fully dressed, sitting on the edge of her bed thumbing her shabby notebook. I sat next to her and asked her to put her notebook aside. She put her notebook on the top of her pillow and said, "I knew what you were going to say. You would ask me, how we should receive Jameela?"

I smiled and said, "Typical Ashu. The subject was perfect, but the conclusion was wrong."

Ashu leaned backwards and asked, "What else did you have in your mind?"

To attract Ashu's full attention, I pressed her right hand with my right hand and said, "Listen to what I was going to say amiga. Either Jameela wouldn't be able to recover her British passport, or she would come with her passport in her hand. In each case, it would be one of two different scenarios to follow. In the first case scenario, that was to say, Jameela could not recover her old passport, I would be confident that Mulla Abdul Rahman would use his contacts and the photocopy of my passport to issue a new travel document for Jameela. Mind you that would be a long process, it could take weeks, or even months. But if Jameela would come with her old British passport, then we could request Sister Nashmeea to arrange one flight for us to London in the same airplane."

Ashu opened her eyes wide and said loudly, "Great, let us hope." We both went silent for a while. Then we realised that we had run out of subjects, or there was not much left to discuss. We moved down to the cafeteria. Once we got there, we both, simultaneously noticed that there was a fourth chair occurred around the dining table. We smiled optimistically at each other.

Ashu put on a serious face and said, "Now what two chairs we should occupy and what two chairs we should leave empty?"

I reacted with a wide smile, "No hard debate, Ashu. The middle chair would be for Sister Nashmeea as usual. And the one next to it would be for Jameela, from today onward till the day of our departure."

When Suroor came with two handwritten menus, she looked across the table with her nice smile and greeted us as always without showing any surprise in her eyes. Minutes later, Suroor came back with a silver colour tray with four folded silky texture white handkerchiefs on top. When Suroor put that try on the table Ashu and I just looked at the tray and looked at each other again without any comment.

However, when Suroor came back to collect the menus, Ashu could not help but to look at the silver tray and ask Suroor nicely, "But excuse me Suroor what was that tray for?"

Suroor nodded her head twice and said, "Forgive me, doctor, I never ask my lady any question. I only would do what she asked me to do." Suroor then smiled and took two steps backwards before she turned her face and disappeared behind the counter of the cafeteria. After munching some food, and sipping some tea, we both twisted our chairs in the direction of the back door of the cafeteria. Watching that door second by second. It took me two flashes to rub my eyes, when I heard Ashu screaming, "Yes, it was her."

We both stood up and fixed our eyes on the back door of the cafeteria. I could see Sister Nashmeea walking consciously from behind the counter of the cafeteria and walking behind her a shadowy figure in a black robe and a headscarf covering most of her forehead. The shadowy figure was moving slowly with a back bag hanging on her right shoulder. That was Jameela herself. I was first to rush to reach her and hug her tightly, repeating, "Jameela, my sister, did you know how much I missed you?"

My tears sprang out beyond my control. I pushed her black headscarf up away from her eyes and looked her in the eye and hugged her again. I noticed that her beautiful wide brown eyes were full of tears as well. Ashu was behind me sobbing and waiting for her turn to hug Jameela.

Sister Nashmeea came from behind and went to the dining table and lifted the silver tray with the few white silky handkerchiefs on top and handed them to me and Ashu. Commenting, "Sorry doctors, we did not have tissues in this land. Everything around her was solid and original." Then it became clear to me the idea of the silver tray and its white contents.

All that was there to dry our expected tears. Kind Sister Nashmeea would not leave anything to chance. The emotional storm lasted for almost fifteen minutes. Then Sister Nashmeea invited all of us to sit down and relax. Sister Nashmeea and Jameela took the middle two chairs next to each other, while Ashu and I twisted our chairs in their direction, I couldn't take my eyes off Jameela as if I wanted to make sure that the lady next to me was Jameela herself.

Every time Jameela noticed that I was staring at her she would look at me and smile through her tears. Jameela's look had changed a lot in comparison with the Jameela who I used to know. She looked thinner and darker and without her loose shiny chestnut colour hair. My first question to Jameela was the reason that delayed her all those days and why she did not join us earlier? Jameela looked around her as if she was making sure that she was no longer under the mercy of Taliban.

Then she looked back at me and said, "You knew, Kameela, my first step to liberty was to move to Grandmother Haida's house. The old lady knew me through the times I visited her in the company of the late Sheika Shahnaz, but those visits were not regular. The old lady liked me very much and she showed me love and affection in her house. The problem with the old lady was her hearing. I tried to talk to her in Dari. But I couldn't communicate with her properly.

The number of times, I told her that the package that was trusted with her by the late Sheika contained a document that belonged to me, and I would like to recover it if that was possible. Instead of responding to my request, the old lady used to tell me stories about her cousin Sheika Shahnaz and how close to each other they used to be. She used to tell me that the late Sheika was not just a cousin, but much more than that. She used to repeat that the Sheika was like her sister, a very close sister.

However, I continued trying to explain to her what I wanted. Eventually, with the help of her housekeeper, Grandmother understood what I was on about.

Then she pulled her walking stick and led me to her bedroom. There she asked her housekeeper to pull out an iron box from under the bed. Once the box was out, the old lady pulled a small key from her pocket and asked the housekeeper to open it. When the box was wide open, I could see a lot of things scattered at the bottom of the box.

On the top of some small packages, I could see my old passport sitting there just as I trusted it with Sheika Shahnaz years ago. I picked my passport up and thanked the old lady by a sign of my hand. The old lady smiled at me and asked her housekeeper to lock the box again and push it back to a place, as it was under the bed."

Then Jameela reached down to her backpack and produced to us her British passport. We all gave her a round of applause to the point that the two Suroors appeared clapping and smiling from behind the counter of the cafeteria, without knowing the cause of our celebration.

Sister Nashmeea looked at one of the Suroors and said, "I think we should add some sweets to our celebration."

Both Suroors retreated through the backdoor of the cafeteria. Two minutes later, both came back, one was carrying a tray of baklava, and the other one carrying a fresh pot of tea. Jameela looked surprised to see the tray of baklava on our table. Sister Nashmeea smiled and teased Jameela by asking her to hand her the passport to avoid staining it with the sticky syrup of the baklava.

Then Sister Nashmeea said, "I did not know doctors if you had noticed that our baklava was different from the baklava you used to serve in London. Your baklava in London was prepared with sugar while our baklava around here would be prepared with honey."

When Sister Nashmeea finished her sentence, Jameela looked left and right and asked Sister Nashmeea in a soft tone, "Who was the doctor?" Sister Nashmeea smiled again and said, "You would be glad to know Jameela, that both your sister Kameela, and your friend Ashu were holding a degree as medical doctors."

Jameela looked surprised and screamed rather loud, "Wow, that was a great achievement."

I looked at Jameela and said, "That was the only way that enabled us to reach you, sister. We offered our medical services to the people of our predecessors' land. That was our practical plan to get to you. Mind you sister without the kind support of Sister Nashmeea and her great uncle Mullah Abdul Rahman we would have never achieved our goal."

Sister Nashmeea said, "Please, doctor, I feel so hambled. We did nothing but our human obligation."

Time was passing fast, and Sister Nashmeea stood up and said, "I was so happy for your happiness. Of course, you could stay here if you like, but I would suggest that you would be better off going upstairs and relax in your bedrooms." I offered to help Jameela with her bag, but Jameela thanked me and told me that the bag was not that heavy, it contained nothing but a few garments and some papers and she would have no problem carrying it upstairs.

# Chapter Seventeen

I was amazed to find myself once again, after all these years, together with my sister Jameela and my friend Ashu in the same bedroom. When Jameela took off her headscarf and sat down on the bed's side, I could not resist but to hug her and kiss her again. Jameela kept smiling and showing unusual strong character. After ten minutes, the three of us felt relaxed and settled and our serious talking had started. Jameela's first question was about my parents. She asked me if my parents were, okay? I told her that my father had suffered a minor stroke, but he survived it after six weeks in hospital. She was moved a bit, but she said, "Well, I suppose that was a possible happening in his age. The main thing was that he was still ticking and alive."

Before she mentioned my mother, I added that my mother was still fine cocking curry and discovering new grocery markets every a few weeks. Jameela smiled and said, "Did you know Kameela I miss my mother's curry? She knew how to balance the spices in her dish. I missed everything around Hounslow Central, even the kaput clock in the tube station."

Ashu and I were listing to Jameela. With deep attention. Jameela went silent for a few seconds, and Ashu and I went silent too, waiting for what she was going to say next. She drew out a long sigh and said, "Did you know Kameela. I hold no bad feelings toward my parents. I was young and green, and I had no idea what was going on around me. My parents, I naturally, thought then that they had chosen the best for me. You could say that I had no clear idea about what was planned for me. However, my shock had come later, when I discovered that I was sent to the land of no return. You should not ask me if I had missed you all? Of course, I did but I had no means to reach you. On top of that, the daily events were overwhelming, and I was feeling that I was like a feather in the eye of the storm."

Ashu surprised Jameela with an unexpected question. She asked her if she was saddened by the death of Akrum? Jameela drew out another long sigh and said, "Of course I was, but I was not shocked. What I witnessed at that battleground made me believe that Akrum could lose his life at any minute. I would remind you, Ashu, that my life with Akrum was not what could call it a normal life of husband and wife.

From the first few days we were together, Akrum discovered his impotency. That condition had impacted him profoundly. I kept telling him to seek a medical advice, but he was mixing between an herbalist and a medical doctor. Because of his condition, as he believed, was caused by an herbalist's prescription. Hence, he lost his faith in medical treatment. Instead, he relayed on incantations and magic power without achieving any valuable result. Akrum like most of the villagers of his terrain was a guy of good nature, but he was brainwashed in his early life by the teachings of those ignorant gangsters in those dungeons isolated buildings, so-called 'Madrasas'.

You knew sisters, it is a common word in Dari that meant schools. You might know sisters my knowledge about the religion of Islam was limited. We followed it through the dictation we received its meanings at our early life from our parents. Its concept might vary drastically from person to person and group to group. Kameela. My sister might remember the discussions, or I should say the arguments that used to take place between my father and my uncle during some Friday evenings in our house. She might remember that when their argument would heat up, we used to leave the lobby and refuge to our bedroom. Still, then we could hear some of the words and phrases they used in their argument.

My father used to support his arguments with quotations from the holy Koran, and he used to repcat that the book of Allah all mighty made it very clear that there Should be no compulsion in religion. That Koranic verse stuck in my mind. Hence, I used it in my discussions with Akrum. I asked him once the reason that made him and his Taliban group to fight the Hazards sect. He used to tell me that they were not on a straight path of the teaching of Islam. When I used to quote to him my father's words from the Koran, he used to say that the Koran should be interpreted by a religious authority. However, the authority in his opinion was the one-eyed Mulla."

When Jameela went silent for a few seconds, Ashu looked her in the eye and said, "I am astonished, how did you survive that kind of fanaticism?"

Jameela looked back at Ashu and said, "What were my options? Before the campaign against the Hazards, Akrum's life used to be divided between the training camps and some military duties nearby. At those days he used to come

158

home quite often. I could tell you that we had many sleepless nights talking and discussing. But in the process, I found out that my discussions with him did not help him much. In fact, it used to increase his confusion and his doubts about himself. All that stopped when he was called to serve at the Hazard's front which was more than hundreds of miles away from where we used to live. Then he was obliged to report his marriage to his superiors who ordered him to bring me along with him to serve at the battlefront.

Well, he took me there, where my life became like hell. Bombardments, shelling, gunfire, and blood were everywhere. Akrum used to visit our tent once a week, several times he came with some visible injuries. I used to nurse him with the limited resources we had, such as gauze dressing and iodine for sterilisation used to be distributed among the tents occasionally. Luckily most of the wild animals, like wolves, foxes and wild dogs had fled the area because of the continuous bombardments, but like everybody else, I had to put up with scorpions and reptiles."

When Jameela mentioned the word reptile, Ashu got alerted. Luckily, she did not panic, and the remark passed smoothly. Since then, I was waiting to have the chance to whisper to Jameela not to mention the word snake in the presence of Ashu. I had that chance when Ashu went to her room for a few minutes to change her shirt. Jameela was rather astonished and told me that she was glad that I told her about Ashu's phobia. She said, "I would avoid the word even if I see one creeping on the floor of our room."

Jameela waited till Ashu had come back. Then she said to both of us, "when we got the news about the severe illness of his mother Akrum, did everything possible to get me special permission to go home to nurse the ailing old lady."

Then Jameela drew a long sigh again and said, "My story would not finish in one night, it might take weeks and months to cover what I had gone through. Hence you should tell me what you planned for me?"

I liked the way Jameela had asked, and I thought it was time to put her mind in peace. So, I said quietly, "You would know my sister, I believe everything would go very well. We arranged for you a good special plan as part of our main plan. All would depend on Sister Nashmeea's preparation. I thought that should you know that Ashu and I had been brought to this land by a charity organisation, known as Ready Doctors for Overseas Volunteering and Raising Donations. Initially, our assignment was set up for three months, with the possibility of extension if necessary. I would think that Ashu was holding the record of the dates of our moves. At any rate, I believed that we were still within the time range of our assignment. All would depend on Sister Nashmeea and her efforts to urge her well-connected uncle to issue you a new passport by the British consulate in Islamabad. Once you would get your passport, we would be able to fly to London together."

Ashu said, "All the dates of our movements were recorded in my little notebook, but I believed that we just passed a month and one or two weeks of the time of our assignment."

I said, "No worries then, let us discuss the issue with Sister Nashmeea. I would think that she would do everything within her reach to sort out the matter. By the way, would you know the time?"

Ashu looked at her watch and said, "Oh my God it was four-thirty in the morning. I knew we would not sleep tonight. Tomorrow, I would look like a zombie. You excuse me to go to my room and get a few hours of sleep before the morning."

After Ashu left us and went to her bedroom, I rested on my back and stared at the ceiling. I relived the times when Jameela and I used to share the same room in our house in Hounslow Central, waiting for our mother to call us for breakfast in the morning, except that the ceiling was of a different colour. It was white, not blue.

Suddenly, Jameela interrupted my thoughts and asked, "How long did it take you to finish your medical studies after secondary school?"

I told her with my eyes still fixed on the ceiling, "Well Jameela that was hard seven-year. Ashu was a great encouragement. We used to revise our subjects together and exchange the notes that we used to take during the lectures."

Then we both went silent trying to catch up on some sleep. The first thing I heard after, were some lights knocking on the door and the voice of Sister Nashmeea calling Doctor Ashu it was one-thirty in the afternoon. Most likely, Sister Nashmeea had forgotten once again that Ashu and I had exchanged rooms the first night we moved into the centre. I surprised her by saying, "Yes Sister, we would be downstairs soon."

Sister Nashmeea heard me and got closer to the door and said, "Great, that was a good sleep."

I went next door and told Ashu to be ready to move as Sister Nashmeea was waiting downstairs. Ashu responded with a deep sleepy voice and ask me to wait for her to get ready. In less than fifteen minutes, the three of us took the stairs down to the cafeteria. Sister Nashmeea was already there, taking her seat at the dining table. When she noticed that we were approaching, she stood up smiling and welcomed us one by one. We took our seats around Sister Nashmeea and went silent for a few seconds till Sister Nashmeea said, "I bet you did not sleep much last night."

Ashu smiled and said, "You were right Sister, but we had to compensate for that by sleeping more than half of the day."

We did not realise that Sister Nashmeea had arranged for us a generous festivity till the two Suroors started to bring plate after plate full of grilled meat. Chicken, rice, curry, and a variety of local dishes that we didn't know their names. The food festivity lasted for about twenty minutes and finished with the usual tea and homemade cake.

Sister Nashmeea took a few sips of her tea and said, "Now I think the serious business should start. All that we need were some planning. The first obstacle we should overcome would be the renewing of Jameela's passport. That would be when my uncle would plan his next visit to Islamabad.

He would take Jameela's passport with him. Of course, he would ask an official to approach the British consulate in Islamabad to find out what was the requirements for its renewal. Most likely they would demand to see Jameela in person, and they would ask her the reason behind neglecting the document all these years. That could require the presence of some witnesses. In that case, we should be all there with Jameela to finalise the renewal process."

Then Jameela stood up and said, "Excuse me, Sister, my passport was upstairs in my back bag, should I go and retrieve it for you?"

"Sister Nashmeea told Jameela that there was no need to rush. And explained that her uncle didn't plan his trip to Islamabad yet. That might take a few days of preparations. You could get it down tomorrow, and I would find out from my uncle whether Doctor's Kameela documents would be of help in the process."

Jameela looked a bit puzzled and said, "You would know Sister my passport was used only for couple of trips. One was with the school to Europe, and one was from London to Islamabad. It didn't contain any address in Islamabad. I hope that would not raise some suspicion against my parents, or me. I could be accused of being a member of Taliban or any other violent group."

Sister Nashmeea smiled in confidence and said, "Jameela daring, you are a British citizen, and you were attending your embassy to renew your passport after being trapped all these years in a troubled part of the tribes' land. I would leave all the explanations to my uncle Mullah Abdul Al Rahman, as he would be your advocator in the presentation."

Jameela looked much more relaxed and poured herself a fresh cup of tea. Ashu looked thoughtful. After a short gap of silence. Ashu thanked Sister Nashmeea for her help and kindness. Then she asked her if she could estimate the time that it would take us to start our trip to Islamabad. Sister Nashmeea adjusted her seat and said, "In a few days. Tomorrow I would know the exact day of my uncle's departure for Islamabad. Then we would time our trip to take place two days after his departure. That would give him sometimes to test the ground with the officials to initiate the case for renewing Jameela's passport. Everything would be under a strict planning and control." After that Ashu looked satisfied with Sister Nashmeea's answer and commented, "We wouldn't have much to pack, our few garments in our back bags. A few minutes and we would be ready to move."

Sister Nashmeea found Ashu's comment encouraging. She smiled and said, "Great, but please Doctor Kameela, do not forget to bring your passport and Jameela's passport down tomorrow, so I could hand them to my uncle before he would commence his trip."

I smiled back at Sister Nashmeea and assured her that the documents would be with us in the cafeteria tomorrow morning. Then Sister Nashmeea stood up and wished us a wonderful day and vanished through the back door of the cafeteria.

A few seconds later, one of the Suroor came out from behind the cafeteria's counter, greeting us and asking us if we need any further service. Ashu thanked her very much, and we moved in the direction of the stairs. We settled for a few minutes in my bedroom till Ashu suggested that we should have an afternoon nap, to meet later in the evening. After Ashu had gone to her room, I noticed that Jameela had dozed for a while, but not me. I was exploring the future with my silent thoughts and waiting for Jameela to wake up so, I could debate with her what would be coming next.

# Chapter Eighteen

An hour had passed on me turning around and around in my bed. When Jameela lifted her head and noticed that I was awake, she rubbed her eyes and said, "You would like to know Kameela, because of my bad experience in the military camp, I cannot sleep continuously for long hours. On some occasions in the camps, the shootings used to come near enough to my tent to the point that I used to think that we were almost being taken over by the opponents. To be honest with you Kameela, I would not know if I would get used to normal life again?"

I sat in my bed and told Jameela not to worry and explained to her that time would be a good healer. To calm her further I said, "If you would face some difficulties in the future, we would get you some anti-depression tablets to use for a short time till you get back to your normal self."

A light knock on the door. Must be Ashu liked to join our conversation. I said a bit loudly, "Come in Ashu. The door was open."

Ashu entered the room in a dancing mode, she was moving left and right and backward and forward. Then she stopped and said, "You know girls, I would love to listen to some music."

My comment was direct. "That would be my promise, Ashu. Once we get home, I would invade your brother's shop and select some dancing songs and keep them in my room discreetly and wait till my father would be taken to his physiotherapy and my mother vanished in her shopping trip. Then I would play the music and you would have the chance to dance your head off."

Then Jameela looked at Ashu and said, "I hope your brother would still stock Abba cassettes in his shop."

Ashu smiled and said, "Oh well, even if he wouldn't stock them anymore, he would get them for us."

Jameela put on a sad face and said, "You know girls that playing music, any kind of music under the rules of Taliban considered to be illegal (haram). That was to say it would not be allowed and it was punishable by public flogging."

Ashu's reaction was a kind of disbelief, she put on a serious face and said, "Oh my God, that was trouble. Where did they find this heresy to attribute it to Islam?"

Jameela looked at Ashu and said, "You would be surprised to know that so many things, we considered as normal in life they considered them to be illegal or (haram). Under Taliban's rules, music, TV, pictures. football, toys, and monuments were all considered to be the work of the devil and punishable sins. I can list for you in that category so many other things, even things you cannot think of. Worse than that was their attitude toward women. For example, a woman under the rule of Taliban cannot venture out to the street without putting her burqa on. She could not go to the hospital without the company of a man of her immediate family, a husband or a father or a brother. They had gathered us on one occasion to witness the public execution of a lady simply because she attended a clinic for treatment on her own."

Ashu suddenly whispered, "Stop it please, please Jameela, I cannot take it anymore."

Jameela apologised and said, "Yes Ashu, I knew that was terrifying, but I would think that we should acknowledge it as a fact. For that reason, I would think that our future campaign for human rights should be revealing and exclusive."

My comment was, "I would fully agree with you, sister, but let us deal with the issue back home at the right place and the right time. Where we could seek the support of related organisations."

Ashu suddenly stood up and said, "Listen, friends, I would think that we could talk non-stop till the next day. We had a lot of things to talk about. I would think that we should take it easy and discuss issues according to their priorities. We should get our documents ready for Sister Nashmeea to collect them tomorrow as she promised. Now you would excuse me to go and have some sleep. So that I would wake you up in time in the morning."

Jameela looked at me and said, "I wouldn't think that Ashu's passport would be relevant to the renewal of my passport. Your passport yes, might be as we share names and address, but why Ashu's?" I lifted my head and told Jameela that it could be relevant if the British embassy in Islamabad would require more than one witness to process the case.

However, what I said didn't close our bed conversation. We talked and talked most of the night. In the following morning, I forgot most of what we talked about. The next thing I remembered was Ashu's voice coming from behind the door telling us that the time was nine-thirty, and we better get down to meet Sister Nashmeea and give her the documents. I called Jameela to see if she was awake. Before she answered me Jameela went to the corner of the room to have a quick wash and put on her pair of jeans. I prepared myself too, and in ten minutes the three of us were on our way downstairs to the cafeteria with our passports in Ashu's handbag.

So far, Sister Nashmeea was not there, but Suroor as usual was pleased to serve us a nice breakfast. The plates of fried eggs, the local cheese and the dark colour tea were an extra treat. We finished our breakfast with no sign of Sister Nashmeea. Ashu started agitating and suggested that we should ask Suroor if she had any news from Sister Nashmeea. I told Ashu that was not necessary. Most likely that Sister Nashmeea had an overloaded program, and I should think she would be with us soon. Before I finished my sentence, Sister Nashmeea appeared from behind the counter of the cafeteria, hanging a black bag on her right shoulder.

We stood up and exchanged greeting with her with our smiles and our due courtesy. After a few sips of hear tea, Sister Nashmeea stood up and said, "Friends, you would excuse me today, I wouldn't be able to stay with you for a long time. My uncle's departure to Islamabad would be tomorrow, and my uncle and I had a lot of issues to discuss before his departure."

Then she looked at Ashu and asked her half-joking, "I would like to think that you would be our secretary. I believed you have the documents ready."

Ashu without saying anything just pulled her back bag from under the table and took out our passports and handed them to Sister Nashmeea.

Sister Nashmeea thanked Ashu and put the passports in the pocket of her handbag. Then she put on a step forward and stopped to say, "I forgot to tell you doctors about the nice report my uncle had prepared for you to take to the charity organisation that delegated you to our terrain. It contained the evaluation of your service and expressed our thanks and gratefulness for your kind mission. I would think that you should present a copy of the report to the representatives of your charity organisation when they would arrange for your return flight at Islamabad airport. In the meantime, I would like to let you know that my uncle promised to do his best to merge your flight with Jameela's flight so that you could board the same plane. Tomorrow, I would not be able to see you, I would be quite busy, but the day after tomorrow, I hope you would be ready for our trip to Islamabad. Please, pack up your suitcases and leave them outside the rooms."

After Sister Nashmeea wished us a lovely day and vanished behind the counter of the cafeteria, we went on staring at each other silently for a few seconds. Jameela broke the silence and said, "What would we prepare for the trip? All that we would prepare were our small bags. It would take us a few minutes to pack them and go." I nodded my head in agreement with Jameela's comment, but Ashu looked a bit absent-minded. I gave Ashu a soft look trying not to provoke her.

I knew that she would come up with an explanation regarding what was disturbing her. As I expected, when Ashu noticed that I was looking at her continuously, she looked back at me and said, "Would you know Kameela, travelling around in that troubled land would scare me to death. From what I heard from Jameela's stories made me to believe that fighting could irrupt anywhere, anytime."

I had to agree with Ashu. In the meantime, I thought I should choose my words very carefully. I went quiet for a while to come up with a suitable comment. When I noticed that Ashu was looking at me, waiting for my response. I looked back and said, "Yes, Ashu, but we were lucky to have Sister Nashmeea with us, she was a good planner and wonderful at setting up a strategy. I believe that we would take the same routes that would be tested by her uncle Mullah Abdul Rahman, a day ahead of our journey." Ashu listened very carefully and looked less anxious.

Jameela supported me in my comment and said, "I had great faith in Sister Nashmeea, and I would go anywhere she planned to take me without worries. After all, that would be our only option, otherwise, we would stay here forever."

Ashu felt that she had lost her argument. Two against one, plus the planner, Sister Nashmeea herself we all considered her to be an iconic guide. Ashu stared at the table and said, "Should we go upstairs? I feel I would like to relax for a while." We took on the stairs cautiously.

Ashu went straight to her bedroom, while Jameela and I went to my bedroom. Jameela took off her headscarf and sat on the side edge of her bed. I sat next to her and teased her by touching her hair and said, "Since we used to be teenagers, I used to be envious of your hair. It was time to give me your secret of the treatment you used."

Jameela smiled and said, "No treatment Kameela, just avoid chemical shampoos and use herbal ingredients. Mind you I had noticed the other day that a few grey hairs had invaded my head already. I wonder how my mother would react when she would see my grey hair?"

I smiled and said, "Do not worry, Jameela. There were only a few grey ones, and you might remember that my mother was not that observant. It might take her a while to recognise your face first. My worries would be her reaction when she would meet you in person. I should think that we should telephone her from the airport and worn her that you are in London, and you were coming home. I would think that would be a wise way to save her a possible heart attack."

Like the night before, we talked, and talked, and talked, till we passed out and went silent. The next thing I heard was Ashu's voice grumbling next to the door repeating that it was late in the morning, and asking if we had decided to sleep the whole day? I lifted my head to find that Jameela was awake already. Thus, I answered Ashu from my bed. I told her to give us a few minutes. We would be with her soon. Ten minutes later, we took our daily way downstairs to the cafeteria.

Suroor rushed to serve us our breakfast, but today something was missing that affected our mood. Sister Nashmeea would not be with us today. We realised that her presence which we took for granted had a great impacted our mood. She would give us hope, confidence and optimism. We felt that we had many things to talk about, but there would be no point to keep Suroor busy if we could talk and discuss in our rooms. Hence when Ashu stood up and yelled, "Thanks Suroor for everything. Have a lovely day." Jameela and I followed her to the stairs.

In my bedroom, after a short silence, I asked Jameela what I thought was a provoking question, "What would you say to my mother when you meet her?"

Jameela contracted her eyebrows and said, "Basically I would let her know that I held no bad feelings against her. She did what she thought was the best for me." Then I asked her opinion about my father's attitude then? "Because I believed that my father was neutral, he did not know what the right attitude was to take." After a few seconds of silence, Jameela lifted her head up and said, "The only person in our family who would take my blames would be my uncle. He was one of those people who would impress you with his progressive thoughts in the way he would advocate women's rights and how they should participate in social life, but in a situation, he would lean to defend his interests though that would be against his principles."

Ashu was relaxing her body behind me, but when she heard Jameela's comment, she sat down and said, "You shouldn't worry Jameela, when we succeed in setting up an organisation that would defend young girls against forced and arranged marriage. I would oblige your uncle to pay the costs."

Jameela smiled and said, "I would tell you Ashu, my uncle was not a mean person, but we should know how to put him in the corner and make him pay our expenses willingly." I agreed with Jameela, and said, "Conspiracy, planning that what it would take to make my uncle pay."

I would not remember what we had talked about after Ashu had left us and gone to her bedroom, but I remember her husky voice early morning and she was reminding us that we should go down as early as possible. By nine o'clock in the morning, the three of us were down there in the cafeteria, dressed as required in public, headscarves on our overall black robes down to our feet. Our early appearance did not bather Suroor at all, neither it affected her morning greetings and usual curtsy. Though I believed the three of us had very little appetite. Nevertheless, we had our breakfast and more than one round of tea.

Ten minutes later, Sister, Nashmeea appeared from behind the counter of the cafeteria, dressed just like the way we were dressed. We stood up and exchanged the morning greeting as we always did. The first thing she said was that her uncle was already in Islamabad, and she was hoping that all of us would be with him soon. Then she explained that there would be plenty of room for us in Aunt Shabnam's house and would be enough rooms to accommodate a tribe. Then she explained that we would commence our journey by eleven o'clock that day along the gangway that would take us about five hours to Islamabad.

Jameela looked a bit puzzled and couldn't help asking Sister Nashmeea about the meaning of the gangway. Sister Nashmeea said, "That meant we would move along the south leg of the triangle of the borders till we get to the end of the nook, then a few minutes of driving and we would be in Pakistan."

Jameela looked satisfied with that explanation, but Ashu looked still uncertain about the trip. It was ten forty-five when Sister Nashmeea picked up her handbag and moved toward the backdoor of the cafeteria. I followed her and Ashu and Jameela followed my steps. On the left side of the high wall that separated the building of the sunflowers field, was an iron door. Sister Nashmeea pulled a key from her pouch and opened that door. Outside the building there was a military van, most likely it was the same van that used to transfer us from the bungalow to our present place. The van was parking by the end of the farm road facing outward in the direction of the main road.

The little man with the white turban appeared once again carrying our relatively small suitcases and placing them next to the back of the van. Then he opened the back door of the van, and in a smart move, he squeezed himself jumping up into the van and pulled out the wooden steps and fixed them between the floor and the back of the van. The three of us were standing there watching and waiting for Sister Nashmeea's next move. Sister Nashmeea waited till the little man pushed our suitcases inside the van. Then she climbed into the back of the van and leaned down in our direction. Then she asked Jameela to lift Ashu to receive her and pulled her into the van.

Neither Jameela nor I had any problem climbing up into the back of the van taking one side of the seats facing Ashu who took the opposite seat on the right side. Sister Nashmeea waited till the little man pushed the wooden steps up into the van. She pushed them under the left seat and took the middle seat in the back of the van behind the driver.

We could feel from the lousy movement of the van that we were going through a rough unpaved road and sensing some dust around. There was not much talking between us because of the high-level noise of the engine of the van. Almost an hour passed in that uncertain atmosphere when we heard a burst of a machine gun. It sounded like it was a distance away. However, the second burst sounded close to us.

Our van came to a halt at the side of the road, and we could hear our driver engaged in a conversation. Sister Nashmeea looked behind her and pulled a small slide of glass that separated the body of the van from the compartment of the driver. I tried to listen intently to the talking between Sister Nashmeea and the driver. With my broken Dari, I understood that Sister Nashmeea asked the driver about the number of the intruders. I would think that he told her they were five of them.

Three stayed in a military vehicle and two armed men were approaching us very slowly. She told him to tell them to identify themself and their reason to stop us. He told her they said that they were a mobile unit of Taliban, and they would like to know if we had any authority to go across the border. Sister Nashmeea told him to tell them that our vehicle belonged to Mulla Abdul Rahman, and we had the authority to move around.

The driver said, "My lady, they asked if we had any proof?"

169

Sister Nashmeea asked the driver about the distance between him and the guy approaching. He said, "Approximately ten metres." She told the driver to ask the guy if he was the commander of the unit. The driver said, "Yes, he confirmed that he was the commander of the unit."

Sister Nashmeea opened her handbag and pulled out an old folder. She opened that folder and pulled out a letter and handed it to the driver. She told the driver to ask the guy to come closer and read that letter. When the guy read the letter, he saluted us and wished us a safe journey. When the drama was over and we moved again, I looked around to see Ashu had stuck her body under the seat. When she looked at me, I whispered to her kindly, "Please Ashu, hold yourself together. We did not have so many spear knickers anymore."

I was not sure if Ashu was serious when she said, "Too late Kameela. It was burning already."

# Chapter Nineteen

We were on the move again and I was wondering how to help Ashu discreetly with her wet knickers. Sister Nashmeea was occupied watching through the sliding window behind the driver. She didn't hear or rather she did not know the subject of the fragmented conversation that I exchanged with Ashu. Our vehicle speeded up a little. I felt that we started moving on a better road. Jameela had been closing her eyes for a while as if she was not paying attention to what would happen next. Ashu was back in the seat closing her legs firmly. She looked at me and whispered once more, "Don't worry, Kameela. It was just a little."

Sister Nashmeea looked back and said, "We passed the hard part of the journey." I thought she heard Ashu saying just a little, and she thought that I asked Ashu if she was tired.

After approximately an hour in the move, our vehicle slowed down. Ashu got apprehensive again. Sister Nashmeea looked back again and said, "Don't worry ladies, we were approaching the borders. The border's guards would identify our vehicle, but there would be nobody around most of the time, but you never know, we might be lucky."

Five minutes later our van picked up speed again, and it was obvious that we started moving on a better-paved road. After another one hours in the move, our vehicle slowed down again. Sister Nashmeea looked back and said, "We were going to enter the city, but there was a long queue of cars in front of us. No problem, we would find a way to overcome the situation."

Sister Nashmeea pulled the same letter she used before that helped us to pass Taliban patrol and told the driver to show it to the military police who was inspecting the approaching cars. The officer read the letter and diverted our vehicle away from the queue and led us to a side gate where we had entered the city through an empty road.

Jameela looked sleepy. She used to open her eyes occasionally just for short times, while Ashu looked a bit tense. She closed her legs firmly again. And everything looked fine under the black overall robe. I was the only one who squeezed herself close to the end of the back seat trying to share Sister Nashmeea the limited view from behind the driver. Sometimes, Sister Nashmeea used to move aside to give me more room to see the landmarks on our way. I couldn't see much, but I relied on Sister Nashmeea's comments now and then that gave me some information about the milestones of the city.

Though I felt as if I lost my sense of time, I thought at least two hours had passed when I felt that our van had come to a halt. I sneaked a glance to see that we were close to a high fence with a huge rusty metal gate insight. Suddenly, the gate was opened, and our van entered inside through that gate. I couldn't work it out who had opened the back door of the van, but once it was opened, Sister Nashmeea pulled the wooden steps from under the seat and handed them to the guy who was waiting nearby.

The first one to get down was Sister Nashmeea. Then she asked Jameela to hold Ashu from under her arms, facing backward, and put her legs first, down to the steps. Ashu was relieved to be on the floor and went looking in all directions. Then Jameela went down easily. When I got down Sister Nashmeea disengaged the steps and slide them up to the back of the van. Sister Nashmeea then led the way and we went in the direction of the main building. On our right, inside the fence, I could see a villa-like that was separated from the main building. Sister Nashmeea looked at that villa and said, "There where my uncle used to stay when he would visit Islamabad."

When we got close to the main building, another door was opened and an attractive nicely dressed middle-aged lady putting on a headscarf came out with her arms wide opened. She gave Sister Nashmeea a patient hug and kissed her several times on her cheeks. I was so impressed to see Sister Nashmeea lifting the right hand of the lady and kissed it twice. Then Sister Nashmeea took one step backwards and said, "My lovely aunt, lady Shabnam." Sister Nashmeea introduced us to the lady one by one who was smiling and inviting us to come in. While we were still at the door a guy came with our suitcases, and lady Shabnam gave him a direction to a room where he should drop them.

Lady Shabnam directed us to the left side of the house and said, "Here ladies there were two identical rooms. Each of them had two beds, a shower, towels, and a table and you chose how to share them. You would wash and relax for the next two hours till we would call you for the dinner."

I gave Sister Nashmeea a meaningful look and said, "Sister, I would give you the company of Jameela tonight, while I would keep the company of Ashu to calm her down." Sister Nashmeea nodded her head twice agreeing with what I said. Both rooms were on the ground floor adjacent to each other. Without any further comment, I pulled my suitcase and Ashu's suitcase and entered the first room on the left. Ashu entered behind me. Once we were inside, I shut up the door, opened my back bag and handed Ashu her knickers which I previously kept in a plastic bag. Ashu looked at me asking for an explanation. I told her to use the soap in the showroom and wash them up properly and hang them near the window till they dry up.

In the meantime, I would lend her a pair of mines till further notice. Ashu took the plastic bag and with a broad smile on her face and went into the shower room. I took off my overall robe and hanged it on a hanger on the wall and threw myself on the top of the bed on the left side of the room. I had no idea about the time Ashu came out of the shower room. When I heard Sister Nashmeea calling next to the door that it was almost time for dinner and requesting us to be ready.

I opened my eyes to see our window was decorated with two black knickers and Ashu next to them announcing that they had dried up nicely. I looked at Ashu and said, "Please Ashu. You should be more careful. We would not have the facilities to cover up your predicament all the time." Ashu looked back at me and said, "Sure, I would promise, if you would promise no more shocks."

Ashu and I left the room to find Sister Nashmeea and Jameela waiting for us close by. Sister Nashmeea greeted us with a smile and said, "Follow me doctors to the room of festivity. It was a tradition here to treat gust on their first evening with an extravagant feast, and thereafter the food would be helped yourself sort in the kitchen."

We followed Sister Nashmeea through a side corridor till we came to an opening that led to a wide opened room. The room was furnished with a nice silk carpet that covered all its middle area. The carpet was surrounded by brocaded pillows decorated with beautiful colourful patrons. The pillows arranged in the form of a circle around the middle area of the room. Several of the people that I didn't know before were invited to join the feast. One of them was Shinwar, a pleasant gentleman introduced by Aunt Shabnam as her husband. Plates of all kinds of appetising food were arranged in the middle of the circle.

Sister Nashmeea, Jameela, Ashu, and I took our places at the bottom line of the circle. The top of the circle was left unoccupied for Mulla Abdul Rahman.

Nobody would touch the food till the opening Koranic verses by Mulla Abdul Rahman. Minutes later Mulla Abdul Rahman appeared at the entrance of the room. Mullah Abdul Rahman greeted everybody in the room with the traditional Islamic greeting, al-Salam Alaykum. Everybody in the room stood up and returned the Mulla's greeting. The Mulla lifted his right hand and lower it several times saying, "God blessed you. Would you sit down, please?"

Nobody touched the food till Mulla Abdul Rahman sat down and said, "By the name of Allah, the most gracious, the most merciful." Then he picked a piece of bread and tested it. That was a sign to everybody around the food feast to start eating. The food was great and delicious. The feast lasted more than half an hour.

After dinner, Ashu and I went to our room. We tried to rearrange it and would make it a bit tidy as we left it in a mess earlier. Ashu collected her knickers from the hangers and folded them back into her suitcase. Then she looked at me and said, "Do you think tomorrow we would attend the British embassy to get a new passport for Jameela?"

My answer was, "No, Ashu. Tomorrow would be Friday. That was to say it would be a holiday. Friday was not a working day in Pakistan, and I think even foreign missions would follow that rule." Then I suggested that we should go next door to Sister Nashmeea's room to find out what would be planned for us. We left our room to find Sister Nashmeea and Jameela sitting chatting in their beds and their door was wide open. Sister Nashmeea waived us to come in and we did.

After exchanging a few words, Sister Nashmeea said, "You might be aware doctors that tomorrow would be Friday, and it was not a working day in Pakistan. Therefore, we wouldn't be able to apply for Jameela's passport. As a pleasant alternative, Aunt Shabnam requested her husband to drive us around Islamabad to show us some nice landmarks of the city." Ashu got excited and asked the time we would start the tour.

Sister Nashmeea smiled and said, "That would be late in the morning. The city would start opening late on Fridays."

Ashu smiled and said, "Please Sister Nashmeea, I would love to know if Aunt Shabnam owned a camera? It would be very nice if we could get a few snaps together to keep them as a memory of our visit of the city."

Sister Nashmeea responded with a smile and said, "Thank you, Doctor Ashu, for putting this idea in my head, I would think that Uncle Shinwar got a nice camera, and he loved photography. He called himself an amateur photographer, I had seen some great shots in his collection."

For two hours we had talked about everything and nothing, but when I noticed that Sister Nashmeea started yawning, I hinted to Ashu that it was time to go to our room. Back in our room, Ashu looked excited and happy, and she said, "Wow, our pictures in Islamabad! I think we should keep in touch with Aunt Shabnam to get copies of our exceptional pictures."

We were hardly settled in our room when we noticed that Jameela was at our door. She took one step inside our room and said, "Excuse me, sisters, Sister Nashmeea looked sleepy, so I thought I better leave her alone for a while so that she could get a good rest. Also, I thought we could explore a few ideas regarding our plans in London."

Ashu nodded her head and said, "Well Jameela, I should think that you were the one who should furnish us with ideas and be the most active to implement them."

Jameela replied seriously, "Sure Ashu, but definitely, I would need your support and your valid pieces of advice."

Hence, I thought I should say something constructive and realistic. I directed my words at Jameela and said, "If you would try to set up an active organisation that would be capable of attracting important human rights activists and reach out to MPs and officials, you would also need to run a few seminars in tv channels and radio stations, in the forms of interviews and public meetings. All that my sister would cost money, and you would need a financial supporter."

Jameela sat down on the edge of my bed and said, "I was fully aware of that, and the person I had in my mind would be my uncle. He was rich and it was time for him to pay for his mistakes."

I was astonished to see Jameela's confidence and determination to realise her dream. After all, she was the victim who went through hell because of these social rigid attitudes. I nodded my head and told Jameela, that I fully agreed with her. I said, "Yes, my sister, you got it right. You would have my full support without hesitation."

Hence, Ashu stood up and said, "And my support too. I would be your right hand in your project. Together we would succeed and achieve our objectives despite all the obstacles."

Jameela looked very pleased with our comments and went on to tell us, "What had happened to her was not accepted, and it should never happen again to any young girl in our community and beyond."

Ashu sat down next to me again and said, "The principles of protecting young girls from their family's oppression should be universal. I heard that underaged marriage of girls arranged by families was common in a lot of parts of the world."

Jameela said enthusiastically, "Yes Ashu I would fully agree with you, but as the proverb specified rightly that charity would start at home, and when we succeed in setting up our organisation, then we would expand our activities to other parts of the world."

Our debate went on till the late hours of the night. We realised that when Ashu reminded us that we should be ready for the city's tour that was promised by Shabnam's husband in the morning. Ashu and I didn't talk much after Jameela had left us to her room. After ten minutes of silence, the usual shrill whistling of Ashu's nose had started. An indication of her deep sleep. The thoughts stayed with me till I passed out. What had happened next was Ashu's voice buzzing in my ears, "Get up, get up Kameela, it was nearly nine o'clock."

We both prepared ourselves and went next door to meet Sister Nashmeea and Jameela. The room was empty, "But where were they?" Ashu asked.

I told Ashu that they would be in the kitchen as Sister Nashmeea said yesterday. Ashu looked a bit puzzled, she looked at me and said, "Fine but where would be the kitchen?"

"I told Ashu that it would be easy to find it, we should get close to the dining room and keep sniffing around till we would get there." Near the dining room, we didn't smell anything, but a few steps to the left of the dining room and we could hear Sister Nashmeea and Jameela chatting and giggling as if they had been there for a while. We greeted them and entered the huge well-organised kitchen. Sister Nashmeea had already fried some eggs and she was busy frying some more.

Jameela was applying some jam to her bread and sipping some tea. Sister Nashmeea pulled a clean plate from a nearby buffet and invited me to fill it with fried eggs and offered it to me wishing me a bone appetite. Then Sister Nashmeea poured me some tea and directed her attention to Ashu and ask her if she would like something. Ashu was searching for the main buffet of the kitchen, and suddenly she said, "Wow I found it. My best honey."

Everything was pleasant in Aunt Shabnam house and the food was nice no matter if it was a big feast or a self-service in the kitchen. We certainly had enough time to feel satisfied when Aunt Shabnam appeared at the door wishing us a good morning and telling us that Uncle Shinwar was already in his car waiting for us outside the gate. Ashu and I rushed to our room to put our shoes on, otherwise, everything was fine. Our headscarves were on, though it was not mandatory in the city, it would help to avoid the staring eyes of the people in public places.

Aunt Shabnam took the lead till we all got through the main gate to reach that silver colour Mercedes six-seat car and uncle Shinwar was waiting behind the wheel. We all greeted him by wishing him a good morning while Aunt Shabnam went swiftly to occupy the front seat. Ashu and I took the side seats in the back, and we allowed the middle one for Jameela and Sister Nashmeea. My impression was that Uncle Shinwar, Aunt Shabnam's husband was a refined gentleman. He held a high-rank position in the local government. He drove slowly so we could explore the city nicely. His radio in the car as Aunt Shabnam told us was tuned to a local Dari station.

Hence, Aunt Shabnam explained that he respected our company and didn't bother to switch it on. After we went out of the complex of the buildings, we entered a beautiful green city. It looked like one large orchard decorated with trees and gardens. We passed a lot of shrines and mosques with beautifully garnished minarets and dooms with patrons and Arabic amazing calligraphy. I expressed several times my astonishment and admiration about the harmony of the colours of those minarets. My eyes never stopped wandering between the people in the streets, and the so many landmarks in the city. I was aware that the city was moderately populated, but I was amazed to see the way people were dressed.

Apart from the slight variation in the colours of their clothes, they looked as if they were in uniform. Uncle Shinwar interrupted my thoughts when he suddenly said, "I would show you a place that you would never forget for the rest of your lives."

Uncle Shinwar drove over a slop of a hill, and he continued driving upward till we got over the other side of the hill, telling us the hill was called Margallo hill, a well-known landmark of the city. Then he explained that when we would get to the other side of the hill, we would see one of the wonders of the city. That was right. At the foot of the hill, we could see an astonishing structure. It was a mosque that was modelled in the shape of a desert tent. The mosque was with four decorated conical minarets as high as the eye could see.

Uncle Shinwar explained that the mosque was known as Shah Faisal Mosque related to king Faisal of Saudi Arabia who ordered to build it in 1986 to be the largest mosque in South Asia. Then uncle Shinwar elaborated to say, "The mosque and so many other projects financed by King Faisal and his successors of Saudi Arabia after the financial windfall that was generated by the energy crisis in wake of the Arab Israeli war in 1973."

Sister Nashmeea couldn't stay silent. She added, "The mosque and so many other projects were erected in the country by the Saudi Royalty to promote their sect of Wahhabism, a fanatic Bedouin version of Islam that was adopted by the movement of Taliban as a form of rigid anti-social dictatorship." Uncle Shinwar nodded his head in agreement with Sister Nashmeea's comment.

Aunt Shabnam suddenly said, "Please Shinwar, whatever the story behind the mosque I would think that it was the best spot to take some pictures to keep the memory of the visit of our guests."

Without comment, Uncle Shinwar drove around to find close-by parking. We all walked to the foot of the building of that amazing mosque, and there was Uncle Shinwar with his camera playing click, click more than seven times. Aunt Shabnam suggested to us to go across a nearby square, stating that she had a surprise for us. On the top of the square. She said, "There was a nicely decorated building with a light illustration of a Dari word on top, meaning restaurant."

Aunt Shabnam was looking at the place and said, "This is one of the most recommended chains of restaurants in the city. I would like to invite you for a dinner in this place today. I hope they would have a table for six without delay." She was right. The minute we got in, a nicely dressed guy led us to our table. Under soft light and music, we enjoyed a very relaxing two hours and tested the most delicious food. I had to admit it was the first time in my life I learnt that there were so many types of biryanis.

Back at home, the four of us went to Sister Nashmeea and Jameela's room talking and repeating the names of the landmarks of the city particularly the amazing Shah Faisal Mosque and trying to define the difference between the lahara biryani and the sindhi biryani.

# Chapter Twenty

It was Sunday, and the time was ten o'clock in the morning. We all had gathered in that open-plan kitchen chatting and revising our last Fridy pleasant tour of the city. It was the early days of October, and we can sniff the breeze of the Autumn through the wide-open back window. Most likely there were one or two fast showers that had taken place over the night. Sister Nashmeea was telling us some facts about the extreme fluctuations of the weather in her country. She said, "We could have a very cold winter sometimes. It might snow heavily in some parts of the country, but Islamabad usually would enjoy a relatively mild temperature all over the year." Jameela nodded her head, While Ashu and I were expressed a little astonishment.

As we were on that subject, Aunt Shabnam appeared at the entrance of the kitchen. Aunt Shabnam, despite her smile, looked a bit serious and apprehensive. She wished all of us a good morning. However, she directed her attention to Sister Nashmeea and said, "Hello Sister. Uncle Mulla Abdul Rahman requested your presence in his villa for some consultation when you were ready." Sister Nashmeea's response was prompt, "Fine, my aunty, I was ready right now."

Nothing unusual for Sister Nashmeea to be called by her uncle. Just because we were anxious regarding the renewal of Jameela's passport, Ashu and I started speculating, guessing, and exploring several possibilities about that early morning meeting. Wise Jameela was the one who avoided any pointless debate. She put her right hand up and said, "Listen, sisters, there would be no point to tax your brains. We should go to the bedroom and relax and wait for Sister Nashmeea to come out of the meeting with her uncle. Then we all would know what the meeting was all about."

We both agreed with Jameela. We looked calm on the surface, but I believed we both continued to be somewhat anxious. A few minutes after we had settled in my room, Aunt Shabnam appeared at the door carrying a large tray with a pot of tea, mugs, and a large plate of cakes. Jameela jumped and helped Aunt

Shabnam by taking the heavy plate of the cakes from the tray and put it on the side table. Aunt Shabnam thanked Jameela and said, "I thought that the cake would be the sweet means to keep you busy while Sister Nashmeea at the same time busy discussing with Uncle Mulla Abdul Rahman."

Ashu thanked Aunt Shabnam for her kindness and invited her to stay around to give us an idea about the subject matter of that uncle's meeting with Sister Nashmeea. Aunt Shabnam stayed for a short while, apologising for being unable to give a direct answer to Ashu's question. She responded with a nice smile and said, "You might know friends that there were so many issues around, and the Mullah had met so many people during the last few days. Most likely, he wanted to discuss some of those matters with Sister Nashmeea."

Aunt Shabnam wished us a good day ahead and left us as we were before. Jameela went to the side table and started serving us tea and cakes repeatedly. That nice gesture from Aunt Shabnam helped us to pass the heavy waiting time for Sister Nashmeea. Two hours had passed before Sister Nashmeea had appeared smiling at the kitchen's door. Sister Nashmeea came with a large envelope containing our passports and her uncle's report regarding our service in the medical store. She handed the envelope to Ashu and requested her to check its contents.

While Ashu was getting through the items in the envelope, Sister Nashmeea sat on the edge of my bed and said, "Please friends, I would like you to pay good attention to what I was going to say. My uncle was not happy about the overall situation in Afghanistan. He thought that if funds and weapons continued pouring to Taliban from abroad, he would be certain that the future of the country would be very bleak. The only factor that stopped those fanatics from taking over the country, for the time being, was the vicious resistance of the group led by Ahmad Shah. However, my uncle told me that he could see that there were so many conspiracies in the making aiming to get rid of Ahmad Shah. Then my uncle explained that, unfortunately, we cannot do much regarding those facts."

"So, let us stick to our priority for the time being. Regarding renewal of Jameela's passport. My uncle explained to me that after he met with some officials, he was informed that the British consulate headquarters was located within a compound in Islamabad suburb known as the Diplomatic Enclave. Then he had told me that the enclave was not opened for the public except for those with official reason. The entry would be arranged by a formal unit that run a shuttle bus in and out of the enclave. He also found out that the enclave was a few miles away from where we were. My uncle suggested that Uncle Shinwar could drive us tomorrow to the station of the shuttle bus service close to the Diplomatic Enclave."

"There you could explain your reason for the visit and ask for pass tickets for two, one for Jameela as an applicant, and one for Kameela as a witness. You might get an appointment from the shuttle station to enter the enclave within one or two days later. My uncle also explained that the bus service would be chargeable, so you would better have some rupees on you. My uncle also would like to remind you that you should take with you a photocopy of Jameela's passport, the expired Jameela's passport, two copies of Jameela's photographs, and Kameela should carry her passport together with some evidence of the charity assignment."

Then Sister Nashmeea said, "Please try to remember what my uncle had suggested to you, word by word. Any mistake would complicate the issue and might cause us unnecessary delay."

Ashu volunteered to say, "Do not worry Sister. I memorised what you said, word by word."

Sister Nashmeea was pleased with Ashu's comment and said, "Great, leave the rest to me. I would arrange with Uncle Shinwar to drive the four of us tomorrow to explore a possible arrangement for Jameela and Doctor Kameela to obtain an entry to the Diplomatic Enclave, enabling them to put an application for Jameela's passport to the British consulate."

Sister Nashmeea noticed my excitement when she mentioned that we would enjoy another tour in the city of Islamabad.

I found everything in that city was new and fascinating, from the landmarks to the people to the landscape. Even though the season, was getting close to the end of summer we found it fascinating to go around the city that was still green. Sister Nashmeea left the room to organise with Aunt Shabnam tomorrow's arrangement. The three of us spent most of the evening in Jameela's room. We never stopped talking about tomorrow, and our high expectation to get so close to our target. We considered so many possibilities except the possibility of failing to renew Jameela's passport. Most likely we avoided negative thoughts.

Ashu asked an important question, "Where we would find a photographer and a document copier for Jameela's photographs to copy Jameela's documents?"

I thanked Ashu for her logical question, and I told her that, "Logically, those facilities should be available nearby the Diplomatic Enclave, where Embassies and High Commissions were functioning around."

At that stage, Sister Nashmeea came back smiling and told us that everything had been arranged for the next day. Sister Nashmeea and Jameela decided to stay in the kitchen for some tines, While Ashu and I went to our room. Ashu and I never relaxed that night. We kept talking about what would happen the following day. It would be our first practical step in our plan to get Jameela home.

After a long meaningful and meaningless debate, Ashu went silent. Then it was my time to struggle to get some sleep. The first thing I remember then was Ashu's voice telling me it was nine in the morning, and it was time to move. Ten minutes later Ashu and I moved to the kitchen to find Sister Nashmeea and Jameela were already there.

I believed that the four of us had something to eat already when Aunt Shabnam appeared at the entrance of the kitchen to tell us that Uncle Shinwar would be ready to drive us to the Diplomatic Enclave within half an hour and asked us to be ready to move. By half-past nine, Aunt Shabnam appeared on the doorstep of the kitchen again to tell us that Uncle Shinwar was waiting for us near the main get in his car. Once Aunt Shabnam left the kitchen, Sister Nashmeea led the way to the gate followed by the three of us to find uncle Shinwar was already in his car behind the wheel and Aunt Shabnam was next to him holding a primitive colourful map. The three of us climbed into the back of the car, giving Sister Nashmeea, as usual, the middle comfortable seat.

Well, the Diplomatic Enclave was a few miles away as we were told, but not all the roads from the city's centre outwards were easily accessible. Nearly three hours on the road before we glanced at the smart protected compound of the Diplomatic Enclave. The shuttle bus station was very noticeable, not too far from the main gate of the enclave. I enjoyed that ride again, and I was rather unpleased when uncle Shinwar parked the car in a nearby square. We all got off the car and we walked a few steps further, when uncle Shinwar noticed that there was very inviting tandoori restaurant on the corner of the square. Uncle Shinwar asked us if it was okay to invite us for a tandoori lunch later.

Jameela said, "Wow. It was my favourite dish." In the restaurant uncle, Shinwar suggested to Jameela and Kameela go first to a small bureau close to the bus station where Jameela could get her photos and a copy of her old passport, while Kameela could copy her documents. Then they could go to the bus station to buy their tickets for the shuttle trip to the enclave.

Uncle Shinwar opened his wallet and said, "I had learnt from a source in my office that a return ticket for the shuttle bus would cost approximately two thousand rupees. That would be, just above ten Pounds sterling or could be about fifteen dollars."

Uncle Shinwar pulled a note of twenty thousand rupees and offered it to Jameela. Kameela took the note from Jameela and gave it back to Uncle Shinwar, thanking him for his kindness and explaining that they had some piety cash in dollars, and it was time to spend some of it on that occasion. Uncle Shinwar took the rupees back and said, "The problem doctor, you would not get the change back in dollars, you would get it in rupees."

Kameela smiled and said, "That would be fine uncle, I would keep them as a souvenir."

The shuffle station was a walking distance from the restaurant, and it took Jameela and me five minutes to get to the station and back to the restaurant smiling and weaving our pass tickets to the Diplomatic Enclave. I was happy to tell our waiting friends in the restaurant that our appointment was for the day after tomorrow. That would be Wednesday, eleven o'clock in the morning. Aunt Shabnam smiled and said, "Thank goodness for that, let us enjoy the tandoori and prepare ourselves for next Wednesday. Nevertheless, we had a wonderful picnicking day."

# Chapter Twenty-One

Time was running fast, as my mother used to say whenever she was late to do something. That was what I thought when Ashu woke me up at seven o'clock that morning. I almost panicked when she reminded me that the day was Wednesday, the promised day for Jameela's interview at the British consulate. I looked through the window to see something beyond any expectation. It was pouring with seasonal rain. Once I was dressed up and ready, I went to Jameela's room. I did not find anyone there. Steadily I went to the kitchen to find that Sister Nashmeea and Jameela were there, while Aunt Shabnam was standing at the entrance. When I wished everyone good morning, Aunt Shabnam noticed that there was a grim on my face. She looked at me and said, "No, no doctor. Do not apply London's culture to Islamabad. We consider the rain a sign of blessing and prosperity. All that we would need to do was to allow some extra time for our trip to the Diplomatic Enclave. Be ready as early as possible."

Uncle Shinwar had his breakfast at six-thirty this morning in the mini kitchen that was adjacent to our bedroom. By seven o'clock, he told me that he would be ready to move as soon as the ladies would be ready.

Ashu said, "We would be ready within fifteen minutes, but we would like to have Sister Nashmeea come with us, in case there would be an issue with the application."

Aunt Shabnam said, "That would be fine, but you excuse me today if I wouldn't come with you as I don't feel very well."

By seven-thirty, we took the road in the direction of the Diplomatic Enclave. Sister Nashmeea was in the front seat while Jameela and I were in the back.

Pity I couldn't see much of the road as the car's glasses were all misty. By ten-thirty, we had arrived at the enclave. After Uncle Shinwar had parked the car, he said, "I would think it was too early for lunch, hence we would wait for you in that corner coffee shop which was close to the shuttle bus station."

Jameela and I rushed to the waiting bus. I was holding the envelope of our documents, while Jameela was weaving our passing tickets to the driver. We requested the driver to drop us close to the British consulate. He nodded his head twice and said, "With pleasure." When we got off the bus, we found that the entrance of the consulate was fortified by a metal gate and there was a white button on the left side of the gate. When I pressed the button, a nice inviting voice came through an intercom. "Please identify yourself and the purpose of your visit."

After we passed the gate, and the first door we found ourselves in a wide room with seats and tables, one of them was loaded with forms and several ballpoint pens. We made sure that we had collected the right form and filled it out carefully. Step by step. After fifteen minutes, one of the officials came out from a door behind a counter. He examined our completed form thoroughly. Then he asked us: "who was Jameela?"

Jameela stood up and said, "It was me, sir."

Then he appointed on her form and asked, "Was that your signature?"

Jameela answered, "Yes sir." Then he looked at me and asked, "How did you recover your sister?"

I told him that was through the rehabilitation centre of Mulla Abdul Rahman. Then he asked me the name of the charity organisation that delegated me and my friend to the area. He was ticking on the back of the form all the time. Then he handed me a receipt that would entitle us to enter the Diplomatic Enclave again. He wished us good luck and told us to attend the consulate for the result of the application early morning next Wednesday. Jameela and I were pleased with the accomplishment of the interview. We rushed outside the building to find out that the rain had stooped, and the sky was clear with blaring sunshine. It was no more than ten minutes waiting to take the shuttle bus back out of the Diplomatic Enclave.

We went straight to the coffee bar where Sister Nashmeea and Uncle Shinwar were waiting for us anxiously. They looked relieved to see us smiling and in high spirits. We joined them with some fresh coffee and explained to them how the interview had gone and why we were optimistic about the result. Although most of our conversation was about the interview, Sister Nashmeea wisely suggested discussing another topic. She said, "Listen friends. Between now and next Wednesday, we could do a lot of things. For example, we could approach the authority at Islamabad International Airport to find out the most suitable flight for you to return to London. On the other hand, we could approach the representatives of the charity organisation that financed your trip and explain to them Jameela's issue to find out if they would be willing to pay for her ticket to be send home as that was her natural right."

Uncle Shinwar said, "That was a great idea. The airport was over fifty miles from our house. So, please, if you make up your mind, let me know one day ahead so that I would arrange for one day off from my office to devote my day to you."

Sister Nashmeea said, "Jameela's air ticket cost would not be a big deal. When she would hold her passport in her hand, then everything would be easy and attainable."

Back at home, we all gathered in the kitchen area where Aunt Shabnam started serving homemade cack and tea. Ashu had the sense of celebrating feeling that our trip to the consulate was a success. Yet, she insisted to know the details and the exact outcome of our interview. Jameela volunteered to give her a full account of what had happened there. Aunt Shabnam was listening enthusiastically and came with a very optimistic comment. She said, "Great, it sounded good. Let us hope for the best."

After the kitchen party, we all moved to Sister Nashmeea's room talking and exploring our visit to the British consulate time and time again. When Sister Nashmeea mentioned Uncle Shinwar suggestion to contact the charity representatives in Islamabad airport to find out if they were willing to help with the cost of Jameela's air ticket to London, Ashu opened her eyes wide and said, "Yes, why not. What were we going to lose? If they wouldn't help, then we consider an alternative."

I agreed with Ashu and asked her if she would remember the place of the office of the charity organisation at Islamabad International Airport? Ashu was fast to say, "Of course. It was in the arrival lounge, number one, on the first floor."

Sister Nashmeea put on a serious face and said, "Fine, Tomorrow would be Thursday. It was a half-day of work in Pakistan. It would be a suitable day for Uncle Shinwar to take the day off and drive us to the airport. Let me rush to Uncle Shinwar and find out if it was okay with him to take us to the airport tomorrow?"

Sister Nashmeea left the room for five minutes and came back smiling to tell us that Uncle Shinwar told her that he would be ready for us to move by eight o'clock tomorrow morning.

Then I asked Ashu to prepare our papers, a copy of our service report, our passports, and our return air tickets to the UK, and be ready in the morning. Sister Nashmeea suggested that she should join us on our call to the airport just in case we might need something. Ashu narrowed her forehead and said, "I wondered Why we were jumping the gun. Why shouldn't we wait till we would get Jameela's passport in our hands then we would explore the situation sensibly?"

Sister Nashmeea disagreed with Ashu's comment and said, "The earlier we would know, the better it would be for us."

# Chapter Twenty-Two

We all went to bed that night dreaming about our first practical move toward reaping the goal of our mission. By fifteen pasts seven in the morning Ashu and I rushed to the kitchen. It was a surprise to see Sister Nashmeea and Jameela were already there. Every one of us went to her favourite breakfast, including a fresh cup of tea that was already brewed by Jameela.

When Aunt Shabnam popped in wishing everyone a good morning. She was amazed to see all of us were together and ready to move. Aunt Shabnam closed the back window of the kitchen and said, "I wished I could join you on your airport trip, but unfortunately I had a lot of things to do today." Ashu told Aunt Shabnam not to worry, it might be next time. Aunt Shabnam smiled and said in Dari "Inshallah. (Hopefully)." Then, Aunt, Shabnam added that Uncle Shinwar was ready in his car outside the main gate.

The trip to the airport was not a very pleasant one. Though Uncle Shinwar knew all the shortcuts in the area, we spent the first two hours struggling among the heavy traffic to get out of the city centre. Eventually, after we got to the airport area, Uncle Shinwar drove to a parking spot and stopped his car there. Sister Nashmeea suggested to Uncle Shinwar to drop us just there, and when we finished, he would find us at the coffee bar on the first floor. Ashu led the way as she remembered very well the location of the door of the court where we had our meeting with the charity representatives upon arrival to Islamabad the first time.

Ashu approached the security guard at the door of the charity court and showed him a copy of our assignment together with our passports. The security guy was pleasant and welcoming and requested us to wait for a few minutes at the door. He went inside for about three to four minutes then he opened the door and asked us to get in. For Ashu's eyes and my eyes, everything was familiar. The table, the chairs, and the atmosphere. Even the middle-aged smart lady who interviewed us last time was still there. We tried to be short and precise.

However, we explained everything regarding Jameela's case and asked the lady if her organisation could pay for Jameela's air ticket to send her home to London.

The lady showed a lot of understanding and promised to do her best. She collected some of our documents and disappeared through the back door of the court. She came back after ten long minutes and said, "I would be sorry to tell you that it was not within our authority to pay for a passenger's air ticket locally. We could write to our head office in London to authorise us, but that would take a month or even longer in exchange for letters. Alternatively, you could fill out a form with some information regarding the claimant. Then we could provide the lady with a voucher that would entitle her to a thirty per cent discount of the cost of her ticket."

Ashu thanked the lady and asked her if it was possible to get a copy of the discount form so that we might fill it with the related information and would bring it back accordingly. The lady's response was, "Sure. That would be no problem."

She went through the back door again for a short while and came back with a large brown envelope and said, "Here was your form. Please read it carefully, fill it up and you could bring it back to collect your voucher any time you like."

We wished the lady a lovely day and went straight to the coffee bar. Uncle Shinwar was already there waiting for us. He received us with a smile and said, "I hope everything went well." Ashu explained to him all what happened with the representative of the organisation.

Uncle Shinwar said, "That was not too bad. At least something good had come out of it." After a short while, we headed back home to find that Aunt Shabnam had prepared a lovely feast for us. Of course, she wanted to know the story of our airport trip. When we told her about the organisation's to apply a discount on the cost of Jameela's air ticket She smiled and said, "Good. That would be affordable."

Between Thursday and next Wednesday was a world of expectation of anxiety, and hope. We talked, we discussed, and we dreamt, sometimes separately and sometimes together without plans, except for Jameela who asked Aunt Shabnam to provide her with a pencil and a blank notebook to draft an important plan. Once Jameela got her tools, she started outlining and preparing her future in London.

It looked like that Jameela was very confident that she would get her passport renewed, but I was so worried about the possible disappointment if that hope wouldn't be fulfilled. In the meantime, I thought it was time to consider with her some aspects of her plan. Her response was a devotion with confidence and determination. She said, "What had happened to me should never happen to another young girl again. A campaign, Kameela, a big campaign to deplore all the oppressive practices of underage marriage, enforced marriage and arranged marriage. All should be condemned as an evil practice of the past."

I could see the difficulties that Jameela would face to fight against those reactionary traditions in our societies, but I encouraged Jameela and told her that I would support her all the way. However, when we gathered at the food session, our subject was Jameela's future and her London project. In that conversation, Ashu asked Jameela about the way she would finance such an ambitious venture. Jameela's answer was short and precise. She said, "Donations and contributions of members."

Aunt Shabnam put her right hand up and looked at Jameela and said, "Fine, please Jameela agrees to my payment for the cost of your air ticket as the first donation for your great plan." Jameela thanked Aunt Shabnam and threw a kiss in her direction.

The days were passing fast, and our daily conversation had concentrated on the possibilities of our Wednesday appointment at the British consulate. Eventually, the promised day had come. It was Wednesday and all of us, including Aunt Shabnam, had gathered in the kitchen at seven o'clock in the morning. We all nipped something for breakfast and every one of us pretended to be calm and well-composed except me. I found it too hard to hide my nervousness. It was a great relief for me when Aunt Shabnam left the kitchen for a short while and came back to tell us that it was eight o'clock already and Uncle Shinwar was waiting for us in the car outside the main gate. I was absent-minded on the way to the Diplomatic Enclave.

Upon arrival, Uncle Shinwar showed us the coffee bar where they would be waiting for us while Jameela and I had rushed to the shuttle bus. Jameela was holding the receipt for our appointment in her right hand. The conductor on the pavement had a quick look at the receipt and signalled to the driver to open the door for us. Our journey to the British consulate forward and backwards was no longer than forty-five minutes. I was wondering about the feelings of our friends in the coffee bar would be when they would see us running, or rather flying in their direction, and Jameela was weaving her new passport, and I was weaving the brown envelope containing the voided old passport and the rest of the documents that the consulate staff did not need to keep.

Everybody stood up and hugged and congratulated Jameela passionately. That was a scene that attracted the attention of the few attendants of the coffee bar at that time of the day. While everybody was still standing up, Aunt Shabnam said, "Please don't sit down. Let us get home as soon as possible and plan for the airport trip tomorrow."

# Chapter Twenty-Three

At Islamabad International Airport, Ashu, Jameela, and I went straight on to the organisation's office. The guard on the door recognised me and Ashu and asked if the other lady have personal issues to discuss? Ashu showed him Jameela's application for a discounting voucher and pointed at Jameela's new passport number on the application form. The guard smiled politely and said, "Fine, what about the two other ladies?" He meant Ant Shabnam and Sister Nashmeea. Ashu told him that they don't mind waiting outside till we come out. The guard invited Aunt Shabnam and Sister Nashmeea to sit down on a nearby sofa and the guard opened the door for us to get in. He went inside with us and alerted the lady behind the back door about our presence. The middle-aged smart lady came out of the back door and straight away she marked our return air tickets as they were valid for booking. Then she collected Jameela's application for the discounting voucher. She left us for a few minutes to come back with the most liked voucher. She handed it to Jameela and wished us all a safe pleasant journey.

Outside the headquarter of the organisation, we found that Uncle Shinwar was already back from the British airway desk with all the relevant information regarding their scheduled flights to London for the next two days. Uncle Shinwar said that, "Friday night's flight would be the most suitable arrangement for such a long hour's flight." He explained further and said, "You would fly at one-thirty in the morning. Taking the time difference into consideration, you would be landing at Heathrow airport at about six-thirty in the morning. The time you would pass the passport checking and collect your luggage, it would be just passed seven o'clock in the morning. It sounded like a perfect arrangement."

By ten pm, we all went downstairs to the counter of British Airways. It took less than ten minutes for Ashu and me to book our flight on that journey. Aunt Shabnam had a slight delay to purchase Jameela's ticket, as that needed verification from the head office regarding the discounted price. However, another twenty minutes and the three of us were booked on that flight to London.

The lady on the counter told us that the plane was not so busy so she would be able to seat the three of us in one row. That was after kindly she converted Jameela's ticket to a business class to match our privileged arrangement.

It was about eleven pm when Uncle Shinwar invited us to farewell lunch in a first-class restaurant at the airport. While walking behind Uncle Shinwar on our way to the restaurant, I rubbed my eyes more than three times just to make sure that I was not dreaming, and that Jameela would board the plane with Ashu and me to London. Uncle Shinwar, Aunt Shabnam and Sister Nashmeea insisted to stay with us till we would walk to the plain. The time came twenty minutes after midnight. Hugging us with good wishes were normal, but when I noticed the tears in Sister Nashmeea's eyes. I couldn't help but sob wholeheartedly.

Shortly after the take-off, Ashu noticed that the row of seats behind us was empty. She moved to that row and stretched her legs horizontally. Ten minutes later, her shrill sleeping whistling had started. Jameela was busy revising and perfecting the future project that she would launch sooner after our arrival. I was awake all the way and thinking about my mother. How she would react to seeing Jameela in front of her eyes without any introduction. She was pretending all the time, that as much as she was missing Jameela, she tended falsely to think that Jameela should be happy in the tribes' land and she was happy for her happiness.

One hour before our landing an idea struck my mind. I waited till Jameela lifted her eyes from her project to suggest that we should phone my mother from the airport and tell her you were coming home. Then I added, "That could spare her unnecessary shock." Jameela agreed with me.

After collecting our luggage and having gone through the customs and excise, we went to the nearest public telephone in the airport. I reached for my little purse inside my back bag to get some coins. While Ashu and Jameela were watching nearby. I dialled my home number and waited till my mother came on the phone. When my mother heard my voice, she got over-excited and shouted in a crying voice and repeated. "Hello, darling. I missed you like greatly. Were you in London? I prayed to Allah all the time to bring you back well and safe."

I said, "Thank you mother, but did you pray to Allah to bring Jameela back well and safe?"

She said, "Jameela was okay in our homeland."

I said, "How did you know that she was okay?" My mother went silent for a while till I surprised her by saying, "I brought Jameela with me."

She said with astonishment, "Did Jameela go to Egypt?"

I said, "No, I went to the tribes' land." Then I handed the telephone to Jameela.

When Jameela held the phone and said, "Hello mother." My mother couldn't take it. She dropped the phone and went to the floor. Jameela gave me the phone and said, "Please Kameela. Quickly phone my uncle."

Luckily, my uncle answered the phone promptly. I said, "Please uncle, I was with my mother on the phone, and I believed that my mother went into a coma. As you would know, the sooner you rushed her to the hospital the more likely that she would recover."

When we got home there was only my uncle there. He hugged Jameela and sobbed heavily he told us that he took my mother to the same private hospital where my father used to get his treatment. He said, "They were both there but in a different lounge." Then he explained that my mother's coma was not critical, she was responding already to the doctor's questions.

# Chapter Twenty-Four

The drama that was caused by my mother's coma was not expected. It seemed that the curse of that tragic wedding continued to occur unexpectedly. Conversely, Jameela looked confident about her project. She used to repeat that by endurance, determination, and patience we would achieve our galls and she kept repeating, "No young girl in our society should experience what I went through." A few days passed before my uncle brought my mother home from the hospital. She could hardly talk, she looked weak and lisping in her attempts to speak. She kept staring at Jameela and drying her tears by the ends of her headscarf.

The following Friday was the time when the family managed to get together. I looked around the house to see my uncle and his wife occupying the middle sofa in the lobby. My father was watching from his wheelchair, while my mother was sitting silently in the corner. My uncle stated that he had ordered us a lunch from a nearby restaurant. So, we would have enough time to discuss our guilt and the sin we committed against Jameela instead of preparing our food. "Hence we should start our deliberation openly and frankly."

Jameela said, "No uncle. The family is not complete yet. One member of our family is still absent." Before my uncle asked Jameela to explain further, the doorbell rang. All of us welcomed Ashu into the house. Jameela immediately said, "Now the family is complete, so we can start our meeting."

I was the one who had to go through the whole episode from A to Z. I explained vividly the hell that Jameela went through because of that arranged tragic wedding. Then I touched upon the anguish Ashu and I went through to get Jameela out of that misery. I told my listeners that what had happened to Jameela should never happen to another young girl in our community, or to that end in any other part of the civilised world.

Then I said, "For that aim, I am going to start an active organisation that would use all means, from calling for legislation to utilising education to stop that kind of life-wresting atrocities." My father was sitting there silently, while my mother was staring between Jameela and the wall with empty eyes.

There was no way to read her mind. The only person in the family who was interacting with my words was my uncle. Sometimes he used to nod his head in agreement with what I was saying, and sometimes he wiped his tears with his white handkerchief.

Suddenly, he put on a serious face and said, "Can we hear something from Jameela regarding her reforming project to learn what kind of support we could offer her to make it a successful?"

Jameela stood up and said, "Yes dear uncle. My project would start with calling all members of the community for a conference. At that conference, I would explain to them that their offspring would never share them their nostalgic feeling towards the simple primitive societies they left behind before they had come to this country. Naturally, the young generations had opened their eyes to a different culture. A culture of free thinking, freedom of expression, democracy, and individuality. Hence, unplugging them from their natural habitat by the act of forced or arranged marriage and sending them to live in primitive societies was no less than a criminal act. So, please uncle, if you wish my conference a success, you help us pay for the cost of printing the pamphlets and the cost of hiring court for a running the conference."

My uncle put his right hand on his heart and said, "Promise, promise, my dear niece."

Jameela immediately looked at Ashu and said, "Ashu, please draft for us the invitation that would call for the people of our community to attend the conference as early as next Sunday, and please have it ready for my uncle to get it printed in hundreds of copies."

My uncle cleared his throat and said, "And please Ashu, draft me an advert for the conference so that I would arrange to publish it in the local newspapers."

The following day, my uncle came with four hundred copies of the printed invitation that contained the date and the time of the conference and the address of the charity court in Hammersmith Road. We divided the flyers between the three of us and our campaign of handing them to the members of the public had started immediately. Here came the waited Sunday. And the commencing time as we stated in the advert and the pamphlets should be commencing at one o'clock in the afternoon.

At twelve midday, Jameela, Ashu, and I left our house in Hounslow Central with our files and waived a black cab in the street to the booked and arranged court. Upon getting close to the named court, we were astonished to see the people, jointly and separately walking in the direction of the court. By twenty to one in the afternoon, we took our seats on the stage just like a professional panel. All the seats were taken, and people were standing in their tens next to the wall. A few minutes had passed the one o'clock and all the eyes of the people on the court were fixed on the sage, while our eyes from the stage were fixed on the main entrance of the court.

When Ashu suddenly stood up, Jameela and I stood up too. When my father entered the court pushed in his wheelchair, he got a welcoming attention. Everyone in the court stood up applauding the mysterious visitor who attracted everyone's interest. After the crowd had calmed down. Ashu and I sat down, and Jameela had taken over the stage.

She greeted and thanked the audience for their presence, and said, "Ladies and gentlemen, I would like to go straight to the point. My name was Jameela, and I had invited you to set up Jameela's foundation to stand against the atrocities of arranged and forced marriages. Young girls, even some underage girls were being pushed by parents and relatives against their will to unpredictable dark fate. Ladies and gentlemen, I am not talking to you from theory or a fiction story I heard or read in a book."

"I was a victim of that backward practice. Fifty per cent of my life had been wasted in hell. Without the courageous effort of my sister Kameela, Please Kameela would you stand up, and my friend Ashu, please Ashu, kindly stand up, I would find that all my life had been wasted in a hell."

The crowd stood up and applauded Kameela and Ashu for more than three minutes Jameela then continued to say, "I should not forget the kind help and the indefinite support in that land of death and blood that we received from a lady who happened that she had studied nursery for a short while in the UK. Her name was Sister Nashmeea. By her commitment and the assistance of her wise uncle in that troubled land, we managed as a team to get to our objective."

At that point, I asked Jameela her permission and stood up and said, "What Jameela just said proved to us that when we would know that we were right and defending justice, we would always attract the support of those who shared our thoughts and values."

Then Jameela stood up and said, "Ladies and gentlemen, this conference is just the beginning of a serious continuous campaign that will reach the parliament, the media, and human rights organisations. You can find my address at the bottom of the invitation's pamphlets. For those friends who would like to get involved in our future activities, please get in touch and we will communicate with you." Accordingly, a huge round of applause roared in the court, and we started to pack our papers and shake hands with people who came closer to the stage and greeted us personally.

At home, the whole family had gathered again, including Ashu. The star of that gathering was my uncle, who well tried to rid himself of his guilt in assisting in Jameela's tragic wedding. My uncle handed Jameela his business card and told her that he would instruct his solicitor to include her project in the scheme of his charity funding, community organisation. Then he added that he would help her initially to set up a moderate office, recruiting a few supporters to expand her activities to cover the entire nation.

My father who was silent most of the time started whispering some Koranic verses, thanking Allah for Jameela's return and her accomplishment. My mother who could not attend the public meeting; we found her later sitting in the corner of the lobby of our home with empty eyes. I thought on one occasion she struggled to say something that was not very clear, I believed she thanked her God for the safe return of Jameela. Two days later, while we were in a semi-celebrating mood, my mother collapsed in the kitchen. Ashu rushed to the phone and called for an ambulance.

The following day, my uncle got the bad news. He was very sad, repeating, "God bless her soul. She was a simple honest lady." My father was sitting in his wheelchair reciting under his breath some verses of the holy Koran. Jameela was sitting on the floor sobbing like a child.

Almost the entire community escorted her coffin to her final resting place at Muslim's Hatton Cemetery.

On the way back, when Ashu noticed that I was in control of myself, she whispered in my ear, "The tragic wedding finished in a tragic funeral. Hence, we should close the chapter and move forward to accomplish our task." Then she added, "Did you know that the news of our conference appeared as headlines in the national newspapers yesterday?"

www.ingramcontent.com/pod-product-compliance
Lightning Source LLC
Chambersburg PA
CBHW060503290526
45791CB00001B/250